Our Lady?

For our Mothers,
Laura Keen Longenecker and Gwen Gustafson,
who have raised their children
in the nurture and admonition of the Lord.

"Her children arise and call her blessed..."
(Proverbs 31:28)

Our Lady?
A Catholic / Evangelical Debate

FR. DWIGHT LONGENECKER
DAVID GUSTAFSON

Forewords by Francis J. Beckwith
and Karl Keating

Wanna + Dominic

D Long

STAUFFER
BOOKS

STAUFFER BOOKS
Terra Lane, Greenville, SC

COVER AND BOOK DESIGN
Christopher J. Pelicano

PRINTED AND BOUND IN THE U.S.A.
CreateSpace

ISBN 978-0-9862713-2-8

Contents

Acknowledgments

I thank Robert Stoddart, Edward Froelich, and John Harocopos for disagreeing with me in such generous and helpful ways. Thanks also go to Steve Froehlich, Sheryl Froehlich, Sharon Gustafson, and Adam Gustafson for suggestions and corrections. Thanks to Jonathan Jacobson and Nicholas Lubelfeld for providing valuable resources and encouragement.

David Gustafson.

I wish to thank John Saward for sage advice and sound theological input, and Fr Michael Clothier OSB and Richard Leiter for their helpful insights. I also thank Bob Trexler and Gregg Terrell for their general encouragement and interest as the book took formation. I also thank my brother Don Longenecker for his cheerful encouragement and enthusiasm. Finally, I thank my wife Alison and my children for their support for my writing work, even if it doesn't 'set the best seller lists alight.'

Dwight Longenecker.

Foreword

Francis J. Beckwith
Professor of Philosophy & Church-State Studies, Baylor
University (Waco, Texas)
July 28, 2013, Feast of St. Alphonsa of the Immaculate
Conception

"I can hear a sweet voice gently calling.
Must be the mother of our Lord"

—Bob Dylan, "Duquense Whistle" (2012)

I grew up Catholic, but during my teenage years wandered away from the Church into the arms of Evangelical Protestantism. I was not so much drawn away from Rome as I was attracted to a group of Christians that seemed to me far more serious about Scripture, evangelization, and walking with Jesus than what I had found in my American Catholic community in the mid-1970s.

To a largely uncatechized, theologically curious, teenager who just wanted to follow Jesus, post-concilliar American Catholicism seemed like an incoherent mish-mash in comparison to an Evangelicalism that seemed to have a well thought-out biblical answer for everything. Although I eventually learned—mostly during my years of PhD studies at Fordham University, a Jesuit institution—that Evangelicals sometimes offered conflicting "biblical answers" and that Catholicism had an impressive intellectual tradition with some of the finest minds in the history of Western civilization, I had already become too deeply invested in the Protestant story and its understanding of Scripture and the development of doctrine.

For that reason, it was not until I was in my mid-40s that I began to take seriously the possibility of returning to the Church of my youth. Among the obstacles that I had to overcome was the Catholic understanding of Our Blessed Mother, that seemed, given my commitment to methodological Protestantism, a virtual impossibility. What eventually changed my mind was not a silver-bullet reason that bested all the Protestant arguments, but rather, a paradigm shift in my thinking. Instead of interpreting the Catholic case for Mary as an attempt to add on "man made" doctrines to *sola scriptura*—that is, instead of approaching the question under the aegis of methodological Protestantism—I began to see the Church's Marian beliefs as fully integrated parts of an organic whole that cannot be antiseptically isolated from all its other teachings. It was only when I began to rid myself of the idea that theological beliefs were like individual conceptual commodities that are always under my control—that I somehow have a right to choose each and every one of them as long as they are consistent with what I think is "reasonable" or "biblical"—that I began to realize that my skepticism about the Marian doctrines were the consequence of reading Catholic words while under the guidance of Protestant grammar.

This is why once I saw that the Catholic doctrines that bothered me the most—apostolic succession, penance, Eucharistic realism, and justification—were not only plausible accounts of Christian belief, but can be found deep in Church history and were embraced by Eastern and Western rite Christians alike until the ascendancy of the Reformation, the Marian doctrines and practices just fell into place.[1] For not only do they also have deep historical roots, as

Fr. Longenecker shows in his contribution to this book, they are tightly tethered to the Catholic understanding of the communion of the saints, which in turn is organically connected to penance, justification, and Eucharistic realism. (During the consecration of the Eucharist, the priest acknowledges the participation of all the deceased saints and asks some of them by name to pray for us. This component of the liturgy is ancient.[2]). For this reason, to ask "biblical" questions about the plausibiilty of specific Marian doctrines and devotions—e.g., the Immaculate Conception, the Assumption, the rosary—without any reference to other Catholic beliefs that contribute significantly to the plausibility of those Marian dogmas and practices is like asking someone to justify the purpose of the lungs without any reference to the human body as a whole.

The failure of most Evangelical Protestants to understand the role of Mary in Catholic theology is often the result of another mistake, one so fundamental to Protestant thought that even most Catholics miss it: the idea that divine action is a zero sum game. Because Americans, even Catholic ones, have been shaped so significantly by a Protestant ethos—which is true also of Catholics in other nations that are culturally Protestant—they seem perplexed on how to respond to Evangelical friends who see the Blessed Mother as a rival to Her Son, that it is not possible for a Catholic to pray to Mary or be devoted to her without diminishing the centrality of Christ.

This claim, though superficially plausible, is based on a mistaken view of divine action, a view that in other contexts not even Evangelical Protestants believe! Take, for example, the belief that the Bible is the Word of God. Both Catholics and Evangelicals believe this to be true. Yet, we also agree that all of the Bible's books have human authors as well. So, when a Christian says that St. Paul authored the book of Romans, is he denying that Romans is the Word of God? Of course not. But he is also not saying that if St. Paul or any other human author were not involved with composing Romans then the book would be more God's Word than it is right now, that somehow having a human author diminishes God's contribution. This is because the Bible, including the book of Romans, is 100% God's Word and 100% the work of human authors. Granted, this is mysterious, but if God is omnipotent, he certainly has the power to allow and use human cooperation without diminishing his grace or glory. In fact, and ironically, to say that God *could not* do this would be to suggest a limit on His Providence, hardly the sort of claim that one would associate with champions of God's grace and glory.

So, it is no more correct to say a Catholic takes his eyes off Jesus when he prays to Mary and asks for her intercession, than it would be to say that an Evangelical has abandoned "true worship of the Lord" when he visits people in prison rather than attending a Wednesday night church service. For, as Christ himself states: "Truly I tell you, just as you did it to one of the least of these who are members of my family, you did it to me." (Mt. 25:40 –NRSV)

I have learned from my journey that on the issues over Our Blessed Mother that continue to divide Christians of good will, if we are to have any hope of finding a resolution, our conversations must gravitate, tempered by graciousness and generosity, to those nagging questions—on ecclesiology, divine action, the sacraments, the communion of saints, etc.—that were instrumental in solidifying the schism with which we now live.

This book, I am pleased to tell you, is an example of just that sort of conversation.

Foreword

Karl Keating
Author of *Catholicism and Fundamentalism*,
Apologist, Founder of *Catholic Answers*

A year after the 1957 death of Msgr. Ronald Knox, Fr. Leonard Feeney wrote a newsletter article titled "A Painful Post-Mortem." It was an intemperate castigation of the English convert, scholar, and Bible translator. Feeney, known best for his exaggerated interpretation of the dogma *extra ecclesiam nulla salus*, had a years-long antagonism toward Knox, the origin of which I never have been able to determine. It may have been an example of *odium theoligicum*, or it may have been that Feeney, known for his wit, felt outclassed by Knox's more capacious wit.

Feeney listed multiple complaints against Knox. The final one concerned a line from Knox's book *Off the Record*: "most of the literature about [the Virgin Mary] and the popular devotions connected with her leave me cold." Feeney didn't explain why Knox's admission merited condemnation. Perhaps it stemmed from Feeney's Irish background, the Irish, for the prior century or so, having been recognized as progenitors of treacly hymns and holy cards as maudlin as those produced in Italy.

I mean it may have been nothing more than the clash of Irish and English sensibilities toward the faith, one exuberant and the other subdued, as least as those sensibilities stood six decades ago. However that may be, I sympathize with Knox's comment because I could have made it myself. I too have been put off by some devotional writings about Mary and by some artistic representations of her.

For me a more telling example concerns the Sacred Heart. I never have been able to work up much enthusiasm for that devotion because I never have come across an image, whether sculpture or painting, that seemed to me anything but cloyingly bad, and usually effeminate, art. I admit a lone exception. Years ago I came across a truly fine image of the Sacred Heart, so fine that I was surprised such a thing existed. Alas, I no longer recall where I saw it, and today the only images that stick in my mind are ones that appeal to me not at all. I realize those same images appeal to others, perhaps even to most observers, so I may be the outlier—but surely not a lone outlier. The devotional life is such a personal thing that I have to assume that I'm not the only one who finds most Sacred Heart representations unedifying.

I have similar feelings regarding images of the Divine Mercy. I accept the reality of St. Faustina's visions and the utility of the devotion, but I find the standard images to be uninspiring. Likewise with the statue of Our Lady of Fatima. I know people who consider it the loveliest statue they ever have seen, but it does little for me. (I much prefer Gian Lorenzo Bernini.) I acknowledge the prettiness of the Fatima statue but confess it fails to assist me in prayer.

I have at home two unpainted wooden statues of the Virgin Mary, carved in the last century according to the Gothic style. I find them conducive to meditation. If I were a non-Catholic coming toward an introduction to Mary for the first time, these small statues might intrigue me. I might wonder what it could be about Mary that would induce woodcarvers to produce things so spare yet so fine. Could the attractiveness of the statues suggest an attractiveness in Mary that I soon would be discovering?

On the other hand, if I were a non-Catholic and knew Mary only in terms of art that I find jejune (most of the religious art of the last two centuries, I'm afraid), would I take an interest in her? Would I suspect that if *this* was the best she could inspire in artists that she might not be worth giving much thought to?

That is how I'm constituted. Others are constituted differently. There likely are many who would find my two Gothic-style statues dull and uninspiring but other representations of Mary—those I consider saccharine—spiritually sensitive and emotionally fulfilling. There may be people who like any and all representations of the Mother of the Lord, on G. K. Chesterton's principle that if a thing is worth doing, it is worth doing badly—though I wonder whether he meant that aphorism to refer to public art.

For four decades I have engaged in Catholic apologetics, usually in terms of challenges from Evangelical and Fundamentalist Protestants. I hardly remember a single one who didn't have problems with Mary and the "overemphasis" the Catholic Church places on her. Consider the words of our Lord as preserved for us in the Gospels. In some Bibles they are printed in red, thus "red-letter text." It takes a long evening to read the quotations through with attention and reverence. The words of Mary would take hardly two minutes, so few of them having been recorded. What is the proportion—several hundred to one? Yet it seems to many, even to many Catholics, that the Church gives as much attention to the Mother as to the Son. This "imbalance" is taken as a sign of misplaced loyalties arising from misunderstood theology.

I recall meeting few Evangelicals or Fundamentalists for whom Mary was not a problem. For many she was the biggest problem in Catholicism. The pope? They could see a certain logic to the preeminence of the bishop of Rome, even if they fancied the preeminence to have arisen accidentally, through political maneuvering, rather than from Christ's overt intention. The sacraments? Acknowledging the reality and necessity of grace, these Protestants could entertain the argument that grace could be passed along through physical things such as water, oil, bread, and wine. But Mary? Wasn't she just a woman, certainly specially favored and with an indispensable role in salvation history—but the patriarchs had indispensable roles too and had far more scriptural acreage devoted to them, so why so much attention to her?

Most of my Evangelical and Fundamentalist interlocutors never became Catholics, so far as I know. A few made the Tiberian swim. Most hesitated at water's edge, second guessing whether they should plunge in and strike for the far bank. Almost always the thing that held them back was Mary. Never was it outright antagonism toward her. That was unthinkable. Yet they remained somewhat put off, even after having been walked through the standard responses to the standard arguments.

I am not a convert to the faith, a fact that makes me something of a rarity among Catholic apologists. I grew up in a milieu in which devotion to the Virgin was unexceptional. While no one in my family was particularly devout in that regard, there was no familial sense that Catholics in general were overdoing it with respect to Mary, although there always were a few people at church who seemed to think the Mass was more about the rosary than about Calvary. My upbringing means that I never have been able to put myself squarely in the shoes of the non-Catholic, whether Protestant or unbeliever, who tries to make sense of Mary's role as seen by the Church in its theology, popular devotions, and art—even the bad art.

The authors of this book have been and are in such a position and thus have certain advantages over me. (I like to think I have advantages over them in having never been anything but Catholic.) Dwight Longenecker once was Protestant and now is Catholic—even a Catholic priest. David Gustafson remains Protestant. They came together to discuss that most contentious woman, the Mother of Jesus: not contentious in herself, of course, but the object of so much contention by others over the centuries.

In this book the contention is good-natured, even winsome. The writers are frank with one another and with their readers.

They acknowledge their own rethinkings, their own unsureness, their own strong attachments to the Christian faith. In many things they are in full agreement; in many not. Even with respect to Mary they agree on much, but their disagreements are many and are not trivial. Each represents his position well and cordially. These are men you would be willing to take a transcontinental road trip with, with no fear of boredom or claustrophobic annoyance.

Over the years I have read innumerable books in which opposing parties went at it with all they had. Usually all they had was anger and exclamation points. Occasionally I found books in which both participants, no matter their views, were men I wish I could have known. I have in mind particularly exchanges in which the Catholic side was represented by Ronald Knox or Sir Arnold Lunn, each a convert to Catholicism and each a master of the pointed but courteous rejoinder. I repeatedly am reminded of Knox and Lunn as I read the pages of this good-natured book.

Introduction

Dwight: It was like throwing a bottle out to sea with a note in it. Only the sea was the Internet, and the note went up on the bulletin board of a religious forum. I wrote asking if there were any Bob Jones University graduates out there who wanted to discuss religion. I wondered if I would get any reply at all. I never guessed I would actually hear from a good acquaintance from my college days.

David: It was a co-worker who showed me your "message in a bottle", because he knew that I had graduated from BJU. (In my world, being from BJU is a status that is, well, distinctive—inspiring reactions something like those you might get if people learned that you used to fight for the Taliban, or that you grew up Amish.) My co-worker asked me if I knew the sender of the message, Dwight Longenecker, and indeed I did.

Dwight: When I got an email from you the next week, I was surprised and delighted. Almost twenty years had passed since we had left college. I remembered you as one of the golden boys. You were a "faculty kid" who knew the system and were three jumps ahead of the rest of us freshmen who were just learning our way around campus. You were a natural leader: you were elected president of the class weren't you? You were smart, but you were also a singer, debater and actor. I first met you when you had a speaking role in the Shakespeare play and I only managed a walk-on part. The last I'd heard about you was from my sister, who had stayed in touch with your sisters. She said you'd done a law degree at Duke and got a decent job at the Justice Department. When I saw who the email was from, I wouldn't have been surprised to find you'd become a Senator.

Instead you had moved your way up the ladder at the Justice Department, had six kids with one on the way, and wanted to talk religion. For my part, I saw God's hand in our re-established friendship. I'd been going through a rough time and had asked God some weeks before to provide me with a friend of my own age and background. I didn't know he would answer my prayer in such a literal way through the wonder of the Internet. I've enjoyed our friendship over the last six years, and been glad to get together for what has become a ritual meeting at the International House of Pancakes during my regular visits to the USA.

When we got back in touch were you surprised to discover that I had become a Catholic?

David: Surprised, but not shocked. In the straight-laced world of BJU, you Longeneckers had always seemed a little--how can I put it?—unpredictable, maybe? One of your sisters had married an artist, which maybe says it all. Your other sister liked to buy beautiful old clothes from consignment shops and thrift stores--almost antique clothes that must have been very stylish decades before and now made the wearer seem like she had stepped through a time warp. (She took two of my own sisters through that time warp.)

You, too, were a striking personality in college—intellectual, literary, artistic. You had a sharp wit that was sometimes sardonic, and a wry, critical way of looking at the world around you. Because you were active in speech and drama, I supposed you would end up teaching in the drama department of a college or high school.

I was wrong about you, though: I heard later through the grapevine that you had moved to England to study theology at Oxford, and that you had become a priest in the Church of England. Since my own horizons are pretty narrow (and I've still never traveled to England), this sounded very exotic to me. Little did I know that my information was a bit out-of-date, and that your trajectory had taken you even further, to the Roman Catholic Church.

Spiritual journey

Dwight: My dalliance with things liturgical had actually started at Bob Jones. We were allowed to go to a little breakaway Episcopal Church deliciously called "Holy Trinity Anglican Orthodox Church". From a background where churches were called "Calvary Baptist" or "Berean Bible Church", the little Anglican Church was exotic, risqué even. There we used a prayer book, lit candles, wore robes to sing in the choir, and knelt to pray on little padded kneelers.

This attraction to the Anglican Church was linked with an acute case of Anglo-philia. I was drawn to all things English and was entranced by C.S. Lewis, J.R.R. Tolkien, Oxford, and the Inklings. When the chance came to study in England, I jumped at it. I see now that I was being drawn even then to an expression of the Christian faith that was ancient, historical, and rooted in European culture. I spent fifteen years within the Anglican Church—ten of those as an Anglican pastor. I will always be grateful for both my Bible Christian upbringing and the years I spent in the beautiful, historic, and magnificent Church of England.

By the early nineties I was married with two young children. I was ensconced in a beautiful old vicarage as a country parson in England. I loved my ministry, my people, and my two 1,000-year-old churches. Increasingly, however, I was questioning the authority of the Anglican Church. She seemed to be unsure what she believed, and she was drifting ever further from the "Mere Christianity" which I sought to follow. At the same time my interest in Catholic spirituality, liturgy, and Catholic history was growing. I discovered that more and more of my best friends were Catholics, and that I had less and less in common with my Anglican colleagues.

In 1995 the journey culminated in me and my family being received into full communion with the Catholic Church. One of the final obstacles in becoming a Catholic was the problem of Mary. I had accepted basic Marian devotions in my spiritual life, but still had trouble with the theological dogmas that Rome expected us to sign up to. In the summer of 1994 those final problems fell away and I realized there was nothing to stop us entering the Catholic Church. How this happened will probably come out later in our discussions.

For now I stand here calling myself an evangelical Catholic. I value, and thank God for, the Evangelical customs and traditions in which I was brought up. I want ordinary Catholics to become more aware of the riches of that Evangelical tradition, but I am also keen to share with Evangelicals more of the riches of the Catholic faith. One of these treasures of the faith is Mary, the Mother of Our Lord. This is not based in a desire to trash Evangelicals or prove anybody wrong. Catholicism is not something different from Evangelicalism. It is something more than Evangelicalism. So my intention in these discussions is not to prove you wrong, but to challenge you a little. If the Catholic faith is my home, I'm inviting you to come and visit and meet my Mother.

The Old-Time Religion

David: I understand and sympathize, at least in a general way, with your being on a spiritual journey that has taken you away from some aspects of your childhood religion. I think some of the same things that influenced you have influenced me. I grew up in a Christian subculture where the phrase "the old-time religion" is said with a straight face. In some ways, that "Fundamentalist" movement may be, from the broad perspective of Church history, a novel creature of 20th-century American Protestantism. However, that movement sees itself as—and resolves to be—none other than the old-time religion of Jesus and His Apostles as reflected in the Bible, "the Faith that was once for all entrusted to the saints" (Jude

3). I don't agree with everything I was taught as a child, but I still do retain that resolve: I want to know and affirm the authentic, apostolic Christianity. Over the last twenty years, that desire has led me to a study of the historic Church. Not as a historian or a theologian (which I am not), but as a layman. So it is as a serious student of the Church that I am trying to discern and affirm the old-time religion.

My particular sub-subculture had another distinctive that I loyally retain: It was decidedly non-denominational. The early 20th-century "fundamentalists" had seen across their denominational differences to recognize that the real common enemy was a "Modernism" that denied cardinal truths like the inspiration of the Bible, the deity of Jesus Christ, and His bodily Resurrection. Disagreements on lesser issues (such as mode of Baptism and eschatology) were set aside, and the "fundamentals" were affirmed and defended. They didn't call their consensus "mere Christianity", but that's what it was. I grew up hearing, and believing, that what mattered was not what denomination you belonged to, but whether you were trusting in Jesus Christ for your salvation. We knew that in heaven there would be Baptists, Methodists, Presbyterians, Lutherans, whatever— even, at least hypothetically, a few Roman Catholics, though not because of but *in spite of* their Church. (Probably also a few Eastern Orthodox, though from my vantage point they looked like another kind of Roman Catholics.)

Can you see how this prepared me, however ironically, for a genuine "catholic" interest? The first time I remember hearing the Apostles' Creed was when my family was visiting an Episcopal Church where a friend of my parents was the pastor. I might have been about ten years old. Unfamiliar with the liturgy, I was following along as best I could and glancing to my parents for cues about when to kneel, when to stand, when to sit. It was all rather alien, but one tries to be polite and not stick out. I remember well, though, my confusion and dismay when, as we recited the Creed, I saw my parents say that they "believe ... in the holy catholic Church." For sure, we were *not* Catholics. What were they saying? After the service, I asked.

My mother explained to me that *catholic* means "universal", "world-wide"; the "catholic Church" is the Body of Christ, all the people who, whatever their denomination, are joined to Christ by faith. That was when I began to know that I am a "catholic" Christian, in one Body with all the other true believers. You call yourself an "evangelical Catholic"; well, I call myself a "catholic Evangelical".

Over the years I have developed an increasing desire to understand what Christians over the centuries have believed and done. I read and believe the same Bible they did, and I know I have much to learn from them. The old-time religion was not invented in twentieth -century America, nor in sixteenth-century Germany. It was invented, so to speak, in A.D. 33; and our task as believers is not to make clever new insights but to receive the Faith and pass it along faithfully. I have ended up in an Episcopal parish (a very conservative one), because for me that is the church best suited for worshiping as Christians have always worshiped and studying the Bible in light of what Christians have always believed.

Dwight: It was my desire not only to understand the ancient Church, but to be a part of it which has led me finally to become a Catholic. As you've hinted, and as I've experienced, American Evangelical religion is largely cut off from the grand sweep of Christian history from before the Reformation. As I began to look more deeply into the writings of our fathers in the Faith I discovered how the early Christians believed and behaved.

In our discussion I will be quoting from these writers from the first four or five centuries of the Christian experience. It is too often the case that Protestant Christians have simply dismissed the ancient extra-biblical writings as "Catholic legends." There are some ancient writings that are fanciful legends. Others are full of heretical teaching. However, the respected writings from this earliest period of Church history are deeply Spirit-filled and full of wonderful insights. I should make it clear that I do not quote from these documents as if they bear the authority of Scripture. I use the letters, sermons, hymns, and theological writings from the first five centuries to show what the early Christians believed. I quote them for their historical authenticity and authority—not because they are the inspired word of God.

David: Thanks for the clarification—and I'll hold you to it. I, too, have learned an enormous amount by discovering the writings of the Church fathers. In some respects, my study has made me more sympathetic to the beliefs of my Roman Catholic friends, or at least has smoothed off some of the harder edges. In other respects, however, the differences persist or have even gotten greater, the more I've learned. Sadly, one of these persistent difficulties is the subject of our Lord's mother, Mary. If Jesus Christ loves His mother—and I know He does, more than any fallen son ever loved his mother—then our errors and divisions on this subject must sadden and displease Him. I wonder whether you've been a Catholic for so long that you've forgotten what a scandal she has become.

Dwight: I don't think so. I still understand the Evangelical mentality, and I understand the deep-seated suspicion of things Catholic. But when you ask me if I've forgotten what a scandal Mary has become, it strikes me in a strange and paradoxical way. When I had put aside my own prejudices and really looked into the question, I discovered that devotion to Mary dates from the very earliest days of the Christian Church. I found that the vast majority of Christians both now and down through the ages have seen devotion to the Mother of the Lord as a natural and simple part of their whole faith. Therefore we Catholics find the Evangelicals' *neglect* of Mary to be a sort of scandal--a late invention by a small segment of Christianity which has diminished the historic faith in a significant way.

Iron sharpens iron

For my part, I hope in these discussions to show what a joy it is to include Mary in the whole range of our love for the Lord. I want to show how ancient and universal the Marian devotions and doctrines are. I hope our Evangelical readers will think again about Mary, and come to share in this beautiful and venerable dimension of our shared faith.

I expect we'll exchange some sharp words now and again. That's okay. Iron sharpens iron. I know we'll do so in fraternal charity and I hope the debate will bring us both closer to that Truth which promises to set us free

David: I join you in that hope, and I resolve to listen. And for my part, when it's my turn to speak, I hope not just to assert a negative—a minimizing of Mary—but to hold up a positive ideal of undistracted devotion to our Lord. And speaking of being positive, it would be a big mistake to forget or ignore the substantial agreement we have about so much that concerns this subject. That agreement becomes obvious when we turn to the question of what the Bible says about Mary.

1

I Stand Alone on the Word of God

The Biblical Evidence about Mary

David: "The Bible says almost nothing about Mary"—that's what the Evangelical is supposed to say at this point, right? But in fact, when I review the Biblical data, it does prompt me to make a concession to the Catholic: The four Gospels say a lot about Mary, and they place her in the middle of the crucial events in the life of Jesus, which are the crucial events in our redemption.

In fact, it's even fair to say that the New Testament begins with Mary—that is, with Mary's conception of Jesus, as revealed to Joseph. (Matthew 1:18-25.) Mary's pregnancy, and her giving birth to Jesus, are given more attention than any other pregnancy and birth recorded in the Bible. That Virgin Birth had been prophetically foretold. (Isaiah 7:14.) The angel Gabriel's "annunciation", Mary's "visitation" with Elizabeth (when Elizabeth and her unborn child John attested Jesus' deity), the late-pregnancy trip to Bethlehem, where "there was no room for them in the inn", the birth in a stable, the visit of the shepherds after they saw and heard the heavenly host (Luke 1:26-2:20)—all Christians know these Marian stories in great detail, and we prize the details. Isn't Mary's song, "The Magnificat" (Luke 1:46-55), the longest song recorded in the New Testament? It was Mary who, with Joseph, took the baby Jesus for His presentation at the temple, where Simeon and Anna blessed Him. (Luke 2:22-38.) Mary witnessed the visit of the wise men, went with the child Jesus and Joseph to Egypt, and returned to Nazareth. (Matthew 2.) Mary took 12-year-old Jesus to Jerusalem, grieved when He was missing on the return trip, and found Him in the temple, "about His Father's business." (Luke 2:41-52.)

Any mother's presence and involvement in the life of her child diminishes as that child becomes an adult, and this was true for Mary and Jesus. However, Mary's presence and involvement in Jesus' life did not by any means cease altogether: It was Mary whose request prompted Jesus' first miracle—the turning of water into wine. (John 2:1-12.) Most notably, Mary was with Jesus at the cross, when most of His followers had fled; and even in that climax and culmination of human history, Jesus did not forget his mother, but made provision for her to be cared for by His young disciple John. (John 19:25-30.) After Jesus' resurrection and ascension, Mary was present in the Upper Room with the Disciples (Acts 1:14), where they awaited the coming of the promised Holy Spirit.

If the stories in the Bible are not mere entertainment, but were "written for our instruction"(Romans 15:4), then any of the incidents the Bible records from Mary's life could be a worthy subject of reflection and meditation. However, there is one incident that may be the most important; and in further concession, I'd like to return to it for a moment: Mary's famous *fiat* (Latin for "Let it be") was spoken by her when Gabriel revealed that God had called her to be the mother of the Messiah: "Let it be unto me according to thy word", she said. (Luke 1:38.) God is sovereign, but He uses human decision-making as a means for working out His plan. Mary's "Let it be" is one of the critical choke-points in salvation history. Mary's monumental decision put her in a class with Abraham. Centuries before, Abraham had heeded God's call to leave his ancestral home and go out "to a land which I will show you". (Genesis 12:14.) By his trust and obedience, Abraham became the father of God's chosen people, the Jews, and became (the Apostle Paul said) a "father" to all those who share Abraham's faith in the one true God. (Romans 4:11-12.) Likewise, Mary can fairly be said to be a "mother" in the faith to all those who, like her, accept Jesus as Messiah and Savior and Lord. She may, in fact, be the first "Christian"—the first to trust in Jesus Christ as the promised Savior.

Given all this Biblical information about Mary, it is obvious that she is an important person in our faith. I'll confess this: I sense that Protestant thinking about Mary is disproportionately negative, too much simply a reaction against Roman Catholic devotion to Mary. While I deny that we have a Mary-phobia, we do seem to be very emphatic about what Mary is *not*, but we fail to appreciate all that she is. We should change.

Dwight: You've started out by giving ground. I can see the seasoned debater in you—granting the strength of the other guy's position and so cutting the ground out from under him. I don't suppose you're going to go on in this vein.

Downplaying Mary?

David: You see right through me. Indeed, that's where my concessions end and my disputes begin: The New Testament is also remarkable for its overt de-emphasis of Mary. One of the strangest things about the life of Jesus is his relationship to His mother. On the one hand he was an obedient child (Luke 2:51), and to the bitter end He thought of His mother and provided for her (John 19:25-30). But on the other hand, He seemed to deliberately downplay her maternal connection to Him, on at least four specific occasions:

First, when Mary requested Jesus' intervention at the wedding in Cana—a request He eventually granted—His reply nonetheless seems distant: "Dear woman, why do you involve me? My time has not yet come." (John 2:4.) Even Pope John Paul II acknowledges Jesus' "apparent indifference" to her request.[1] Is Jesus saying that

3

Mary has no special standing to make requests of Him?

Second, when he was twelve years old, and Mary very forgivably chided Him for not keeping up with their caravan—"Son, why have you treated us like this? Your *father* and I have been anxiously searching for you"—His reply to Mary would have been almost impudent from any other son, and must have been especially startling to Jesus' legal father Joseph: "Why were you searching for me? Didn't you know I had to be in my *Father's* house?" (Luke 2:48-49.) Was Jesus down-playing his connection to his earthly family? Any adoptive parent can tell you how painful such a comment might be.

Third, and most remarkable, is an event recorded in all three synoptic Gospels, on an occasion when Jesus was teaching publicly:

> Then Jesus' mother and brothers arrived. Standing outside, they sent someone in to call him. A crowd was sitting around him, and they told him, "Your mother and brothers are outside looking for you." "Who are my mother and my brothers?" he asked. Then he looked at those seated in a circle around him and said, "Here are my mother and my brothers! Whoever does God's will is my brother and sister and mother." [Mark 3:31-35[2] = Matthew 12:46-50 = Luke 8:19-21.]

If you treated your mother that way, I would correct you. I would not correct Jesus, but I would certainly observe His deliberate subordinating of his family relationships to the spiritual family that His salvation would create.

Fourth, and perhaps most pertinent to our consideration of Mary, is another incident that took place when Jesus was teaching: A woman in the crowd called out raised her voice and said to him, "Blessed is the mother who gave you birth and nursed you!" This is a blessing of Mary to which (correct me if I'm wrong) the prevailing spirit of Marian devotion in the Roman Catholic Church would say a hearty "Amen!" Jesus, however, did not give that response, nor otherwise endorse this woman's sentiments. Instead, He said,

"Blessed rather are those who hear the word of God and obey it." (Luke 11:27-28.) Again, Jesus seems to deflect attention away from His mother, to keep her from being a distraction, and to focus attention on other things (here, the hearing and obeying of God's word).

The Gospels do not show Jesus creating for Mary a place of attention or special honor. They do not record Him commending Mary to His followers, promoting her intercession, or holding her up as of continuing importance to them (or even to Him). He seems, in fact, to have done the opposite.

Protestant prejudice?

Dwight: I don't want to interrupt your flow too much, but I can't help making one or two points. First of all, you say the gospels evidence an "overt de-emphasis on Mary". If you don't mind me saying it, this is your prejudice showing through. Catholics don't think these passages de-emphasize Mary at all. Let me show you these passages from our perspective.

First, you mentioned the conversation between Jesus and Mary at the wedding in Cana. I'm glad you used the New International Version because it is more accurate when it quotes Jesus as referring to Mary as "Dear woman." The King James Version has him saying "Woman." And to modern ears this sounds coarse— rude even. In fact, the New International Version expresses the fact that the term "woman" is used in tenderness in Jesus' culture. It is a common reference of a son to a mother. It is the same term Jesus uses for his mother from the cross for instance. (Jn.19:26.) Forgive me for laboring over one word, but when Jesus calls Mary "woman" it is also a reference to the fact that she is the second Eve, for Eve is called "the woman" and "Mother of All the Living." (Gen.2:23;3:20)

David: There's a little tension, isn't there, in saying that "Woman" is a conventional, familiar son-to-mother form of address *and* saying that "Woman" is a word charged with specialized theological meaning?

Dwight: Not necessarily. Words carry many levels of meaning, and we may use a word in an ordinary way, yet it carries other levels of extraordinary meaning. For example, Jesus says, "You call me master, and so I am." The word "master" has a simple meaning and theological meaning. Let's look at the rest of Jesus' question. Again, the King James Version uses the words, "What have you to do with me?" (which sounds rude) but the New Jerusalem Bible translates, "Woman, what do you want from me?" and as you've quoted, the New International Version says, "Dear woman, why do you involve me?" In other words, Jesus is not rebuking or marginalizing Mary at all. He is simply saying, "Yes, mother, what is it?"

The phrase translated "What have you to do with me?" sounds brusque to us, but it was actually an idiom which showed respect and deference. Notice in Luke 8:28 the same idiom is used by the demoniac as he cowers in deference to Jesus. This phrase was used as a mark of humility and honor towards the hearer. So in a more ceremonial culture you might bow your head and speak a word of respect and submission like "Speak, Lord, your servant is listening" or "What have you to do with me?". This being the case, the phrase, "What have you to do with me?" rather than showing Jesus' dismissal of his mother, shows his deference to his mother. This is supported by the context of the story because he then goes on to do as she requests.

Your second problem is when the boy Jesus says, "Didn't you know I had to be in my father's house?" What we can never know is a person's tone of voice. How you envision this conversation depends on your already pre-determined view of Mary and Jesus. If you see them as disconnected, then you may see the exchange as one that exhibits Mary's ignorance and Jesus' impudence. If, on the other hand, you see an intimate relationship between them you will simply see a worried and relieved mother and a young teenager who really was innocent of his parents' worries. This is a natural conversation—like one you might have when your teenager stays out too late playing basketball.

"Son! we thought you'd be home by six. It's now nine. Where have you been? We were worried."

"You shouldn't have worried dad, didn't you realize I was just playing basketball?"

Furthermore, the point of the story is not to reveal some tense relationship between Jesus and his mother, but to show that even at the age of twelve Jesus was aware of his destiny and his special relationship with his heavenly father.

Catholic bias?

Dwight: I know we Catholics view these stories in a pro-Mary way, but doesn't your third incident also reveal your unconscious bias against Mary? The point of the story when Jesus says, "Those who do my father's will are my mother and brothers and sisters" is not to reject his mother or to portray her as inferior. You read this into the story because that was your viewpoint already. In fact Jesus doesn't reject his mother and kinfolk at all. He simply uses their appearance as a chance to make the point that those who are hearing his words and doing God's will are also his family. We know from earlier in the chapter (vv.20-21) that there was tension in his extended family about Jesus' ministry, but there is no evidence that Jesus was rude to his mother or that he rejected her in any way. He simply used her arrival on the scene as a teaching point.

You quote the story in Luke 11:27-28 as evidence that Jesus is de-emphasizing his mother. The woman in the crowd was using a blessing that was formulaic and even casual. It was equivalent in our day to someone who uses "God bless" as a flippant form of farewell. In the context Jesus wasn't saying anything one way or the other about his mother. He was challenging the enthusiastic lady in the crowd to take her religion further than casual catchphrases and popular sentimentality.

Finally, you say Jesus does not commend his mother to his disciples, but that is precisely what he does at the cross when he commends Mary to John. (John 19.25-30) You have already said that Mary might be regarded as our mother in the faith. Here Jesus confirms it. Generally, Evangelicals are quick to place themselves among Jesus' disciples and hear His words as if spoken to them: "Follow Me, and I will make you fishers of men" (Matthew 4:19); "Go into all the world" (Mark 16:15)"—such things spoken to His disciples are taken as for all Christians. Why not "Here is your mother"?

David: I hope I read these Marian incidents fairly, though my preconceptions surely must affect my reading of the Bible (just as yours affect your reading). Here, I'll just say that the texts of these stories will have to speak for themselves, and as readers we have to try prayerfully to determine what they communicate about Mary. In making that determination, we probably ought to be influenced by Mary's place in the remainder of the New Testament, which is a very modest place:

Mary in the Epistles and Apocalypse

David: The Apostle Paul, the preeminent doctrinal writer of the New Testament, makes only one (anonymous) reference to Mary: "When the time had fully come, God sent forth his Son, *born of a woman....*" (Galatians 4:4.) Thus, insofar as Paul's message is reflected in his canonical epistles, that message did not feature Mary with any prominence.

The Apostle Peter's two epistles omit any mention of Mary. If we associate the Gospel of Mark with Peter's teaching (as some do, since Mark was apparently one of his protégés), it adds only two Marian references to the Petrine canon: the incident discussed above, when Jesus asks "Who is my mother?" (Mark 3:33), and a quotation of skeptics observing that Jesus is "Mary's son" (Mark 6:3).

The Apostle John, the disciple whom Jesus charged with the care of His mother and with whom Mary presumably lived for the rest of her life, has surprisingly little to say about Mary: In his Gospel, he describes her role in Jesus' changing water to wine at the wedding in Cana (John 2:1-12), he mentions the skeptics remarking that they know Jesus' mother (John 6:42), and he recounts Jesus committing Mary to his charge (John 19:25-27). In his three epistles, John mentions Mary not at all.

Dwight: You've done a good job of summarizing the New Testament evidence. Let me challenge you on one or two points. It is true that Saint Paul says little about Mary, but then have you ever considered that he actually says very little about Jesus as well? He writes to the churches but scarcely mentions the actual events of the gospels. Instead he assumes that his hearers know the basic gospel facts.

Added to this you must consider that the gospel writer who has the most to say about Mary is Luke. Indeed, the ancient traditions say that Luke received many of the stories about Jesus' life from Mary herself. Remember that Luke was the companion and co-worker of Saint Paul. We can safely assume that Paul knew the stories that Luke recorded. It is true that Peter and Paul are almost silent about Mary, but we can just as easily take their silence on the subject of Marian devotion as tacit approval.

It is more likely that Paul didn't mention Marian devotion because it had not developed by the time he was writing the epistles. The reason it wouldn't have developed was that Mary was still alive. Also, Peter and Paul are writing from a time when the Church was coming to a full understanding of who Jesus was. It was right that the Church should first come to understand the true nature and identity of Jesus, and only later go on to meditate on the full role and identity of Jesus' mother.

The one apostle, who did survive along with Mary for the longest time, is the one who gives us the strongest hints of the already developing devotion to Mary. You say that John is silent, but not totally. John looked after Mary as Jesus asked, and the early traditions of the church say that they lived together in Ephesus as mother and son. John knew Mary well, and as he lived the longest of the apostles, had time to meditate on her true role. He is the one in the book of Revelation who records his vision of the woman who battles against Satan in chapter twelve. I will talk more about her later, but it is clear that the triumphant woman in Revelation 12 is Mary the mother of Jesus. John gives her a very exalted role, and so is not silent about her as you say.

David: To you folks who are predisposed to see her, it may be "clear" that Mary is the woman in Revelation 12. To the rest of us, it is a thorny interpretive question. It is hard to see Mary's biography in verses 5-6 and 13-16, and it seems more likely that the "woman" is Israel, the Church, the people of God.

Dwight: I think most commentators agree that the woman in Revelation 12 *does* represent the People of God (Israel and the Church) and that the "desert time" is the time of persecution at the time of writing. But if the child "who will rule all nations" is Jesus, doesn't the woman who gives him birth have to be Mary? I think she is both, and that the multiple images for the woman are no mistake. I hope we will discuss Mary's relationship to the Church in more detail later.

David: I guess I agree with Pope John Paul II when he said, "according to the sacred author's *primary* intention, … the woman [in Revelation 12] obviously personifies the People of God, both the biblical Israel and the Church", but I'm less convinced with the "Marian interpretation" he defends by seeing Mary as "a type of the Church".[3] That assertion bears more reflection. In the meantime, I'm not really *arguing* from Biblical silence—not yet, anyway. At this point, I mean simply to *observe* the silence. Biblical silence about Mary is a fact that must be reckoned with in determining her place in the Church, which we will attempt in coming chapters. I think it is probably this silence that prompted the Pope to observe that "Mary … does not want to call attention to herself".[4]

Dwight: You've raised a very important point. Mary is a hidden person in the Gospels for two reasons. First of all she is naturally humble (Luke 1:48) and humble people are hidden people. They're natural. They blend in. They don't draw attention to themselves. Secondly, Mary's role is always to point to Jesus and not to herself. This is the role she plays in all genuine Catholic thinking and devotion.

Marian doctrine in Scripture

David: We also need to consider the relative lack of doctrinal significance that the New Testament accords Mary's person and actions. In the case of Jesus Himself, many of the incidents of His life recorded in the New Testament are shown to have enormous doctrinal importance and to apply to all of us: His conception and birth are the Incarnation of God; His earthly ministry is the fulfillment of Messianic promises; His death is the atonement for human sin; His resurrection is the human race's victory over death; His ascension is the drawing up of humanity into fellowship with God; His return will be The End of the World. Thus, while you are right that Paul's epistles say "very little about Jesus" (that is, they do not recount, but assume, the biographical facts about Jesus), I know you'd concede that Paul's epistles (and Peter's and John's) are brimming with teaching about the significance of His person and acts. There is, by contrast, no indication of equivalent doctrinal significance to events in the life of, say, Thomas or Pilate. What about Mary?

In a later chapter we'll discuss the Virgin Birth. With that signal exception, the New Testament seems to me to be devoid of doctrines that pertain immediately to Mary. Admittedly, as I have recalled here, the New Testament gives us many stories of her life–as they bear on the life of Jesus–but it does not teach us that her events, or her person, has over-arching significance for believers generally.

That is the Biblical data about Mary, as I see it. We'll return to some of these passages later as we discuss specific issues, but now I make a generalization about this Biblical data: If Mary has special importance in the life of the believer or the life of the Church, it is an importance not evident in the plain text of the Bible.

Dwight: You've re-affirmed the Catholic position again. You say that the New Testament is devoid of doctrines that pertain specifically to Mary. This is precisely what Catholics have been saying all along. Mary is not the key person. Jesus is. All the things we say about Mary are derived from what we believe about Jesus. As we come to discuss the various Marian doctrines I hope you will see that all of them have grown from our beliefs about Jesus. From the New Testament the church developed certain doctrines and beliefs about who Jesus was and what he accomplished. From that we deduce the real truth about Mary's identity and role in the plan of salvation.

Mary in the Old Testament

Dwight: Let me pick you up on your Biblical analysis. You have explained the Biblical references to Mary in the New Testament, but you haven't touched on the Old Testament. You may not say this, but many Protestant Christians regularly hit Catholics with the charge that "There is very little in the Bible about Mary. Why do you emphasize her as you do?" I'd like to show that contrary to the idea that there is very little about Mary in the Bible, in fact there is quite a lot. Just as Jesus is pointed to in every stage of the Biblical revelation, so Mary is there too, if you have eyes to see.

Before I do this let me ask you a question. You accept, don't you, that the Old Testament is full of pointers to Christ in the form of symbols and archetypes? In other words, Adam is a pointer to Christ as the second Adam, Melchizedek points to Jesus the priest, King David foreshadows Jesus the King, the temple is a picture of Christ's body, Moses the law-giver pre-figures Christ the fulfillment of the law. This is something we agree on, isn't it?

David: I sense a trap—but I'll take the bait. Yes, we properly see "types" of Christ in the Old Testament, and the New Testament makes this explicit. For example, Hebrews 9:24 shows that the high priest's entrance into the tabernacle was a "copy" of Christ's entry into heaven. We have to discipline our type-finding, to keep from *creating* typology and to ensure that we are instead *discerning* authentic types. But there's no denying that the Old Testament Scriptures, read in the light of the New Testament, include symbols and types of larger truths.

Dwight: I agree with you that typology can be a tricky form of Biblical interpretation. In the Catholic tradition it has always been treated seriously because the New Testament writers themselves interpret the Old Testament typologically. However, this form of interpretation is always secondary, not primary. One always has to be cautious.

The point I would like to make is that throughout the Old Testament we are given types not only of Jesus, but of the whole structure of God's plan of redemption. Some of these are explicit. Others are implicit. So the fact that the twelve tribes and twelve minor prophets of Israel pre-figure the twelve apostles is explicit. (Luke 11:49; Eph. 2:20; 2 Peter 3:2; Rev. 4:4.) An example of an implicit type is the story of the patriarch Joseph. He had dreams, went down into Egypt so that the people of Israel might one day be saved. He was a steward and was described as a "just man." All of these details echo in the gospel story of Joseph, the husband of Mary. The connection is implicit, but clear.

Likewise Mary herself is pre-figured throughout the Old Testament. So Eve—the first virgin—points to Mary the second Virgin. Eve said "no" to God. Mary said "yes" to God. All the miraculous birth stories in the Old Testament from Sarah to Hannah and Samson's mother point to Jesus' miraculous birth from Mary. Moses' sister Miriam led a rebellion against God. The new Miriam (the name Mary is another form of the name Miriam) takes the decision that leads the people back to God.

The stories of powerful Queen Mothers in the Davidic dynasty like Bathsheba (2 Kings 2:19-20) point to the role Mary plays as Queen Mother to King Jesus.

One of the most vivid types of Mary is the Ark of the Covenant. The Old Testament ark bore the word of God on tablets of stone. The New Testament ark bears the Word of God incarnate. The Old Testament ark contained the manna—the bread from the wilderness. The New Testament ark (Mary) bears the Bread of Life Jesus Christ. The Old Testament ark was shadowed over by angels (Ex.25:20) The New Testament ark was shadowed over by an angel and the Holy Spirit at the annunciation. (Luke. 1:35) That the ark is a type of Mary is explicitly stated in Revelation 11:19-12:1. There in John's vision the Ark of the Covenant is revealed in the heavenly Jerusalem, and that ark is the triumphant woman spoken about in Revelation 12. The chapter clearly equates the woman's child with Jesus, so the woman must be (at least on one level) Mary.

David: I find the comparison of Mary to the Ark to be problematic. You say that the comparison is made "explicit" in Revelation 11:19-12:1, but I don't find it. Rather, the ark appears (in 11:19), and the "woman" appears (in 12:1), and that's all; to make your point, one must both see the woman as Mary and also make the (big) step of equating the Ark and the Woman.

Dwight: Remember the chapter headings in the Scriptures were imposed by medieval scholars for the sake of convenience. When you read the verses straight through the text says, "Then God's temple in heaven was opened and within his temple was seen the ark of his covenant...a great and wondrous sign appeared in heaven: a woman clothed with the sun with the moon under her feet..." That Mary is the woman in this passage is an interpretation followed in the fourth century by Saint Ambrose, Saint Ephrem of Syria and Saint Augustine. Saint Athanasius, in the mid-fourth century, refers to Mary as the Ark with these words, "O noble

Virgin…who is your equal in greatness, O dwelling place of God the Word? To whom among all creatures shall I compare you, O Virgin?…O [Ark of the New Covenant] clothed with purity instead of gold! You are the Ark in which is found the golden vessel containing the true manna, that is, the flesh in which divinity resides."[5]

Discerning vs. inventing

David: Perhaps we can gain inspirational profit from a comparison such as Mary and the Ark, but are we discerning, or inventing? When we try to extend the comparison, it must break down at some point. For example, you observe that Mary carried the (incarnate) Word, as the Ark carried the (written) Word. In a sense that's right; but more specifically, the Ark carried the Law (Exodus 25:16, 34:28-29), whereas Mary carried, well, Grace. Even if the comparison is warranted, we can't necessarily learn more about Mary by studying the Ark.

Dwight: I accept that typology is a poetic form of interpretation, and it is easy to pick holes in it. To do so misses the point. Your literalism here is like a person who interprets the line from the poem by saying, "But we know that a young lady is not really like a red, red rose at all. A rose is a plant with thorns. A young lady is nothing like that." Typology expresses truth in a poetic way. It does not prove truth in a prosaic way. I'm picking nits here. My main point is that Mary does not just drop out of nowhere. She is an integral part of God's plan of redemption from the dawn of time. (Gal. 4:4.) As Saint Augustine said, "The New Testament is hidden in the Old and the Old Testament made manifest in the New." The Scriptures are a rich and intricate tapestry. The symbols and types of the Old Testament point to Jesus, but they also point to many other details in God's great drama of salvation. From them the Catholic Church from the earliest centuries has deduced the true role and function of the Lord's mother in God's plan for the human race. That role is humble and lowly, but it is also exalted and magnificent. This is why Catholics, along with Eastern Orthodox Christians, have always honored the Blessed Virgin and encourage other Christians to do the same.

2

God's Mother?

Holy Mary, Mother of God

Dwight: I can remember soon after I moved to England (and still a convinced Evangelical) hearing a German Catholic refer to Mary as *Mutter Gottes*. I don't know German and thought he was calling Mary "Mother Goddess". I was suitably horrified and not really surprised that this Catholic actually referred to Mary as the Mother Goddess. Only when I expressed my dismay did a friend explain that I had misunderstood. The German was using the term "Mother of God". I tell the story to make two points. First is the reminder of how easy it is to misunderstand the viewpoints of others. We often disagree with what we think they believe rather than what they really believe in the same way that I disagreed with what I thought the German said, rather than what he really said. This instant disagreement based on our honest misunderstanding can then stymie any further discussion. The second reason I relate the story is because it introduces the term "Mother of God." It was a term he used naturally, but which I still recoiled.

I was dismayed by the term "Mother of God", but I probably hadn't stopped to ask myself why. I suppose some Christians are dismayed by our use of the term "Mother of God" and imagine that we Catholics elevate Mary so much that we even think she was pre-existent to God the Father. This is not what Catholics believe. The logic for our use of the term is simple. Jesus was God in human flesh. Mary was his mother. Therefore Mary is termed "Mother of God." This term *theotokos* was affirmed at the Council of Ephesus in the year 431. The Council upheld the title as a way of defending the true nature of Jesus Christ the God-Man.

History and mystery

Dwight: In 431 the Council of Ephesus affirmed the title "Mother of God" or "God-bearer", but they didn't invent it. John the Baptist's mother Elizabeth calls Mary "Mother of My Lord" (Lk. 1:43) Furthermore, the theological term had already been in use for hundreds of years before the Council of Ephesus. For example, around the year 189 Irenaeus writes, "The Virgin Mary, being obedient to his word, received from an angel the glad tidings that she would *bear God*."[6] It's important to remember that Irenaeus knew Polycarp who had been instructed by the Apostle John, so this is a very early and important witness to the attitude of the early church to Mary. The teaching of the apostles was still echoing clearly in Irenaeus' day. He wouldn't have taught anything contrary to their teaching.

When the title the "Mother of God" was first formally affirmed by the church it was a bulwark to the right doctrine about Jesus. This is a very important point because we believe as Catholics that the correct understanding of Mary's role and identity continues to be a strong support for the proper understanding of Jesus' identity and role. If Mary is ignored or side-lined it is easy for Christians to treat Jesus as merely a good man. Graham Leonard has put it this way, "It is a fact of history that, if true honor is not paid to Mary as the Mother of God, people put Our Lord in her place as the highest of creation rather than adoring him as God Incarnate."[7] Isn't it sometimes the case that in popular Christianity we get so chummy with Jesus that we forget he is also the incarnate God? It is true that Jesus is our friend and brother, but it is also true that he is Lord and God. (John.20:28)

The mystery of Mary being the Mother of God is reflected in the mystery of every human birth. As we contemplate the mystery of conception, gestation and birth we are taken into the mystery of the incarnation in a fresh and profound way. We are not separate from our mothers. Instead our lives are intertwined with theirs. Our mothers make us who we are. In Jesus' case Mary contributed to his genetic make-up. She conceived, carried and bore him. She nursed, nurtured and loved him.

If we really believe that Jesus was the God-Man we believe that he was half-Mary. As the early Christians meditated on this truth they came to understand the true importance of Mary. She was an integral part of God's plan of salvation. So Hippolytus, around the year 217, writes, "To all generations they [the prophets] have pictured forth the grandest subjects for contemplation and for action. Thus, too, they preached of the advent of God in the flesh to the world, his advent by the spotless and God-bearing [*theotokos*] Mary in the way of birth and growth, and the manner of his life and conversation with men."[8]

Early Christians like Hippolytus came to see that Mary was an integral part of who Jesus is. It is true to say that we would not have Jesus without Mary. Because of this we want to challenge non-Catholics about their historic neglect of Mary. She is honored by the vast majority of Christians in both the Catholic and Orthodox traditions, and has been from the beginning of the Christian Church. Why do non-Catholics neglect Mary so much? Do you think it is simply part of the Protestant reaction against Catholicism, or is there a deeper reason?

David: I've already observed that, in my opinion, Evangelical neglect of Mary is an over-reaction to what we think of as Catholic excess, so that's my rather dull answer to your question.

Dwight: Rats. I was hoping for more of a scrap.

Back to Basics

David: Sorry to disappoint you. But *Theotokos* is indeed a good place to explore our very different attitudes since we agree, at least in large part, on doctrine, but diverge pretty seriously in application.

Let's get back to basics. Jesus is God. Evangelicals are emphatic about that. The so-called "Modernism" and "Liberalism" of our day are no better than the Arianism of centuries ago when they deny Jesus' deity. In contrast, Evangelicals affirm Jesus Christ to be true God and true Man. For that reason, Evangelical objections to *Theotokos* and "Mother of God" usually soften after a short discussion. We understand the syllogism: Mary is the Mother of Jesus; Jesus is God; therefore, Mary is the Mother of God—or, as Elizabeth said, "the Mother of my Lord" (Luke 1:43). Moreover, we learn that *Theo-tokos* is transliterated as "God-bearer" (with "bear"-ing here meaning not mere "carrying" but "bearing (a child)". Certainly it was God whom Mary bore, so we gladly affirm: Mary was indeed the "God-bearer".

There's a bit more to learn from the title *Theotokos*: It was not actually Arianism (denial of Jesus' deity) that the Council of Ephesus addressed with this title, but a later heresy, "Nestorianism"—the idea that Christ in effect contained two persons, God the Son and the human Jesus. Because the Incarnation is so mind-boggling, the "two-person" theory of Christ was a handy way to avoid some difficulties: "No, 'God' didn't die on the cross, since God can't die; rather, it must be that the human 'Jesus' part died." It's true that God can't die, and that we properly view Jesus as experiencing death in his human nature; but the Church perceived that splitting Christ into two persons effectively denied the Incarnation.

If Jesus Christ was not a single person (with divine and human natures), but instead was two persons (one human and one divine), then God the Son was not really born as a man, and did not die as a man; He only accompanied a man, and watched him die.

The Council of Ephesus rejected this error. As I understand it, the Council invoked Mary's title *Theotokos* to show that Christians had always known that whatever is true of Jesus is true of God. The child born of Mary was God. The victim on the cross of Calvary was God. The risen victor on Easter morning was God. And all the Evangelicals said: Amen.

Dwight: And all the Catholics too.

David: Still, when we hear the English phrase, "Mother of God", we Evangelicals pause. Why? I think there are three reasons, and I'll lead with the *least* important one.

Misgivings about "Mother of God"

David: First, the translation "*Mother* of God" prompts a question. As you well know, I'm no Greek scholar, but I have it on good authority that the ordinary Greek word for mother is not any form of -*tokos* but is *Meter*. The most direct way to say "Mother of God" in Greek is *Meter Theou*, and in fact we do see that Greek phrase (or its abbreviation) on Greek icons of Mary. If the early Christians, and the Council of Ephesus, called Mary *Theotokos* rather than *Meter Theou*, perhaps "God-bearer" *is* the better translation of *Theotokos*, and "Mother of God" may have connotations that weren't anticipated or intended by the earliest Christians.

Second, it is no insult to the Council of Ephesus to suggest that *Theotokos* should be used with some clarification. The Council's actual statement was that "the holy virgin is the mother of God (for she bore *in a fleshly way* the Word of God become flesh)". Likewise, when the Council of Chalcedon re-affirmed *Theotokos* twenty years later in 451, it called Mary "the virgin mother of God *as regards his humanity*".

Thus, both councils found it expedient to make it clear that Mary was the mother of Jesus' humanity, and of course was not (nor could be) the mother of His deity. Mary is, of course, a creature of God, not the mother of the Trinity, nor God the Father's wife by whom He eternally begot God the Son. It makes me feel a little creepy to state that, even for the purpose of denying it, but perhaps it's useful to be specific: As hard as it may be for Catholics to understand, the phrase "Mother of God" inspires that same creepy feeling in most Evangelicals. We wonder whether someone calling Mary the "Mother of God" thinks she must be "Mother of the Trinity", or "Wife of God the Father", or in some other way antecedent to God the Son. And then, when one hears Mary called "our heavenly Mother"[9] (which feels parallel to "our heavenly Father"), or reads references to Mary as the "Spouse of the Holy Spirit", those fears are aggravated.

Third, whatever its denotations, the *connotations* of the phrase "Mother of God" seem to us to be calculated to exalt Mary, at the expense of Christ. We prove that Mary was the Mother of God by that simple syllogism (Mary is the Mother of Jesus; Jesus is God; therefore, Mary is the Mother of God). Once we learn that logic, however, we could as well say that Anna and Joachim (Mary's parents) were the "*grandparents* of God", that John was the "*Baptizer* of God", that Herod was the "*King* of God". And all those statements are true in what they denote.

What they connote, however, is rather confusing. If we did use such statements, we would qualify and explain them. Such statements, however, are rare—except in the case of Mary as "Mother of God". The use of the unique title *Theotokos* is a selective honor peculiar to Mary, without analogue to any title for any other who bore any relation to Jesus as God. This presents us with a tension: The title "Mother of God" is defended (at least by contemporary Catholic apologists like yourself) as a Christological affirmation, but it seems actually to be used as an honorific to Mary.

Higher than the Cherubim

David: Just yesterday I read a portion of the Eastern Orthodox communion liturgy that reflects such honor being given to Mary.

You tell me if this would fit in Roman Catholic worship:

CHOIR:We praise Thee, we bless Thee, we give thanks to Thee, O Lord, and we pray unto Thee, O our God.

PRIEST:Especially for our Most-Holy, most pure, most Blessed and glorious Lady, the *Birth-giver of God* and Ever-Virgin Mary.

CHOIR:It is right, in truth, to glorify Thee, the Birth-giver of God, the ever-blessed, wholly immaculate, and the *Mother of our God*. More honorable than the Cherubim, and beyond compare more glorious than the Seraphim. Thou, Who without defilement gave birth to God the Word, true Birth-giver of God, we glorify Thee.

Dwight: This is a beautiful and ancient hymn to the Virgin Mary. However, I realize that a hymn like this cuts across the cultural grain of most Evangelicals.

David: That's putting it mildly.

Dwight: So be it; but similarly, a cradle Catholic or Greek Orthodox Christian might be taken aback were he plunged into a full blooded hell-fire and brimstone revival meeting. But if you read the hymn closely you'll see that it is properly addressed as praise to God, and only secondarily to Mary. It expresses the view that Mary was the highest and holiest of created beings. If Mary was who we believe she was, then this view follows logically.

At Ease

Dwight: We will talk more about these implications later: in the meantime let me take your points one by one. You suggest that "God-bearer" would be a clearer term than "Mother of God." But as you've said earlier, the idea of "God-bearer" does not so much mean "one who carries God" but "one who gives birth to God."

The one who "gives birth to God" has to be the "Mother of God" doesn't she?. That being the case, "Mother of God" is clearer than the somewhat ambiguous "God-bearer", isn't it?

Second, I grant you the point that the term "Mother of God" may be both culturally and theologically confusing for some Evangelicals. But you answer your own question when you say that the Councils of Ephesus and Chalcedon take trouble to clarify the term. The Church Fathers of the time also take care to clarify what they mean by the term in all their writings. Furthermore, Catholic teaching from that time onward has always been careful to express its meaning precisely and guard against distortions.

Third, you grumble that this is an honorific term for Mary. Why don't we honor Mary's parents as the "grandparents of God" or John the Baptist as "Baptizer of God"? We Catholics *do* honor the other good people who are close to Jesus. That's why we have feast days to celebrate the life of Saint Anne and Saint John the Baptist. (You'll understand that we don't have a special feast day to honor King Herod, though.)

Finally, you don't like terms like "our heavenly Mother" or "Spouse of the Holy Spirit". You find them "creepy". I accept that these terms are disagreeable and alien to the ordinary Evangelical. Its easy to misunderstand these terms (especially if you've been trained to have an anti-Catholic bias). It's a side issue, but does it occur to you that Catholics find certain Evangelical catch phrases distasteful and alien? When a fervent Evangelical asks a cradle Catholic, "Are you saved?", or "Have you heard of the Four Spiritual Laws?" or "Are you ready for the rapture?" the Catholic is dismayed and turned off. To him these extra-Biblical terms sound like the secret language of some creepy sect. This is not the religious terminology he uses. Much of this is simply a difference in religious culture and theological language. Instead of rejecting the terms we find disagreeable, and assuming that the other side must be in serious error, doesn't it make more sense to find out what the other side really mean by the terminology we find alien

Discovering what the other side believes might actually enrich both parties. "Spouse of the Holy Spirit" and "our heavenly Mother" (along with many other titles we use for Mary) follow logically from reflecting on who Mary is and how she co-operated with God. All of the terms are fully orthodox and most of them are rooted in Scripture. So when the Holy Spirit overshadowed Mary (Luke 1:35) there was a kind of mystical marriage. We believe Mary is our Mother, and she is in heaven, so we sometimes refer to her as "our heavenly Mother." (Rev. 12:17.)

These terms are part of the honor we ascribe to Mary. I think it's important to recognize that the honor paid to Mary was part of our devotional life *before* it was ratified formally at the Council of Ephesus in 431. So the term "Mother of God" was used in a devotional context before it was affirmed in a theological context. Apocryphal writings like *The Protoevangelium of James* were circulating from the middle of the second century. These were pious stories about Mary's birth and family life which were meant to inspire the faithful and nurture their love and respect for the Mother of Jesus. There are sacred paintings of Mary in the catacombs dating from the early second and third centuries. These indicate the Church's very early devotion to Mary. From the early fourth century we have the beautiful hymns of Saint Ephraem the Syrian which praise Mary the Mother of God, and from the same time period we have prayers asking the intercession and prayerful protection of Mary. The vast majority of the Church fathers of the first five centuries honor Mary in lovingly devotional terms.

A revolutionary rejection?

Dwight: The historical record shows that the early Christians honored Mary the Mother of Our Lord. The worship, prayers and devotions from that time are congruent with present-day Catholic theory and practice. We believe and pray as the early church did. You seem happy to accept the theological term "Mother of God" from the ancient church and yet you reject the devotional practices that those same Christians celebrated. Isn't that inconsistent?

David: Not at all. We'll take up those "devotional practices" in a later chapter; but as for the English phrase "Mother of God", I've explained my unease with it, and I've explained that I accept the early councils' theological term *Theotokos* because the councils qualified and explained its use. I am uneasy with today's use of the term because it comes with elaboration, rather than qualification, and because I do not hear any reassuring explanation accompanying its use in practice.

Dwight: Hold on. Catholics themselves agree that devotion to Mary can sometimes be distorted and excessive—a subject we'll address later[10]—but we're talking here simply about honoring Mary with the title *Theotokos*.

Try to look at it from the Catholic perspective: here is an ancient and venerable devotional practice loved and used by the vast majority of Christians around the world both now and for all ages. It is a practice that is in no way contrary to Scripture or orthodox Christian doctrine, yet a relatively small (but vocal) breakaway group grumbles about it and demands "correction". Although we listen patiently, I hope you'll see that many Catholics consider it a rather eccentric grumble similar to that of the Seventh Day Adventists who think that Sunday worship is a later innovation and insist that we all return to Saturday worship. I don't say this to dismiss your concerns, but to show you how it looks from the Catholic point of view.

In search of the Early Church

David: Part of your answer to my "grumble" about honor being paid to Mary is to say that these honors have been paid for many centuries. That is, you defend the disputed Marian attitudes and practices by invoking the beliefs and practices of the early Church— and the closer to the Apostles, the better. This is a good instinct, from the Evangelical point of view. The Church is indeed built on "the foundation of the apostles and prophets" (Ephesians 2:20), so we want to know what those foundational teachers taught. But if we do resort to the unquestionably ancient, authentic, apostolic, authoritative, divinely inspired Scriptures, we get no warrant for praise being given to Mary; we get only the silence that we observed before. Even the Woman in Revelation 12, whoever she is, does not receive any praise or honor from the hosts of heaven.

Dwight: I don't know. She sounds pretty glorified to me: She is clothed with the sun, has the moon beneath her feat and wears a crown of twelve stars on her head.

David: Let's assume (as you would assert) that not all the Apostles' teaching was committed to the canonical Scriptures, and that some of the genuine apostolic "traditions" were passed on orally (*see* John 20:30, 21:25; 2 Thessalonians 2:15). If that were true, and if the alleged teaching was well-attested, was early enough, and was widespread enough, then we might well justify Marian doctrine or devotion (in this case, using the title "Mother of God" as a deliberate honoring of Mary) by the example or teaching of the early Church— That is, we could presume that the early Christians were doing what the Apostles had taught orally. However, reconstructing apostolic-era practice doesn't really seem to be the Catholic method for regulating Marian devotion. Instead, the Roman Catholic Church is frank to admit that its understanding of Mary, and its devotional practices related to her, have evolved. Luigi Gambero, a Catholic writer, summarized it this way:

> During the first centuries, the Fathers and other Christian writers rarely speak of Mary apart from Christ.... As the centuries passed, especially from the second half of the fourth century on, the Fathers and other Christian writers began to pay more attention to Mary, although we must grant that the quantity of Marian literature produced in that period is fairly modest.... After the Councils of Ephesus (431) and Chalcedon (451), there is a sharp increase in the level of Marian doctrine and devotion.[11]

The Second Vatican Council said the same.[12] The Catholic Church does not attempt merely to replicate apostolic-era teaching and practice about Mary; rather, it consciously *builds* on them.

Dwight: Gambero recognizes the subordinate role of Mary in the early church, but he also makes clear, that "faith, devotion, and interest in the ineffable mystery of the Mother of the Lord were never lacking among the people of God, even though the manifestations and expressions of faith and doctrine may vary in different historical periods."[13] I agree that the Catholic understanding of Mary's role and identity has developed and matured over the years, but the same can be said of many aspects of Christian practice and theology. I don't mean to skirt the issue, but this is a very important point and I think we ought to give it more time later.

Keeping Christ first

David: Good idea. My essential point, however, is not and must not be merely to stifle praise to Mary. No one was ever brought near to God just by *not* glorifying Mary. The reason we care about paying her honor is that we are concerned that it may detract from the honor due to God alone, particularly as revealed in Jesus Christ, God the Son. The Evangelical's point must be that Christ is to be glorified, and that "in everything" He must "have the supremacy" (Col. 1:18). Any means genuinely well ordered to that end can be employed; any means inimical to it must be set aside.

Dwight: Catholics would agree with you. That's why from the beginning the Catholic Church has always been careful to establish the right teaching about Mary and to moderate the devotion paid to her. So around the year 400 Saint Epiphanius writes, "Let Mary be held in honor. Let the Father, Son, and Holy Ghost be adored, but let no one adore Mary"[14] This shows two things: first that a fervent devotion to Mary was part of Christian practice *before* the Council of Ephesus (else why would Epiphanius warn against its excess?). Second, it shows that from the early centuries of the church, this devotion to Mary was accompanied by clarification and control against distortion and excess.

The terminology employed is quite precise. The Greek words *latria, dulia,* and *hyperdulia* are used to distinguish the different types of adoration or honor in Christian worship. *Latria* is that adoration and worship due to God alone. *Dulia* is the honor due to great people. In the Christian context it is the proper honor paid to the saints and martyrs. (Rev. 14:1-5) Finally, *hyperdulia* is that special honor due to Mary as the highest and holiest of God's creatures. These terms express the clear distinction between the honor we pay to Mary, the saints and the angels and our total adoration and worship of God.

David: I understand these three categories as a logical, academic matter. What concerns me is the practical difference—or lack of difference—among these categories, in the actual devotional lives of individual Christians.

Dwight: It's difficult for an outside observer to make this judgment, isn't it? What might look like divine worship to you may actually be a proper form of lesser devotion.

David: Judging another individual's subjective interior experience is not just difficult but impossible (and is not our job), whereas we can form judgments about what a church objectively teaches and encourages. You can take another shot at this *latria-dulia* distinction in our later chapter on veneration.

"Blessed are you!"

Dwight: I'll do my best. In the meantime let me pick you up on another point. You are fond of claiming that the Bible does not show honor to Mary as Mother of God, but this is precisely how Mary is welcomed by Elizabeth when Mary goes to visit. When she sees Mary, Elizabeth exclaims, 'Blessed are you among women, and blessed is the child you will bear! But why am I so favored that the mother of my Lord should come to me?" (Luke 1:42-43) For Elizabeth—a good Jewish woman— "her Lord" was none other than God himself. Thus, when she calls Mary "Mother of My Lord" she is not only recognizing the unborn Jesus as "her Lord" but also honoring Mary with the title "Mother of God".

When we Catholics honor Mary under the title "Mother of God" we are expressing that same wonder and joy at the miracle of the Incarnation. Like Elizabeth, in Mary and her Child we recognize and rejoice in the mystery of Mary Mother of God. The Madonna and Child give us a beautiful picture of the reality of the incarnation, but we also have an excellent image of the relationship God wants to have with each of us. As a mother and child are interdependent in love, so we are called to an intimate union with the Father.

David: Elizabeth, as an example of honoring Mary, is interesting and helpful, though we must ask whether the contemporary Christian believer who has never confronted Mary in person is to be compared to Elizabeth, who did. After all, if *my* mother entered your house, I know you would honor her (though with something less than *dulia*); but I wouldn't expect such honor to be paid to her by someone who never met her. And Biblically speaking, the "image of the relationship that God wants to have with each of us" is not the Madonna and Child but the marital union of Christ and His Bride, the Church.

Dwight: Yes, this is the predominant image of the divine and human unity that God wills for us, but the image of Mother and child is not alien to Scripture. Psalm 131 speaks of our relationship with God in terms of the intimate bond between Mother and child, so does Isaiah 66:13 and Luke 13:34. Nevertheless, I'll concede that in Catholic customs the image of Madonna and Child has been used far more than the image of the Bride of Christ. This is probably because of the immediately accessible nature of the Mother and child image. Ordinary people were attracted to the Madonna and child as an image of that creative love which lies at the heart of our faith.

David: I can join with Elizabeth in confessing that Mary is "blessed ... among women", and "Mother of her Lord" so I can admit that some measure of attention to Mary can redound to the glory of Jesus Christ. I don't see how this can fairly be denied. In future chapters we may see the extent to which we disagree on just how much Marian[15] attention is well-ordered to that end. Before that, though, we have a little more agreeing to do, on the one cardinal doctrine as to which Mary is front and center, and which unquestionably redounds to His glory: the Virgin Birth of Jesus Christ.

3

All in Favor

The Virgin Birth

David: Several years ago, there was a TV talk-show program entitled, *Surprise! I'm a Virgin and I Want You to be my First.* The show was *not* about brides and grooms and wedding nights. Instead, it was about teenagers who were deciding that they had delayed sex for long enough, and that the fun should now begin. While the mindset on display there does assign a sort of value to virginity, it is a distorted value—not more than a consumer value, with sex as a recreation and virginity as a sort of novelty or bonus. If virginity is outside of that context, this mindset sees virginity as a deprivation, or as prudery.

Christianity assigns a real, positive value—to virginity. Virginity involves purity, wholesomeness, wisdom, innocence, health, obedience, restraint, perseverance, patience, trust, and loyalty. And for Christians, when we speak of "*the* Virgin", we are of course speaking of Mary of Nazareth, whose virginity embodied all these virtues.

Dwight: I'm glad to hear you say that, because I think some Christians regard Mary's virginity as simply the biological fact that she had never had sexual intercourse. Mere sexual abstinence, however, doesn't necessarily imply holiness.

The popular definition of virginity is a negative definition: A virgin is someone who has *not* done something. Catholics see Mary's virginity as a positive character trait. So "virgin" implies not only an unspoiled sexuality, but an unspoiled character. On the positive side "virgin" indicates a natural wholeness and goodness not only physically, but mentally and spiritually too. The early church writers are unanimous in seeing Mary's virginity as a character trait as well as a biological condition. Saint Ambrose in the middle of the fourth century expressed the attitude of the early church in a long passage picturing the character of the Virgin Mary. He summed up by saying, "she was a virgin, not only in body but in her mind as well, and never mixed the sincerity of her affections with duplicity."[16]

The Scriptural basis

David: Mary's virtuous character certainly does shine brightly through Luke's account. However, giving to Mary the title "*the* Virgin" may be more remarkable than we sometimes realize. We are well accustomed to the idea that Mary is "the Virgin", but there is in fact another virgin so much more important to our faith—the Lord Jesus Himself.

Nevertheless, we think of "*the* Virgin" as referring not to Jesus, but to His mother Mary. Why? I think the reason is this: Mary's virginity was emphatically given to us by God as "a sign". The prophet Isaiah had written, "The Lord Himself will give you *a sign*: the virgin will be with child and will give birth to a son, and will call him Immanuel", which means *God with us*. (Isaiah 7:14.) The Gospel of Matthew tells us that this prophecy was fulfilled in Mary's virginal conception of Jesus.

Matthew's Gospel begins with the genealogy of Jesus through his legal father, Joseph; but when the list comes to its climax, it does *not* follow its set pattern and conclude with "Joseph the father of Jesus" but, instead, concludes with "Joseph, the husband of Mary, of whom was born Jesus, who is called Christ". (Matt. 1:16.) Matthew 1:18-24 then tells the story of Jesus' conception from the point of view of Joseph, the "righteous man" who learned the disturbing news that his fiancé was pregnant. While he was considering what to do about Mary's apparent immorality, "an angel of the Lord appeared to him in a dream and said, 'Joseph son of David, do not be afraid to take Mary home as your wife, because what is conceived in her is from the Holy Spirit.'"

Mary's point of view is presented in great detail in the event we call "the Annunciation", in the Gospel of Luke (2:2638). Providence thus assigned a doctor (Col. 4:14) to inform us of the Virgin Birth. Since Luke says that he "carefully investigated" the facts that he had learned from eyewitnesses" (Luke 1:2-3), we think he probably learned the story from Mary herself: The angel Gabriel appeared to Mary and told her, "You will be with child and give birth to a son", the Messiah. Mary asked, "How will this be, since I am a virgin?" Gabriel explained, "The Holy Spirit will come upon you, and the power of the Most High will overshadow you. So the holy one to be born will be called the Son of God." Mary responded with her decisive "Let it be unto me according to your word." Thereafter, Luke says that Jesus "was the son, *so it was thought*, of Joseph." (Luke 3:23.) But in truth He was "Mary's son" (Mark 6:3; John 6:42).

Matthew and Luke's clear teaching of Mary's miraculous, virginal conception of Jesus sheds light on other Bible passages also relevant to the doctrine of the Virgin Birth: The Savior that God promised to fallen Adam and Eve in Eden is called there "the offspring *of the woman*" (Genesis 3:15). Paul says that "God sent His Son, *born of a woman*," and he likens Christians to Abraham's son Isaac, "the son born by the power of the Spirit". (Gal. 4:4, 4:29.) In the prologue to John's Gospel, Jesus is the champion and forerunner of "children [of God] born not of natural descent, nor of human decision or a husband's will, but born of God." (John 1:13.)

The doctrinal significance

David: If someone asks an Evangelical, "Why do you believe Jesus had a 'Virgin Birth'?" his first answer is likely to be, "Because the Bible says so", in light of the Biblical teaching set out here. However, we *do* have a little more to say on the subject. Without being hostile to the Bible, one could still ask, "Why does the Virgin Birth matter?—couldn't God have used a virtuous *married* woman to bear His Son?" Another way of asking that question is: "Of what is the Virgin Birth 'a sign'"? In answering that question, may I cite your 1994 catechism, *The Catechism of the Catholic Church*? or, for an Evangelical, would that be cheating?

Dwight: What's a good Evangelical man like you doing reading the Catechism of the Catholic Church? Not going soft on us, are you?

David: Never! But the Catechism is a very good resource, and I consult it often. It's useful not only to find out the distinctive Roman Catholic position on controversial issues but also to find out the agreed, historic Christian position on undisputed issues. It is loaded with footnotes that give useful citations to Scriptural and extra-Scriptural support for its assertions. It has numerous excellent indices in the back. If your home theological library is going to have as few as ten books in it, the Catechism of the Catholic Church should probably be one of them.

Dwight: Thanks for the commercial break.

David: Don't mention it. Where was I? Oh, yes—The Virgin Birth is a sign, as your Catechism well says, of "God's absolute initiative in the Incarnation." (CCC, 503.) The Virgin Birth assures us radically that Christ's advent was God's doing. The Virgin Birth is also a sign that, in Christ as the "New Adam", God is "iinaugurating the new creation." (CCC, 504; 1 Cor. 15:4550). It is also a sign that, despite Eve's being the first to fall,

God would particularly use "the woman" to bear the Redeemer. (*Cf.* 1 Timothy 2:1415.)

Dwight: The Virgin Birth is also a sign of our own ultimate destiny isn't it? You quoted the prologue to John's Gospel, which bears this out. If a sign is a pointer, then when Christ is born of a Virgin, He points the way for all those who will be born "not of natural descent, nor of human decision or a husband's will, but born of God." (John 1:13.) By doing this he opens the way for us to be born again of "water and the Spirit." (John 3:5) If this happens, then we really are the children of God (I John 3:1) and co-heirs with Christ (Rom. 8:15-17).

David: Exactly.

Dwight: Can we take this further?—In order to be born again of the Holy Spirit in a similar way to Christ's birth, then we too need to have a Virgin Mother. We will discuss this in more detail later, but this is why we see Mary as a type of the Church, because the Church is our Virgin Mother. She stands for that "glorious Church without spot or wrinkle" (Eph. 5:27) which brings us to new birth, and nurtures us spiritually. As Cyprian of Carthage wrote in the third century, "He cannot have God for his father who has not the Church as his mother."[17] How does Cyprian's aphorism sound to Evangelical ears?

David: Well, the Church is indeed a virgin, but she is presented in Ephesians 5 as a virgin *bride*, and in the New Testament the believer is described as a *member* of that bride, not a daughter of her. On the other hand, the imagery of a Christian as a child of the Church is perhaps suggested in Paul's striking words to his converts that he was "again in the pains of childbirth until Christ is formed in you" (Gal. 4:19), so perhaps the metaphor has some Biblical warrant. But I sense that there may be ecclesiological issues looming here that are too big to address in the context of the Virgin Birth.

Dwight: We'll tiptoe around that minefield, shall we?

Avoiding original sin

David: Let's keep it for the sequel. While the Virgin Birth was a sign, it may also have been a spiritual necessity, if humanity was to be saved. Even though our mother Eve was the first of our first parents who disobeyed (Gen. 3:6; 1 Tim. 2:14), it is because of the sin of our father Adam, and through him, that our race inherited the curse of sin. (Rom. 5:1219; 1 Cor. 15:2122.)

We do not understand enough about theology or even anthropology to elaborate or be dogmatic, but we do infer that sin is somehow transmitted from *father* to child, and not from mother to child.[18] In the case of Jesus, this deadly transmission of "original sin" from a fallen father was forestalled by His virginal conception. His only Father was the all-holy God. Consequently, unlike us, Jesus could say that Satan "has no hold on me" (John 14:30).

Dwight: I think the Virgin Birth *was* a spiritual necessity if we were to be saved. That's why I am so keen to get down to a deeper vision of what Mary's virginity is all about. I'm not at all denying the importance of Mary's physical virginity, but I'm even more interested in Mary's whole character. You asked why God chose to become incarnate of the Virgin Mary and not from a godly married woman. We agree don't we, that God chose a girl who was virginal in body, mind, and spirit because that woman was going to be the source for his Son's human nature?

The Apostles' Creed is one of the most terse statements of cardinal Christian doctrine, and yet it makes space to affirm that Jesus Christ "was conceived by the power of the Holy Spirit, and born of the Virgin Mary". Likewise, the Nicene Creed affirms that "by the power of the Holy Spirit he was born of the Virgin Mary, and was made man." During the controversy over just who Jesus was, the theologians were willing to battle over prepositions. The Creed, like the New Testament (Gal. 4:4), says that Jesus was born "of" a woman and not just "through" a woman. This was a vital distinction because certain heretics were saying that Jesus only seemed to be a man, and that God simply used the Virgin Mary as a channel for his Son to come into the world.

So in the third century Origen writes, "Therefore it is wise to accept the meaning of Scripture and not to pay attention to those who say that [Jesus] was born through Mary, not of her... Observe that he [the apostle Paul] did not say 'born *through* a woman, but rather 'born *of* a woman.'"[19] In the middle of the fourth century, Cyril of Jerusalem says of Jesus, "He was made man, not in appearance only or as a phantasm, but in a real way. He did not pass through the Virgin, as if through a channel; rather he truly took flesh from her and by her was truly nursed, really eating and really drinking just as we do." Then he makes the vital point: "For if the Incarnation were a mere appearance, such would be our redemption as well."[20]

Extraordinary purity

Dwight: Cyril states the absolutely crucial truth, which you suggested, that for our redemption is to be real, the Incarnation had to be real, and for the Incarnation to be real Jesus had to have taken human flesh from his mother. If this is true—that Jesus took his sinless human nature from his mother—then it follows that his mother could not be just any good married woman. In such a case it would have been assumed that the child was conceived in a natural way, and the birth would not be a "sign". If Jesus took his human nature from Mary, then she could also not be just any ordinary young girl who had not yet had sexual intercourse. If Jesus took his human nature from his mother, then Jesus was half Mary. If Jesus' human nature was from Mary, then her virginity had to be of an extraordinary kind didn't it? In fact, not only did her purity have to be extraordinary, it had to be unique in human history. Do you agree with this, or am I starting to take the logic too far for your liking?

David: I wouldn't say your position takes "logic" too far; I'd say it takes speculation too far. Yes, as you say, Jesus certainly was born "of" Mary rather than merely "through" her; He really took on human nature from a human mother. As the Athanasian Creed puts it, Jesus Christ is "Man, of the Substance of his Mother." However, we are and must be ignorant of the spiritual and physical mysteries involved in the Incarnation. Whether Jesus' sacred humanity, conceived by the Holy Spirit without a human father, *also* required a mother of a particular degree of holiness, only God knows. It has not been revealed to us.

Here we approach one of the problems of debating about Mary. When the Catholic speaks in loving and superlative terms about the virtue of our Lord's mother, the task of demurring becomes very delicate. Who would denigrate her?—not me. But the question you put is—Do I agree that Mary's purity had to be unique in human history, in order for her to be the mother of the Incarnate God?—and if I must answer that question, then I must say that it would be pious speculation to say yes.

Dwight: Hold on a moment. I hear what you're saying about our "loving and superlative terms" and "pious speculation". It sounds a bit condescending to me. I admit we speak glowingly of Mary (who doesn't love and speak well of their mother?), but in this context I was being the prosaic, theological one. I wasn't using poetic, superlative language about the Blessed Virgin. I was simply laying out the logic: Jesus was the sinless Son of God. He took his sinless human nature from his mother. For that human nature to be really human and really sinless its human source must have been uniquely pure. This seems to be a simple, logical and modest claim.

David: If I sounded condescending, it's because I didn't express myself well. I was actually just trying to be diplomatic, while undertaking the delicate task of suggesting—since you asked—that Mary might not be as supernaturally high and holy as

Catholics describe her to be. I actually had in mind an observation C.S. Lewis made in *Mere Christianity*, to the effect that "there is no controversy between Christians which needs to be so delicately touched as this. The Roman Catholic beliefs on that subject [Mary] are held ... with the peculiar and, as it were, chivalrous sensibility that a man feels when the honor of his mother or his beloved is at stake."[21]

I want to be polite, but I really do want to answer the question honestly and candidly. No, I don't think one can say that in order for Jesus' humanity to be pure, its "source" (His mother) had to be uniquely pure. Rather, the Incarnation and Virgin Birth was a miracle involving the direct intervention of the Holy Spirit of God. We simply don't know the boundaries or the mechanisms of that miracle. Your reasoning here is something like trying to infer Neanderthal politics from old pottery shards; we just don't know enough to make the necessary extrapolations. There's too much speculation in the project.

Dwight: You wish to avoid "speculation", but it was this same sort of logical speculation (otherwise called deduction) by which the church worked out the intricacies of the doctrine of the Incarnation and the Trinity. If the church had kept to your limitations and mode of operation those doctrines would not have been developed and defined.

David: I have to disagree with you. You're opening up the question of the so-called "development of doctrine", which we will address head-on later. For now let me say just this much: Unlike the Marian ideas that I here call "speculation", the doctrine of the Trinity and the Christological doctrines associated with the Incarnation are derived directly from, and are provable from, authentically apostolic sources—the Scriptures. I don't object to doctrinal inferences being drawn from the apostles' teaching; I do object when the apostolic basis for a proposed doctrine is flimsy or absent.

My point here is this: For all we know, the conception of Jesus by the Holy Spirit without a human father was enough to ensure the sanctity of His sacred humanity. For all we know, Jesus' holiness did not depend on the holiness of His mother. It is no insult to Mary to say that *no* human mother could possibly have been *worthy* to bear the Incarnate God; no matter how excellent Mary's virtues were, it was an indescribable, unfathomable condescension for God the Son to enter Mary's womb and thereby "make Himself nothing, taking the very nature of a servant". (Philippians 2:7.)

Here's an analogy: We know it would be a great fallacy to try to infer facts about Jesus' birthplace by trying to imagine what sort of a palace would be fitting for such a birth. If someone had studied the Ark of the Covenant (the box in which the written Word was laid), and considered the Ark to be a "type", he might have made grandiose suppositions about the cradle of the Messiah— the box in which the Incarnate Word would be laid. But in fact, God chose a manger in a stable, defying what anyone would have predicted. By the same token, we may err just as wildly if we try to infer facts about Mary's nature by trying to imagine what sort of a mother would be fitting for such a birth. He chose someone not fitting, since none could be fitting. God chose to do, in the Person of Christ, that which, by human reason, was *not* fitting but was instead a scandal. (1 Cor. 1:23.) I think we cannot know how to quantify the holiness of Mary.

Dwight: And I think you're sidestepping the logic because you don't like where it leads. But let's leave it there for now. I'll come back to annoy you with it later!

Evidence from tradition

Dwight: I do agree with you that we mustn't speculate on our own about the details. But the subject of Mary's special purity was not all ungrounded speculation. In the early church, in addition to the New Testament writings, there were other oral and written traditions about the events surrounding the life of Jesus. Saint Paul mentions certain apostolic oral traditions, (2 Thess. 2:15) and Saint John refers to extra Biblical oral traditions when he says, "Jesus did many other things as well. If every one of them were written down I suppose that even the whole world would not have room for the books that would be written." (John 21:25.)

David: The only "traditions" that Paul sanctions are "the teachings [or "traditions"] that we [the Apostles] passed on to you, whether by word of mouth or by letter." (2 Thess. 2:15.) The oral teaching *of the Apostles* was tradition to be held to firmly, because it was "the word of God" (1 Thess. 2:13).

Dwight: One of the early traditions about Mary's life and family background was thought to have originated with the Church in Jerusalem. These stories were written down in the early to mid second century. (Remember this is only about fifty or sixty years after the death of the apostle John.) These stories about Mary were gathered together in an attempt to support the doctrine of the Virgin Birth.

This document is called *The Protoevangelium of James* because the apostle James was thought to be the main apostolic source.

David: More precisely, it was called "of James" because of its stated claim that "I James ... wrote this history in Jerusalem". Well, James didn't write it, as everyone pretty much agrees now; and the people who thought he did were mistaken. The writer attempted to bolster his book with James's reputation, but it was a fraudulent attempt. But I interrupted, and you were saying?—

Dwight: Yes, the literal attribution to James was added as a post-script to bolster the book's credentials. (Remember the book's credentials were being bolstered for a good reason—to defend the virgin birth.) Nevertheless, the book was not written by James, but the scholars do say that it was compiled from earlier oral and written sources, which may very well have originated from the church of Jerusalem of which James was the leader. The book is clearly a conflation of different stories, and some segments seem more reliable and ancient than others. There were other "apocryphal gospels" in the early centuries of the church, but unlike the *Protoevangelium* they are later, sometimes weird, and often heretical.

The *Protoevangelium of James,* on the other hand, is totally orthodox. We are told about the circumstances of Mary's birth and early life. Her parents were called Joachim and Anna. They were infertile and prayed for a child whom they then promised to God. According to the *Protoevangelium,* Anna conceived miraculously (but naturally) like Sarah, Hannah, and Samson's mother in the Old Testament. Her parents dedicated Mary for service in the temple at the age of three, and she served there as the boy Samuel did. (1 Sam. 1-2.) There may have been an order of "temple virgins" who were like young nuns or girls in a convent school. The story of Jephthah's daughter (Judges 11:29-39) suggests that a Jewish girl (like a Jewish boy) could be offered to serve in God's house as a virgin for life. (Some people think Jepthah killed his daughter after promising her as a burnt offering, but it's interesting to note that Jephthah's daughter and her friends lamented the fact that she would never marry—not the fact that she was going to be brutally sacrificed.)

The story of Simeon and the widow Anna (Luke 2:25-38) indicates that there was a kind of religious community in the temple during the time of Christ. Did Simeon and Anna recognize the Christ child because they already knew his mother? Had they been Mary's guardians during her childhood days serving in the temple?

Now this *is* speculation, and I don't offer it as gospel truth; nor do I suggest that the *Protoevangelium of James* is on a level with Scripture. I bring it up for two reasons. First, the basic story of Mary's childhood in the *Protoevangelium* rings true. It is a very ancient account based on older oral and written traditions. The story is congruent with the Old Testament and fits in with what we know of the gospel account.

More importantly, however, I am introducing this ancient documentary evidence to explain why the first Christians regarded Mary more highly than we might from the Gospel record alone. From the very earliest times the followers of Jesus understood that His saving work began with God's grace active in Mary's life. At a time before the canon of the New Testament was established, *The Protoevangelium of James* was read as Scripture. As a result, the early Christians believed Mary's own birth was miraculous. Her virginity was more than simply the fact that she was an unmarried young woman.

The early Christians believed Mary had been dedicated to God by her parents, and that she served as a dedicated virgin in the temple. I'm introducing *The Protoevangelium of James* not as an extra gospel, but because it is an important ancient document which shows us what the early Christians thought about Mary. It therefore influenced the whole development of the Church's understanding of Mary, and as a result it still colors our discussions today. Do you agree that this tradition needs to be dealt with?

"Test everything"

David: Your artful description—"some segments seem more reliable and ancient than others"—sounds like a euphemism. Put plainly, does the *Protoevangelium* feel to you like a mixed bag—some of it maybe true, and some of it baloney? I skimmed it, and that's how it struck me.

Dwight: Some parts strike me as baloney, but much of it rings true. That's why I want to de-emphasize the *Protoevangelium* on the one hand, but on the other I want to sniff out what might be authentic about it. The difficulty of the extra writings is nothing new. In the third century Origen wrote about the problem, "We must therefore use caution in accepting all these secret writings that circulate under the name of saints... because some of them were written to destroy the truth of our Scripture and to impose a false teaching. On the other hand, we should not totally reject writings that might be useful in shedding light on the Scripture. It is a sign of a great man to hear and carry out the advice of Scripture: 'Test everything; retain what is good.' (I Thess. 5:21)"[22]

David: Even so, the *Protoevangelium of James* is hardly the stuff on which to base firm conclusions (much less dogma), even if some early Christians did (as you say) "read it as Scripture". (If they did so, they erred, according to the later Church Councils that defined the real canon of Scripture.) But you're an honest apologist, so when push comes to shove, you say no more than is really justified—*i.e.*, that this book shows how Christian people may have felt and thought about Mary about a hundred years after she died.

Dwight: Whoops. I am actually saying more than that. I'm saying their opinions were based on a second century document which scholars tell us was based on earlier oral and written traditions from the Jerusalem area. This book was written when there were people still alive who may have known Mary, certainly there were people alive who were only one generation removed from the characters in the story. While the book isn't Scripture, and we don't want to base dogma on it, nevertheless, it gives us credible details about Mary's character and family background. As Origen says, it sheds light on Scripture.

David: But why do you need to use it? If the question is, "Was Mary a remarkable, very good woman?", we can confidently answer yes, based on the reliable, authentic Scriptures: Mary "found favor with God" (Luke 1:30), as had previous heroes of the faith like King David (Acts 7:46) and Noah (Gen. 6:8-9). In a crisis, Mary responded quickly with complete obedience (Luke 1:38) and with faith (Luke 1:45). Undistracted by a stupendous privilege given to her, she gives the glory to God and maintains her humility. (Luke 1:46-55.) Her words about her son at the wedding in Cana form an excellent motto that would surely be Mary's message to all of us: "Do whatever He tells you". (John 2:5.) About Mary's character we need go no further—and we *cannot* go much further without speculating or borrowing the speculation of another.

Common ground

David: We will surely pick up again later this issue of Mary's holiness, when we consider the doctrine of Mary's Immaculate Conception, but for now I'd like to return to the common ground. I read once a phrase that, to my mind, combines truths we agree on regarding *Theotokos* and the Virgin Birth: Jesus was without father in His humanity, without mother in His deity. We firmly agree that Jesus was born of a Virgin, by the power of the Holy Spirit.

Dwight: I think we've actually agreed on more than that. We've agreed that Mary's virginity was not just a negative biological condition. We've agreed that Mary was a virgin in character. In other words, she was wholesome, natural and full of faith and goodness. I've suggested that this goodness was also a spiritual quality that was trained and dedicated to God in a formal way. I think our agreement is going to start straining as I go on, but I don't think it needs to. What we believe is not as far out as you may imagine, so let me go on to explain why we think Mary's virginal goodness and wholesomeness extended for her entire life.

Our Lady? : A Catholic/Evangelical Debate

4

Once a Virgin, Always a Virgin?

The Perpetual Virginity of Mary

Dwight: One of the interesting things about our meeting again after a twenty-year gap, was how little either of us had really changed. I don't know about you, but, apart from the waistline and hairline, I found myself talking to the same guy I'd remembered all those years before. It interests me how much anybody's character changes or stays the same. On the one hand I am who I have always been and you are who you have always been. It is written not only in our genetic code, but in the greater code set before the dawn of time. However, while our essential personalities remain, they don't stay the same. If we are continually alive to God's grace, then our essential self can continue to mature and grow to the full statue of God in Christ Jesus. (Eph. 4:13.)

As I said in the previous chapter, when the early Christians used the title "Virgin" for the Mother of Jesus they did not simply mean that she was sexually inexperienced. Instead the title "Virgin" was a sign of Mary's essential character. She was virginal not only in body, but also in mind and spirit as well. (I Cor. 7:34.) Now this essential character trait didn't just disappear. By God's grace, Mary's character matured and grew. She too had to grow up into the full stature of God in Christ Jesus. So her essential virginity became a mature kind of purity. She went from being an innocent young girl of a virgin to be a venerable, pure, and holy matron. From the very earliest times therefore, Mary's virginity (which was a physical sign of her spiritual character) was assumed to have continued until her death. This is what we Catholics refer to as the perpetual virginity of the Blessed Virgin Mary.

A Christian consensus

Dwight: To show what the early Christians believed about this, consider the whole point of *The Protoevangelium of James*. It was written about fifty or sixty years after the death of the last apostle, and it says Mary was subject to a religious vow of virginity, and that Joseph was an elderly widower assigned to be her guardian. As patristics scholar Johannes Quasten says of *The Protoevangelium:* "The principal aim of the whole writing is to prove the perpetual and inviolate virginity of Mary before, in, and after the birth of Christ."[23] This belief appears very early in the Church: "When it comes to the mystery of Mary's perpetual virginity, Origen (c.253) not only has no doubts but seems directly to imply that this is a truth already recognized as an integral part of the deposit of faith."[24] Origen taught, "There is no child of Mary except Jesus, according to the opinion of those who think correctly about her."[25]

We Catholics defend this belief in solidarity not only with the whole of the early church, but also with virtually the whole of orthodox Christendom down through the ages. The Perpetual Virginity of Mary is a beautiful and fitting belief upheld by the Eastern Orthodox as well as many Anglicans and Lutherans. Furthermore, it was defended not only by the ancient Church fathers, but by Luther, Zwingli, Calvin and the classic Anglican theologians.[26] John Wesley also believed in the perpetual virginity of Mary writing, "I believe he [Jesus Christ] was born of the blessed Virgin, who, as well after as she brought him forth, continued a pure and unspotted virgin."[27]

Catholics therefore find it odd when Protestants deny a belief that the founders of Protestantism held firmly. Furthermore, we don't understand the point of denying the perpetual virginity of Mary, a belief that in no way contradicts Scripture or orthodox doctrine. The continued virginity and holiness of Mary up to her death does not distract from the saving work of Christ in any way. Denial of the perpetual virginity of Mary only denigrates Mary. Is there any virtue in this denial? In what way is it a positive thing? All we can conclude is that some Evangelicals dispute this point simply because they think it is "Catholic" and they have to knock it over for that reason alone. Is that it? Surely not.

David: No, I wouldn't say that arguing for Mary's perpetual virginity necessarily distracts from Christ's work. As I'll explain in due course, our principal objections are that the doctrine denigrates sex and marriage, and impugns Christ's humanity. But to take last things first: You ask how Evangelicals explain their failure to follow Protestant luminaries like Luther and Calvin in affirming Mary's perpetual virginity. This is a question that an Evangelical might not even think to ask. By and large, most Evangelicals knowingly disagree with both these theologians on a wide range of important issues—baptism, eschatology, ecclesiology, predestination, free will, etc. Luther and Calvin were no less fallible than any other theologian, and we submit their opinions to the same Biblical scrutiny to which we submit Catholic dogma.

Dwight: Wow! The ease with which you dismiss fifteen hundred years of virtually unanimous Church teaching is breathtaking. So the modern Evangelical waves his hand and says with a straight face, "You see, everybody (including our own founding fathers) had it wrong for the first fifteen hundred years…" And this from the folks who accuse Catholics of altering the historic faith with later distortions!

David: Catch your breath! You overstate things a bit to attribute belief in Mary's perpetual virginity to "everybody" in the early Christian centuries. No less formidable a Christian than Tertullian (d. 220) taught that Mary bore other children (by Joseph) after Jesus' birth.[28]

Dwight: Tertullian's is the only voice from the early church that suggests such a thing.

David: I admit that by the close of the fourth century, the consensus is clearly in favor of the perpetual virginity. However, as instructive as it is to know what Luther, Calvin, Origen, and Tertullian thought about this subject, the critical question is whether we have any Apostolic teaching on the point. A post-Apostolic novelty is a distortion, whether it originated in the sixteenth century or the second. So, no, to learn that Mary's alleged perpetual virginity is another issue on which we disagree with Luther and Calvin is not a great shock.

The holiness of marriage

David: I paused in writing that previous sentence. I hesitated over the phrase "Mary's *alleged* perpetual virginity" for fear that the word "alleged" would sound like sneering. As I write this, I wonder how seriously I am offending Catholics to say that I presume Mary had sex with her husband Joseph after Jesus' birth. My impression is that Catholics wince at such talk. However, I need to be frank, since being too overly delicate on the subject may be tantamount to conceding that there would be some shame or unholiness to Mary's having sex *with her husband.* On the contrary, for Mary (or any other wife) to have sex with her husband would, of course, be shameless and holy, and pleasing to God. I therefore reject the whispering, tip-toeing approach, and resolve to address this question directly and cheerfully: The question is whether Mary had sex *with her husband,* or instead remained celibate, even though she was married.

Dwight: Yes, that is the question, but while we Catholics treat such a delicate subject with respect and decorum, we do not treat sex with the hush-hush embarrassment you imply. We acknowledge that sexual relations between husband and wife are normal and good, but we also say that when celibacy is dedicated to God, that is also a good thing.

David: Paul did teach that it can be *good* to remain single (1 Cor. 7:1, 26); that celibacy can liberate someone to "be concerned about the Lord's affairs—how he can please the Lord" (7:32); that the virgin has a special opportunity to "be devoted to the Lord in both body and spirit ... in undivided devotion to the Lord" (7:3435); and that celibacy is a "gift" (7:7).

I have to concede that in my experience we Evangelicals have a very deficient understanding and appreciation of celibacy (or "consecrated virginity"). There is no special status or honor accorded to celibacy in Evangelicalism; on the contrary, I hear that in many Evangelical churches, single adults find great difficulty just fitting in. Where is the recognition that a vocation of celibacy, with its "undivided devotion to the Lord", is a "gift" to the Church? It's one thing to disavow monasticism, as we have done, but it's another thing thereafter to fail to construct some other means of cultivating and employing this gift.

By contrast, when I read Roman Catholic writing on consecrated virginity, it is obvious that some of the best Catholic minds have contemplated this subject very fruitfully over the centuries, and have come to understand celibacy as a great spiritual gift to the Church. We Evangelicals probably have much to learn from Catholics on this subject.

Dwight: On the other side, I'm one of those Catholics who feel that we have often over emphasized celibacy to the neglect of marriage. We're still struggling with what I personally feel is a misguided discipline of mandatory celibacy for priests for example. There *has* been an element in Catholic teaching that has viewed any sexual activity as degrading, and we have been too slow to promote a mature understanding of the true value of sex and married love. I don't think Catholics have a monopoly on prudishness, but I admit we have had our share. Despite this danger, we still rightly uphold the value of virginity and the sacredness of celibacy.

A higher calling?

Dwight: The reason celibacy is honored is because it's a higher spiritual calling. I know in our egalitarian day we dislike the idea that one way of holiness might be better than another, but this is a gospel principle. Martha served the Lord by giving him a meal. Mary served him by sitting at his feet in love. Jesus praises Mary for choosing the "better way." (Luke 10:42.) Martha isn't condemned for her more practical service; Jesus just establishes that there is a good way and a better way.

In 1 Corinthians chapter seven Paul says that celibacy is a better way. He says it is a good thing not to marry. (vv.1, 7-8.) He recommends single people and widows to stay as they are, and actually calls marriage a "concession" (v.6) because there is "so much immorality" (v.2). From the earliest times, the Church valued consecrated virginity, but this had also been part of the Jewish religious tradition. The Essenes, a Jewish sect contemporary with Jesus, encouraged celibacy; and Philo Judaeus, a Jewish philosopher and another contemporary with Jesus, records the existence of an order of Jewish virgins who give their lives in pursuit of God's wisdom.[29] The Jewish tradition was that Elijah and Elisha were celibate. John the Baptist followed in their footsteps of celibacy, and Jesus said there was no one greater than John. (Matt. 11:11.)

The classic understanding of the Adam and Eve story is that part of their primal perfection was that they lived together in a kind of child-like innocence. That's why, with the fall, they suddenly became aware of their nakedness, and only after the fall did Adam lie with Eve and have children. This indicates that virginity is part of the un-fallen human condition. To confirm this, Jesus teaches that this higher state is what we are destined to return to. This is why there is to be no marriage and sex in the resurrection life. (Mark 12:25)

There are other passages of Scripture that suggest that celibacy is in fact both a special *and* a higher calling. Jesus himself was the consecrated virgin *par excellence*. He actually recommends perpetual virginity as a way of total consecration to God in Matthew 19:12 and so implies that lifelong celibacy is a higher calling. The Book of Revelation also teaches that virginity is a higher spiritual calling. In chapter fourteen John has a vision of the throne of the Lamb before which a great crowd are singing a hymn of glory to the Lamb. "These are the ones who have kept their virginity and not been defiled with women; these follow the Lamb wherever he goes; they, out of all people, have been redeemed to be the first fruits for God and for the Lamb." (Rev. 14:4) Presumably they are "out of all people…the first fruits" because they followed Jesus in the higher way of perpetual virginity.

As Catholics we believe that the Virgin Mary identified with her son by following this higher spiritual calling and remaining a virgin for her whole life.

A celibate marriage?

David: I join in affirming that celibacy can have great value, and celibacy is certainly the better way for those particular people whom God calls to celibacy. In the hope that our readers will check you out on the Biblical examples and passages you cite, I'll resist the urge to go tit-for-tat on your arguments that celibacy is somehow "higher" in a general sense, because I don't think we need even to reach that question: To state what should be obvious, celibacy is a gift for *unmarried* people. It is an exception. God's general will for the human race in this age is to "be fruitful and increase in number; fill the earth and subdue it." (Gen. 1:28.) God repeatedly pronounced His unspoiled creation as "good" and "very good (Gen. 1:431)—with one exception: "It is *not good* for the man to be alone" (Gen. 2:18), so God created woman, and then blessed human sexuality (Gen. 1:28, 2:24). The normative human state is marriage and procreation—even for the clergy (1 Timothy 3:2-5, 11; Titus 1:6); and marital sex is "honored" and "pure" (Heb. 13:4). Even if celibacy were in some sense a "higher" thing, we're discussing here the supposed celibacy of a *married* couple. You haven't shown any reason why celibacy should be higher for *married* people, nor have you shown that Mary is somehow diminished if she consummated her marriage.

Let's be clear about what it would mean for Joseph's wife Mary to remain a virgin after Jesus' birth: Even though, with angelic encouragement, Joseph "took Mary home *as his wife*" (Matt. 1:20, 24) in fulfillment of their having been "pledged to be *married*" (1:18); and even though thereafter Joseph was "the *husband* of Mary" (1:16) and she was his "wife" (1:20); and even though they *lived together* as husband and wife, and as a family together with the child Jesus (Matt. 2:14-23; Luke 2:39, 51)—despite all that, Mary and Joseph supposedly never consummated their marriage. Instead, they lived under one roof but refrained from normal marital relations and vowed themselves to celibacy. So Jesus grew up in a household that we call "the Holy Family"—but which was really more a convent than a family, where the parents were never intimate with each other, and He, out of the corner of His eye, never saw them smile coyly at one another or linger over a kiss.

The basic questions are: What is the evidence for this alleged marital celibacy? and, what was the reason for it? I know of no direct Biblical evidence for Mary's perpetual virginity. We have already observed that Mary was probably the source for Luke's narratives of Jesus' infancy, but Luke—so deliberate and emphatic about the Virgin Birth—finds no occasion to assert that Mary remained a virgin after Jesus' birth. If Joseph was the source for his story in Matthew, then the only recorded information that he gave includes no direct statement as to whether the marriage was consummated after Jesus was born. Thus, these two sources, which seem most probably derived from the only people who really knew, do not report that they remained celibate.

Dwight: Luke and Matthew may not have mentioned the perpetual virginity of Mary because it was assumed. The second century Church documents indicate that this assumption was widespread, and that the matter only needed clarification later. You are right in saying that the Gospels do not report Mary and Joseph's marital celibacy, but neither do the Gospels report that Mary and Joseph *did* consummate the marriage physically. In fact the gospel record is inconclusive on the matter.

Indirect Biblical evidence

David: I admit the Gospel accounts are not absolutely decisive on this point. But recall the *indirect* Biblical evidence that tends against Mary's perpetual virginity: (1) Matthew 1:25 asserts that Joseph "had no union with her *until* she gave birth to a son". (Does this imply that he *did* "have union" with her afterwards?) (2) Luke calls Jesus Mary's "*first*born" (2:7). (Does this imply that others had followed?) And (3) the New Testament includes several references to Jesus' "brothers" and "sisters" (*see, e.g.,* Matt. 13:5556). (Were these Mary's younger children by Joseph?)[30] As a reader of the English New Testament, I find that these details—even if they are not conclusive—add to my impression that Mary and Joseph consummated their marriage.

Dwight: Matthew 1:25 does not necessarily mean that Mary and Joseph did "have union" *after* Jesus' birth, since "until" does not always mean that a change took place after the noted event. (When I tell my children to "be good *until* I return home", I don't mean that they can start being bad when I arrive.) In the fourth century a fellow called Heldivius brought up these same points, and Saint Jerome wrote a long treatise in reply. About the "firstborn" question Jerome answered, "the divine Scriptures are accustomed to call someone firstborn, not because other siblings come after him, but because he is born first."[31] An only child is therefore called "the firstborn" because he is the one who "opens the womb". (Ex.13:2.)

Did Jesus have brothers and sisters? *The Protoevangelium of James* says that Joseph was a mature widower, and that the "brothers and sisters" of Jesus were the children of Joseph's first marriage. Other writers in the early church said they were simply Jesus' cousins or the kinsmen of his extended family. The terms for "brothers" and "kinsmen" in the original languages are ambiguous. Several times in the Bible "kinsmen" are referred to as "brothers." (Gen. 29:10; Gen. 14:14; Deut. 23:7; *et al.*) Furthermore, when Jesus, Mary, and Joseph go up to Jerusalem with the twelve-year-old Jesus, there is no mention of younger brothers and sisters. And when Jesus is dying on the cross, he commends his mother to the Apostle John (John 19:26), something he would not have done if he had younger brothers and sisters to look after Mary.[32]

Pledged to be married

David: I think these arguments from details in the Gospel stories depend on linguistic issues that are beyond most of us laypeople[33]; and these detailed issues may miss the forest for the trees, by ignoring the main Biblical problem with the doctrine of Mary's perpetual virginity: Simply put, sexual union is definitional to marriage,[34] and Mary and Joseph are said to have been "married" as "husband" and "wife". This fact raises a natural presumption that, as a married man and woman, they consummated their marriage. This leaves me assuming confidently that Mary and Joseph did have normal marital relations, and leaves me with no reason to suppose otherwise—unless other credible evidence is brought forward.

Dwight: Your assumptions are natural, and the *Protoevangelium of James* was written partially to address these same questions that the second and third generation Christians had. The *Protoevangelium* explains that Mary was a consecrated Virgin. That explains her surprise at the angel's announcement that she will have a child. She says, "How will this be, since I am a virgin?"

This is not the response one would expect from a typical engaged woman, who would have simply been thankful that in time she would be blessed with a child. Mary's surprise may well show that she did not expect to have a normal marriage relationship with Joseph, despite their engagement.[35]

Mary had been set aside for God in two ways. If she had taken a vow of celibacy, then she was committed to God. According to the *Protoevangelium,* Joseph knew of this commitment and the obligation for the marriage to be a "guardianship" from the beginning. I will get into this topic in more detail in the next chapter, but Mary was also set aside for God by virtue of what happened at the Annunciation. In effect she was "married to God" in an astounding new way, and that also confirmed that her marriage to Joseph could only ever be a legal and pastoral necessity.

I agree with you that sex within marriage is a good and wholesome thing. It is the norm for a husband and wife to make love, but Mary and Joseph's relationship was not the norm. How could their relationship be "normal" when Mary had participated in the totally unique event of the Incarnation of God's Son? Saint Jerome asks, "Would he [Joseph], who knew such great wonders, have dared touch the temple of God, the dwelling place of the Holy Spirit, the Mother of his Lord?"[36]

David: This is another argument based on what may seem fitting (or not), but we simply can't calculate what would be fitting in the event of an Incarnation of God. Would anyone who understood the Incarnation have dared treat Jesus like a human being? But when Peter did the "fitting" thing and declined to have Jesus wash his feet, Jesus chided him. (John 13:8.) Evidently, when God became a man, He expected to be treated as a man. And there's every reason to suppose that He likewise expected His mother to be treated as a woman.

If Mary and Joseph were vowed to celibacy, then just what was Mary and Joseph's betrothal? Even assuming that Joseph was an older man,[37] the relationship that you propose for him and Mary sounds like foster care, or an adoption, not an engagement. What was the "pledge" that Mary and Joseph made when the Bible says that they were "pledged to be married"? It seems, rather, that according to the *Protoevangelium*, and in your view, Mary and Joseph had pledged *never* to be married. Even if the *Protoevangelium* were not a pseudonymous grab-bag of unlikely tales, it would not be sufficiently weighty to overcome this difficulty.

Dwight: This "pseudonymous grab-bag of unlikely tales" was considered reliable enough for the church fathers who lived less than two hundred years from the events described, but not for you who are separated by nearly two thousand years. Who's more likely to be right here?

More evidence for marital celibacy

Dwight: Anyway, I've said before I don't use *The Protoevangelium* as Scripture, but as an ancient document that helps "shed light on Scripture". But it is not the only evidence that points to a marriage that is permanently celibate. Such arrangements were part of the Jewish background of the New Testament Church. Both the classical historian Philo and the Dead Sea Scrolls tell us that permanently celibate marriages were part of the religious customs of the first century Jewish Essene community at Qumran.[38] 1 Corinthians 7:36-38 may suggest that relationships like this were encouraged in order for the couple to devote themselves to prayer and the Lord's service. Paul may also be recommending this type of marriage when he advises "those who have wives to live as if they have none." (1 Cor. 7:29.)

David: 1 Corinthians 7 is a very slender reed on which to balance this argument. The interpretation of the passage is difficult; Paul almost disclaims its authority (v. 25: "I have no command from the Lord"); and it is tailored to an unusual circumstance (v. 26: "Because of the present crisis"). Your view of this passage puts it in some tension with Paul's instructions about clergy properly being husbands and fathers (1 Tim. 3:2-5, 12; Titus 1:6). Most important; the people involved in the arrangement Paul permits are expressly held *not* to be bound by vows, but to be free to marry (vv. 28, 36). The clear, pedestrian teaching about marital sex in this chapter is in verse 5: "Do not deprive each other except by mutual consent and for a time …. Then come together again…." There's little evidence that vowed celibate "marriages" existed in the Apostolic-era Church, and no evidence that Mary and Joseph had such a marriage.

Dwight: I give historical, Scriptural and cultural evidence from first century Judaism and Christianity, but that isn't enough. But consider: What other arrangement could have been made for a young Jewish girl who found herself pregnant? (Especially if she had taken a vow of celibacy.) By all appearances she had committed a heinous sin and the law demanded her to be stoned. She couldn't be sheltered by her family. Joseph had intended to "put her away" but when the angel informed him of the circumstances he changed his mind. But he couldn't just take Mary in and shelter her as an unwed mother. That would have been scandalous for both of them. His going through with the planned marriage and adopting the girl by marrying her was the only option given the extraordinary circumstances.

David: The only option? How about the option the Bible describes?—He took her *as his wife.* If it would have been a scandal for Joseph to shelter an unwed woman, I don't see how the scandal is relieved by his taking her in under a pseudo-"marriage" in which (according to the *Protoevangelium*, chapter 15) it would have been a "grievous crime" for them to have sex. There was still no chaperone.

Dwight: You don't account for the possibility that an older man might just look on a young girl in such a situation as a man might regard a daughter or a niece. Neither do you account for the fact that Mary and Joseph would have been surrounded by an extended family and closely-knit community who would have helped keep an eye on the situation.

David: No, I do understand the concept; I just don't understand calling it "marriage". I don't think any real evidence accounts for this doctrine of Mary's perpetual virginity. It seems, rather, that the "evidence" of a celibate marriage was cooked up to bolster a conclusion that someone had already deemed fitting. And that brings me to the second question, which is, What would be the reason for Mary's supposed perpetual virginity? Your answer is that her continued virginity is a fulfillment of her virginal character. You link—and equate—virginity and holiness. In order for Mary to be *really* holy, she would have to be a virgin; a woman who has had sex—even just with her husband—can't be *really* holy. However, virginity is not *always* a mark of holiness, and for a person who is married but is still a virgin (and there are such people), that virginity may be a pathology (and grounds for an annulment, I think).[39] A husband or wife who deliberately refuses sex to his or her spouse is not holy in so doing; he or she would be selfishly "depriving" his or her spouse. (1 Cor. 7:25.) On the contrary, the ideal for married people is a well-ordered and fulfilled sexual relationship.

You describe Mary in her maturity as "a venerable, pure, and holy matron". I hope you wouldn't say that this status is impossible for a married woman. And yet you said that it "denigrates" Mary to suggest she had sex with her husband. Do we "denigrate" married women—our mothers, wives, sisters, and daughters—if we presume that they have had normal relations with their husbands? Not at all. But it's evidently not enough for you that Mary be morally pure; she must, though married, remain physically a virgin in order to remain *truly* pure. I resist that. It misunderstands sex, marriage, and virginity.

Dwight: It denigrates Mary not because she might have made love with her husband and was therefore "dirty". Instead it denigrates her because it suggests that she followed a lesser way of holiness.

Monks, miracles and magic

David: As I've said, I don't think you can show that marriage is a "lesser" way of holiness. I know that you are not arguing that sex is "dirty", but I can't help thinking that such an attitude was behind the doctrine. One historian observes that the doctrine of Mary's perpetual virginity "spread in close connection with the ascetic overestimate of celibacy, and the rise of monasticism."[40] But what really suggests this to me is that right alongside the teaching that Mary did not consummate her marriage is the strange idea that the birth of Jesus was miraculous in not disturbing Mary's physical traits of virginity.[41] To "prove" this miracle, the *Protoevangelium* tells a most repulsive story (at chapters 19-21). By this light, not only does ideal holiness require abstinence even from marital sex, but also it evidently requires physical resemblance to a woman who has never given birth. There's something almost Gnostic about this abhorrence of natural procreation.

The Bible says that Mary "gave birth" to Jesus (Matt.1:25), and that Jesus was "born of" Mary (Matt. 1:16);[42] and without getting into the obstetrical details, we know what this means. Hypothesizing, instead, a "birth" other than through the birth canal is a self-contradiction, and it impugns Jesus' full and real humanity. It impugns marriage, sex, and childbirth. To put my own position positively, I affirm a full, real humanity for Jesus, not a magical birth that left his mother unaffected, and not a childhood in a stilted environment where his parents had vowed *not* to be a real husband and wife.

Dwight: We *are* referring to a miraculous event here.[43] The whole idea that a woman becomes pregnant by the Holy Spirit is pretty astounding. The belief that Mary's virginity was preserved through the birth process as well as after is not due to some repulsion about sex. The story you refer to is a simple, vivid support for the total fact of the Virgin Birth. The *Protoevangelium* was written to bolster belief in the Virgin Birth, and for good or ill, the episode was included in the *Protoevangelium* for that reason alone. You can't blame this view on sexually repressed monks. The perpetual virginity of Mary was established well before the rise of Christian monasticism in the early fourth century.

The reason for the perpetual virginity

Dwight: Let's get back to the real point. You ask, "What is the reason for Mary's perpetual virginity?" Athanasius, that great defender of orthodoxy in the fourth century, answers your question quite succinctly, "Mary, who gave birth to God, remained a virgin to the end [in order to be a model for] all to come after her."[44] In other words, Mary's perpetual purity was a model and example for all those who would strive for that "better way" of discipleship that identifies most fully with the example of Jesus. In other words, Mary's perpetual virginity makes sense because it reflects the glory of her Son—the virgin *par excellence.*

I can see your worries that this belief denigrates marriage and impugns Christ's true humanity. That might be true if the Catholic Church's teachings generally supported such views, but they don't. On the contrary, of all churches, it is the Catholic Church that has the strongest, most consistent, complete and life-affirming view of marriage, sex, and procreation. Likewise, the doctrine could impugn Christ's true humanity only if the Catholic Church actually took that position. It doesn't. The Catholic Church has been both the definer and defender of the true Christology for the last two thousand years. The only other question is whether the doctrine of the perpetual virginity of the Blessed Virgin must lead to other more unpalatable doctrines about Mary. In other words, is it the thin edge of the wedge?

David: I guess that's one way of putting it. In the fourth century, Basil of Caesarea observed that if Mary had had normal conjugal relations, "That would not have affected the teaching of our religion at all, because Mary's virginity was necessary until the service of the Incarnation, and what happened afterward need not be investigated in order to affect the doctrine of the mystery."[45] Therefore, Mary's supposed perpetual virginity marks the point where Marian doctrine stops being about Jesus and starts being about Mary.

Dwight: You left out the last part of Basil's observation. He goes on to say why he *does* believe in the perpetual virginity of Mary: "since the lovers of Christ [that is, the faithful] do not allow themselves to hear that the Mother of God ceased at a given moment to be a virgin, we consider their testimony to be sufficient."[46] That leads me to end where I started. The perpetual virginity of Mary is a beautiful, fitting doctrine that has been held by the vast majority of Christians, including the Protestant Reformers, at all times and in all places from the earliest days of the Church. The only Christians who deny this doctrine are modern Evangelicals. It is possible, I suppose, that the vast majority of Christians have got it wrong, but I know where I'd place my bet.

David: On this one, we'll have to disagree. However, you do state a good point to leave us Evangelicals thinking about: Are we paying adequate attention to the testimony and wisdom of the historic Church, especially as it relates to a concept—consecrated virginity—on which our own thought, meditation, and experience may be lacking? And if consecrated virginity is an unfamiliar concept for Evangelicals, how much more unfamiliar will be our next subject—the Catholic idea of Mary's espousal to God.

Our Lady? : A Catholic/Evangelical Debate

5

Whom did Mary Marry?

Mary as "Spouse of the Holy Spirit"

David: My seven-year-old son likes me to quiz him on religion. He recently proposed another round, so I posed the usual types of questions. Some of the questions are theological ("How many Gods are there—three or one?"), and some are just about Bible stories. Since this dialogue about Mary was on my mind, I asked my son, "Who was Jesus' mother?" He easily answered "Mary". I then warned him to listen carefully and asked him, "Who was Jesus' *father*?" Avoiding the error of "Joseph", he correctly answered "God". But then he got a funny look on his face, and asked his own question: "Was Mary God's *wife*?"

My young son had pulled me right into an issue that you and I had been avoiding. I complimented him on asking a very good question, and then answered with a solid "no". But your contrary words from the previous chapter were much on my mind: You said that, "in effect, Mary "was 'married to God' in an astounding new way". Pagan gods were sometimes thought to have had sexual relationships with humans. (For example, according to Greek myth, the god Zeus impregnated the mortal woman Alcmene and thus sired the demi-god Hercules.) The Mormon Church teaches a similar, pseudo-Christian myth—that "Christ was begotten by an Immortal Father in the same way that mortal men are begotten by mortal fathers."[47] You're not flirting with this error, are you?

Dwight: Not at all. Catholic theology is clear that the Virginal Conception takes place entirely without seed, congress, intercourse, or marital relations of any kind. It is "the immaterial and transcendent operation of the whole Trinity delegated to the Holy Spirit".[48]

David: Well then, exactly what *did* you mean when you said that Mary was "married to God"?

Dwight: To answer you, I'd like to reflect on an underlying issue that will illuminate our discussion and facilitate my answer. One problem in dialogues like these is that our open disagreements are often only the symptom of much deeper differences. Since becoming a Catholic, I've realized that, beneath our disagreements about particular Scriptural interpretations or tricky doctrinal problems, there lies a radically different way of approaching the Bible and doing theology.

In my memory, Evangelicalism uses the Bible in several different ways: First it is a personal daily devotional guide by which God speaks directly to our hearts. Second, it is an inspirational rulebook, outlining right behavior. Third, it is a theological source book—a mine for proof texts. Fourth, it is a sort of prophetic code, explaining current events and predicting the future. In my Evangelical experience, the Bible was a straightforward religious text that was practical in its everyday application. On the whole, it is a good thing that we used the Bible in such practical ways.

David: I'm glad you still think so, since the uses you describe almost correspond to Paul's statement about the uses of Scripture—"teaching, rebuking, correcting, and training in righteousness" (2 Tim. 3:16).

Dwight: Catholics do use the Bible in the ways I've outlined above; but when I first began reading the theologians of the first four centuries, I was struck with a new way of seeing the Bible. For them the Bible is not primarily a source book for proof texts— it is a drama of characters making cosmos-changing decisions in the battle of good and evil. The early church fathers see Scripture poetically, as a tapestry of interwoven types, images, themes, and symbols. For them the whole of salvation history is re-capitulated in Christ, and the work of Biblical interpretation is to discern how the New Testament is hidden in the Old and the Old is made manifest in the New.

David: As you've indicated, these approaches do not exclude one another. Don't you remember some of that "Catholic approach" in your Evangelical upbringing?

Digging deeper in the Bible

Dwight: Yes, there was some, and I can remember being most fascinated by the typological approach to the Old Testament when it was used. But generally speaking, the Catholic approach to the Bible has been symbolic, mystical, and poetic while the Protestant approach has been literal, practical, and prosaic. These two different approaches tend to confuse our discussions. The Evangelical will look for a good solid black-and-white proof text and think the matter is either proven or not, while the Catholic will be annoyed by this approach, thinking that the whole matter is far deeper and richer.

The Catholic doesn't so much look to the Bible to prove his beliefs; instead he finds his beliefs presented there for contemplation. He will trace his beliefs in the symbolic meanings of the Gospels, find them written in the very actions of the life of Christ, and echoed in the epistles and the history of the Church. Evangelicals will be annoyed by this approach, thinking the Catholic is pulling in inadmissible evidence, and spinning fantastic and unbelievable doctrines out of thin air. In many ways the Evangelical is Paul's man, preferring the straightforward, practical theology of the epistles, while the Catholic is John's man, preferring the subtle, sacramental theology of the Beloved Apostle.

These differences explain some of our own difficulties in communication. Catholicism has always tended to use Scriptural language in a colorful, poetic, and ornate way, because the language of the Bible is itself poetic, dramatic, and full of symbolic meaning. We use Bible-based poetic imagery in our liturgy, hymns, and devotional poems, but we also allow that poetic language to influence our theological discussions. In this discussion, therefore, I am in a bit of a jam. I want to introduce this rich Catholic way of reading the Bible, but I don't want people to confuse our poetic imagery with the hard theological definitions. The subject of this chapter is just such a topic. We use a poetic and romantic turn of phrase when we call Mary "spouse of the Holy Spirit", but what do we mean by it? I'm happy to explain, but has my analysis so far been of any help?

From Poetry to Dogma

David: I think I do understand; but Evangelical Christianity has its own share of the figurative and poetical. The singing of extra-Scriptural songs and hymns, for example, is an important part of our spirituality. Our sermons include poetical embellishments and flourishes. (It's the rare sermon that achieves the poetical excellence of, say, James Weldon Johnson's *God's Trombones*, but the genre is not unknown.) However, admittedly the imaginative features of the Evangelical sermon or song acquire no authority for us; and for our doctrine we always revert to the Scriptures. But for the Catholic, the figure of speech seems to harden into dogma, and our current issue shows that process:

The first known reference to "espousal" between Mary and the Spirit was by the poet Prudentius (348-405): "The unwed Virgin espoused the *Spirit*."[49] As poetry, I suppose this is unobjectionable.

The Bible uses marriage vocabulary to describe God's redeeming love: The Old Testament describes Israel as God's wife (Ps. 45:9-15; Isa. 54:4-5, 62:3-5; Jer. 2:2, 3:1-14, 31:32; Hosea 2:19-20), and the New Testament describes the Church as the Bride of Christ (Matt. 22:1-14; John 3:29; Rom. 7:3-4; 2 Cor. 11:2; Eph. 5:23-32; Rev. 19:7-9, 21:2, 9-10).[50]

Dwight: In addition, the whole book of Hosea gives the extended analogy of God being a husband to his faithless people; and the early church read the Song of Songs as a meditation on God's intimate love for his people.

David: So as poetry, Prudentius's phrase—that Mary "espoused the *Spirit*"—is acceptable. We grant the same poetic license to St. Ephrem the Syrian (d. 373), who referred to Mary as the Bride of *Christ*,[51] and to John of Damascus (b. 676), who referred to Mary as "the Spouse, whom *the Father* had taken to himself."[52] However, since the time of St. Francis of Assisi, [53] "the spouse of the Holy Spirit" has become a settled convention in Catholic usage, and has become a staging ground for *further* reflection and doctrine.

Whether that's a problem depends on how far you go with that imagery. We know that Mary wasn't *literally* the Spirit's wife. For one thing, Jesus Christ's Father is The Father, not the Spirit; but if we make the Spirit the literal husband of Mary, then we make the *Spirit* to be Jesus' *Father*.[54] More generally, Mary's relationship with the Spirit simply can't meet the definition of literal marriage. Literal marriage consists of "leaving" and "cleaving": "Therefore shall a man *leave* his father and his mother, and shall *cleave* unto his wife, and they shall become one flesh." (Gen. 2:24, *KJV*.) That is, literal marriage consists of (1) a public, legal establishment of a new family and (2) a private, exclusive sexual union; but (3) by definition, marriage exists in this life only, and not the next. Mary and the Spirit had no such literal marital relationship—no legal rights, no sex, no termination at death. In addition, since all believers will constitute God's Bride, God's "marriage" to Mary is hardly exclusive. Literal marriage presupposes a parity between partners,[55] not the extreme disparity between God and Mary, who are Creator and creature, infinite and finite. Instead, it was with Joseph that Mary had a literal marriage (at least, you'll agree, in its legal respects), so that Mary is the "Spouse of the Spirit" only figuratively.

Dwight: You've made my point that you Evangelicals are better on the literal thing. And you're right that this marriage is not literal. But we do need to ask in what sense the poetic "marriage" language of the Bible is fulfilled. To use a more familiar example, in the Old Testament God promised to be the "shepherd" of his people. (See, e.g. Ezek. 34.) In the Gospels this is fulfilled in Christ. (John 10:11.) However, Jesus is literally a carpenter. He doesn't tend sheep; he tends people. So while the prophecy is *certainly* fulfilled, it is not *literally* fulfilled. In the same way, the prophecy of God marrying his people is fulfilled in his relationship with Mary. This fulfillment is real, but it is not literal.

We agree that God's being a husband is a thoroughly Biblical concept, and that it is figurative. Can we also agree that this image can apply not only to God's people collectively, but to an individual as well?

David: The Bible applies these marriage metaphors to the people of God collectively, but I see no harm in an individual poetical application. What I think you need to show is that these metaphors can properly be applied to Mary in particular.

Mary and the people of God

Dwight: God's marriage to his people is particularized in Mary for a couple reasons. You stated in chapter one that the mother of Jesus in Revelation 12 represents the whole nation of Israel. At the Annunciation, when God's power "overshadowed" Mary, she became pregnant. At that point Mary became the literal mother of the Messiah and the embodiment of this maternal Israel. If

God had promised to be a husband to His people, and if Mary embodied His people, and if He then conceived a child in her, then a kind of spiritual marriage took place, and this "marriage" fulfilled all the prophecies about God being the husband of the nation of Israel.

Mary also stands for Israel because in a real way she was the culmination of Israelite history. In her, redemption history reached a climax or focus point from which its fulfillment would be born. God had chosen the Israelite nation to be His agent for blessing the world. (Gen. 22:17-18.) More specifically, the women of that nation would bring forth the one who would defeat evil (Gen.3:15)—even more specifically, a woman from the House of David. (Micah 5:2-4.) Then in the fullness of time (Gal. 4:4), the whole history of Israel became focused in that one woman through whom fulfillment would come, in the person of the Redeemer.

The Annunciation as a "spiritual betrothal" is also revealed through Luke's actual language. Using the Septuagint (the Greek translation of the Hebrew Old Testament), we can compare Greek expressions used in the New Testament to their Hebrew equivalents in the Old. At the Annunciation the angel says that the power of the Most High will "overshadow" her. "Overshadow" is used for the glorious creative and protective presence of God (Gen. 1:2; Ex.13:22; Lev.16:2; Ps.17:8 *et al.)* The word is also used for the protective, creative power of a husband for his wife. In the ancient Middle East, a way for a woman to ask for marriage was to ask a man to put his cloak around her (Ruth 3:9, Ezek. 18:6.)—a custom still practiced in the Middle East today.[56] The word for cloak is linked with the words for "wings" and "shadow",[57] so when the man "overshadowed" a woman with his cloak, it was a euphemism for marriage. Ruth's request (3:9) for Boaz to spread his protective power over her was an ancient Hebrew form of betrothal.[58] In addition, Boaz is Ruth's "kinsman Redeemer" (3:9), and this is the same term Isaiah uses for the Lord as husband of Israel. (Isa. 54:5-8.) So when the Power of the Most High "overshadowed" Mary, Luke is telling us that a spiritual marriage took place. We know the gospel writers made such verbal allusions throughout the gospels;[59] this allusion also explains why Ruth is included in Matthew's genealogy of Jesus. Therefore, the Catholic idea that Mary is the "Spouse of the Holy Spirit" is more than the fanciful musings of a fourth century poet. We believe it is true in a real, but not literal way.

Spiritual marriage

David: You have yet to specify the senses in which Mary's relationship to the Spirit *does* figuratively resemble marriage. You've rightly insisted that this "marriage" is *not* literal (with its lack of legalities, sexual consummation, exclusivity, parity, and termination at death). So what does it mean that Mary is the "Spouse of the Holy Spirit"? How about this: We associate with marriage such things as love, fellowship, and child-bearing—and those *are* attributable to this relationship. Is that what you mean?

Dwight: Love, fellowship and child-bearing do come into it, and our own human relationships do reflect divine love. But this is where that mix of theology and poetry come in. "Spouse of the Holy Spirit" communicates not just sentimental devotion but also some very complex theological concepts. The analogy of marriage between Mary and the Holy Spirit is given not mainly to foster extravagant Marian devotion, but to explain the mystery of the Incarnation. It does so in three ways.

First, when we say that Mary and the Holy Spirit are married we affirm that in the Incarnation there is a marriage of heaven and earth. God and man are not just reconciled, but united. The fruit of a human marriage is a child, who is a living union of the two parents. Likewise, the fruit of Mary's "marriage" to God is the God-Man Jesus Christ.

Second, a marriage is indissoluble, as signified by the child it produces. That new everlasting soul who is a union of the two parents is a living sign that the marriage is a perpetual union. Likewise, the union of God and Man in Jesus Christ is perpetual—in fact, everlasting. The Son did not take human form temporarily. He did not possess the body of Jesus like an alien spirit only to leave it again. No—the union of God and Man in Jesus is just as indissoluble as the union of husband and wife as expressed in their child.

Third, in a marriage man and wife become "one flesh." (Gen.2:24; Matt. 19:5; Eph. 5:31.) I said that while Mary's union with the Spirit was not literal, it *was* real. An astounding new relationship between God and Man took place in Mary to bring forth the God-Man Jesus Christ. Saint Ireneaus said that "God became man so that men could become like God," and Mary was the first human to enter into a new kind of intimate relationship with God, and she indicates what is in store for each one of us. We are getting into a very deep and wonderful subject here, one where language begins to fail us. Mary's espousal reveals the full implications of our redemption, and unlocks what it really means to be members of the Church—the Bride of Christ. (Cf. Eph.5:31 –32.)

David: If Mary's relationship with God is something that she has in common with every member of the Church, and if each of us is or will be, in a sense, a "spouse of the Holy Spirit", then applying that phrase to Mary would be less problematic. However, while the Catholic Church calls each believer a member of the "Bride of *Christ*,"[60] it seems pretty clear that it applies the title "Spouse of the *Holy Spirit*" uniquely to Mary. I can affirm with you that love, fellowship, and cooperation existed between Mary and the Holy Spirit; and we can poetically liken that to marriage; but I lack much enthusiasm for the phrase "Spouse of the Holy Spirit", for two general reasons: unsatisfying Biblical exegesis, and inadequate boundaries.

You find that God's marriage promises were fulfilled when the Spirit conceived Jesus in Mary, who supposedly embodied Israel. However, the Bible does not suggest that God (the Father? The Spirit?) will "marry" a wife who will then be the mother of His Son, the Messiah. Instead, the Bible's divine marriage imagery describes a Bride who will marry God the Son, the Messiah. In the great divine marriage, Jesus is the *Groom*, not the *child*: "The kingdom of heaven is like a king who prepared a wedding banquet *for his son.*" (Matt. 22:2.) Jesus is the Groom and His Church is the Bride.

Dwight: I think we're getting tangled up in the three-way cord of the Trinity. Thomas Aquinas offers this wisdom about our problem, "The work of the conception [of Christ] is indeed common to the whole Trinity; yet in some way it is attributed to each of the Persons. For to the Father is attributed authority in regard to the Person of the Son, who by this conception took to Himself (human nature). The taking itself (of human nature) is attributed to the Son: but the formation of the body taken by the Son is attributed to the Holy Ghost."[61]

David: But doesn't that make it all the more problematic to suppose a marriage between Mary and the Spirit in particular? If thinking of the conception of Jesus as a sort of "marriage" of Mary and the overshadowing Spirit is potentially edifying, it is nonetheless not a Biblical idea, strictly speaking. The fulfillment of God's promise to marry His people will occur in the end times. The good news is that the Great Wedding is yet to come—and we will have a part.

Dwight: The Catholic way of thinking is not so much "either-or" as "both-and". To say that the Annunciation was a marriage does not rule out the Church's being the Bride of Christ nor the invitation of all to the wedding supper of the Lamb. As I'll show later, this imagery flows from the Annunciation; it is not contradictory to it.

The teacher vs. the poet

David: I said that the phrase "Spouse of the Holy Spirit" has inadequate boundaries. One who teaches that Mary is the "Spouse of the Holy Spirit" should certainly be clear about what that means, bearing in mind the Apostle's warning that those "who teach will be judged more strictly" (James 3:1). The teacher can't take all the liberties that the poet might take. Regarding Mary's "marriage" to God, we've seen that a misunderstanding (in the case of Mormonism, for example) is entirely possible. Consequently, this notion must be kept it in its bounds.

I have to say that in Catholic usage I see extravagance, not limitation. I have to quickly admit that I am in no position to judge Catholics. All I know is what I read, but some of what I read troubles me. I give two examples from what you'll agree are mainstream Catholic sources.

First, apparently not all devotees of the "Spouse of the Holy Spirit" understand that the "marriage" here is figurative. One author states, in an article on the EWTN website,[62] that Mary's marriage to God, and His conception of Jesus in her, had the same legal effect as if she had committed adultery with another man:

> [A] woman who had know[n] contact with another man, even if by force, was considered no longer fit to be visited by her husband.... [W]hen the angel revealed to [Joseph] that Mary was truly the spouse of the Holy Spirit, Joseph could take Mary, his betrothed, into his house as a wife, but he could never have intercourse with her because according to the Law she was forbidden to him for all time....Joseph knew that God had conducted himself as a husband in regard to Mary. She was now prohibited to him for all time....

This article's mix of literalism and legalism makes God seem to be an adulterer. In my view, this takes "Spouse of the Holy Spirit" much too literally.

Dwight: I agree that this article takes the idea of the "Spouse of the Holy Spirit" too literally. As you say, Mary was betrothed to Joseph but (by this light) God barged in and committed adultery. Let's go easy, though, on this author. It's not always easy to distinguish just what is literal in religion and what is figurative. Besides, his opinion is corrected by the formal teaching of the Church, as I've shown above. I think we can agree that over-literal readings of the Bible are not unique to Catholicism, and that Evangelicalism has its share.

David: Indeed we do, though it still seems clear to me that the Church's teaching on Mary as "Spouse of the Holy Spirit" invites this sort of error.

St. Maximillian Kolbe

David: My second example is from the writing of a man who is admittedly one of the great Christian heroes of the twentieth century. Fr. Maximillian Kolbe was killed in a Nazi prison camp after taking the place of a chosen victim. Pope John Paul II canonized him, after ensuring that none of his writings contradict the Catholic Faith. Fr. Kolbe had a particular devotion to Mary as the "Immaculate Conception" (a subject we will later address), but in this passage, he reflects on her being the "Spouse of the Holy Spirit":

> United to the Holy Spirit as His spouse, she is one with God in an incomparably more perfect way than can be predicated of any other creature.... Among creatures made in God's image, the union brought about by married love is the most intimate of all. In a much more precise, more interior, more essential manner, the Holy Spirit lives in the soul of [Mary] the Immaculata, in the depths of her very being.... In the Holy Spirit's union with Mary we observe more than the love of two beings; in [the Spirit] there is ... all the love of the Blessed trinity; in the other [Mary], all of creation's love. So it is that in this union heaven and earth are joined; all of Heaven with the earth, the totality of eternal love with the totality of created love. It is truly the summit of love....[63]

If among human beings the wife takes the name of her husband because she belongs to him, is one with him ... and is, with him, the source of new life, with how much greater reason should the name of the Holy Spirit, who is the divine Immaculate Conception, be used as the name of her in whom He lives as uncreated Love, the principle of life in the whole supernatural order of grace?[64]

For Fr. Kolbe, Mary's status as "Spouse" is to be mined for all the significance it can yield. "Marriage" is no mere figure of their relationship; rather, their relationship, which is the "*summit of love*", may be the *quintessential* marriage. Fr. Kolbe sees not disparity but parity between the Spirit and Mary, since she takes His name ("Immaculate Conception") as any Bride might take her husband's name. Fr. Kolbe has launched Prudentius's notion of espousal into the devotional stratosphere.

Dwight: As a former Evangelical, I realize just how shocking Maximillian Kolbe's language sounds to Evangelical ears, but when I read his words closely, I actually agree with him. What Fr. Kolbe is saying is not actually that foreign to Evangelical theology, but its Marian context is what Evangelicals find alarming. Let me try to explain.

First, there seems to be undue reverence and veneration for Mary, and I hope you won't think I am ducking the issue, but I will address this later (when we discuss veneration). For now let's think about what Saint Maximillian means theologically. We have to ask again the tricky question of how literal or figurative this marriage or union between Mary and the Holy Spirit really is. You feel that it must be merely figurative. I suggested that it is "real, but not literal".

Union with the Spirit

Dwight: Here is the problem: If the union between Mary and the Holy Spirit is totally figurative, then the Incarnation itself is not real. If the union between Mary and the Holy Spirit is *only* a metaphor, then God simply used Mary as a channel for Jesus to come into the world. If Jesus really was born *of* Mary and not *through* Mary as we've agreed in chapter three, then there was a real union between the Holy Spirit and Mary. I don't see how we can avoid the logic of this. Are you with me thus far?

David: Sorry, but no. The reality of the Incarnation depends upon the reality of the Spirit's conceiving Jesus in Mary; it does not depend upon the supposed reality of Mary's union with the Spirit. You infer the union from the fact of the conception, and you thereby beg the very question we are considering. A conception "entirely without seed, congress, intercourse, or marital relations of any kind" (to use your phrase) simply does not presuppose any particular "union" between the woman and the power behind the conception. If the conception really happens (with or without such "union"), then the Incarnation is real.

Dwight: We both believe that Jesus took Mary's flesh.[65] It seems self-evident that for this to happen there had to be a union of Mary and the Spirit. It is natural for someone who sees such a union to reflect on its implications. This reflection is the basis for Maximillian Kolbe's teaching. While expressed in the context of devotion to Mary, his teaching is thoroughly Scriptural, and when explained, it is something most Christians would not dispute.

While I'm not as fervent in my Marian devotion as Maximillian Kolbe, I *can* appreciate what he is saying. Mary's intimate union with the Holy Spirit is a realization of the whole point of the Incarnation and God's plan of redemption. What happened at the Annunciation points back to the prophecy of Joel 2:28-29 when God promises to pour out his Spirit on all flesh, and it points forward to Pentecost when that same Spirit was sent down to indwell the first Christians.

One of Fr. Kolbe's ideas which sounds shocking is that Mary is united with God. But this is a Biblical concept. Through the power of the Holy Spirit we are engrafted into Christ (John 15:5;

Rom. 11:17); we become part of his body (I Cor. 12:13, 27). By the Spirit we become one with Him. We abide in him and he in us. (John 15:4-5; I John 3:24; 4:13.) This is the language of union, and Kolbe uses marriage imagery for the union of the Christian with Christ, just as Saint Paul did. (Eph. 5:32.) Notice that Fr. Kolbe says Mary is united with God not as a member of the godhead, but as a creature. This is exactly what Jesus promises. If we abide in His love we are united with Him as he is united with the Father. (John 17:21.) To be precise, we are not united with the Godhead, but with the *love* of God. (John 15:9-10.)[66] This is the "summit of love" which Saint Maximillian is referring to—the love of Christ which, when we know it, will fill us to all the fullness of God. (Eph.3:19.) It is therefore no overstatement to say that we are "united with God", for when we abide in that love we actually live in God and God lives in us. (I John 4:16.)

By the power of Jesus' death and resurrection, and by virtue of her union with the Holy Spirit, we believe Mary was the first person to be united with the divine love that Jesus spoke about in John 15. As such she has opened the way for the fulfillment of those promises in the lives of each one of us. Does this cause Kolbe to rejoice? You bet. That's why Jesus shared this wonderful mystery with us in the first place—so that our joy would be full. (John 15:11.)

David: All Christians believe in union with Christ: The most Calvinistic book on my shelf has a chapter entitled "Union with Christ".[67] Union with Christ is a wonderful mystery, but it is hardly "shocking" to Evangelicals.

Dwight: Yes, in this way Kolbe's teaching is not alien to Evangelical thought.

David: But hold on: Kolbe's writing troubles me not because he speaks of a union between God and man but because he describes a *special* union between God and *Mary*—and this brings me to your second point: You suggest that Mary's "union" is something she does or will have in common with all Christians, and this would indeed defuse many Evangelical objections. However, Fr. Kolbe is quite clearly describing a relationship unique to Mary. We will *all*, as you say, be "united with God"; but *Mary*, Fr. Kolbe says, "is one with God in an incomparably more perfect way than can be predicated of any other creature". The proof of this?—Prudentius's poem, and centuries of elaboration on it.

Dwight: The "proof" is not the result of centuries of Marian elaboration. The proof is simply the miracle of the Incarnation. Mary had a unique and "incomparably more perfect" union with God because God dwelled within her for nine months. He took her flesh. He was nursed by her and learned the lessons of love from her. He was one with her as any son is one with his mother. Tom Howard has put it this way: "the Ancient Church increasingly became aware that Mary had been granted a dignity, by God's grace, unparalleled by any other creature in the universe, including the seraphim. There were patriarchs, prophets, kings, apostles, the Fathers, the martyrs, and all the angelic orders. All of these bear witness to the Word: Mary bore the Word. No seraph has ever been drawn into the mystery of Redemption in even a remotely analogous manner."[68]

David: From what you say, her "incomparable union" was with the Son as His mother, not (as Kolbe says) with the Spirit as His Spouse. But what do you think of the second paragraph in the above quotation, and my suggestion that Fr. Kolbe sees not disparity but parity between Mary and the Spirit?

God's grace to Mary

Dwight: This points us toward the next chapter, but very briefly—The parity in this union is the gift of grace. Mary shared in the curse of original sin and needed redemption like everyone else, but the result of her redemption is this parity with the Holy Spirit.

She takes on his name. This is not to say she is the same as the Holy Spirit. This is why marriage is such an apt metaphor. Husband and wife are one flesh, but they are also distinct persons.[69] This gift of parity between Mary and the Holy Spirit is a particular expression of the promise to all believers. In a similar way we are lifted by the action of the Holy Spirit from being faithless wives to become the bride of Christ, and as Jesus Christ's bride we too are honored to take his name—the name that is above all names. (John 20:31; Acts 11:26; Acts 19:5; 2 Thess. 1:12.)

David: It's good that you sound the theme of God's "gift of grace", and I urge its greater implications for this issue. For the Marian devotee, truths about the Incarnation seem to become comments on Mary (and compliments to her): If the Incarnate Christ was holy, then this must mean that Mary was holy enough to bear Him. If the Incarnation was glorious, then this glory must redound to Mary. If the Holy Spirit was the divine agent of the Incarnation, then this must mean that Mary ranks as some sort of partner with the Holy Spirit. Such thinking, however, involves a fallacy:

One might just as soon—but just as wrongly—take the Incarnation as a compliment to Israel. ("God must have chosen a very holy people to produce the Christ.") On the contrary, God persisted in that gracious choice even when Israel proved itself unworthy. Matthew mentions in Jesus' genealogy only four women besides Mary—the incestuous Tamar (1:3), Rahab the harlot, Ruth the heathen Moabitess (1:5), and the adulterous Bathsheba (1:6)—all surprising as Jesus' ancestors. Using the glory of the Incarnation to draw inferences about Jesus' ancestors would take us wildly astray. Matthew teaches us, instead, to let the glory of the Incarnation point us to God's unmerited and unaccountable grace.

In the Incarnation, God crossed an unimaginable gulf: from "the glory of the One and Only, who came from the Father" (John 1:14), to "the likeness of sinful flesh" (Rom. 8:3). This stupendous accomplishment can be explained in one of two ways—either by presuming great virtues possessed by Mary as a fit vessel, or else by assuming an incalculable condescension exercised by God. I admit God certainly could, by His grace, have raised Mary up to some dazzling, heavenly height. But the fact of the Incarnation is no proof that He did. The Apostles describe the Incarnation as proof, instead, that He Himself stooped to an earthly low. God in Christ "made Himself nothing" (Php. 2:7). There's no explaining this by supposing His nation was fitting or His mother fitting or His cradle fitting. They were not and couldn't be fitting. God the Son came down to zero, and then—praise Him—He draws us up with Him to "the right hand of God" (Col. 3:1-4).

I do see that, happily, Marian devotion can result in a focus on, and a deeper appreciation of, the Incarnation. However, this great potential strength seems to carry with it a corresponding risk of a serious error—*i.e.*, that the Incarnation will be explained from a human point of view ("Here's how Mary's nature and character made the Incarnation possible") when in fact the event is inexplicable other than from the point of view of pure divine grace. The uncreated eternal God who could condescend to be the son of even the *highest* mere creature (if that's what Mary was), could just as well condescend to be the son of the most "*humble*" creature (which is what Mary *said* she was (Luke 1:48, 52)). The "overshadowing" of the Spirit at the Annunciation teaches us not Mary's virtues but God's great grace.

Dwight: Once again, you've encapsulated the Catholic view but made it sound contrary to what we believe. We also believe that the incarnation is only understandable from the viewpoint of pure divine, unmerited grace and favor. How this grace was first ministered to Mary in particular we will discuss in the next chapter.

We do *not* believe that God chose Mary because she was some sort of superwoman. He did not choose Mary because of her own merit or personal goodness. Mary was only made fit to be Jesus' mother by the action of God's grace. Yes, she was humble and lowly, but that's exactly the point on which the argument turns. Her total humility does not contradict her greatness; it is the seal of her greatness. God's grace enabled her to be as humble as she was, and that natural humility is the very trait that made her fit to be the mother of God. While Mary understood her lowliness, she also understood that God lifts up the humble. (Luke 1:52) She recognized that it was due to her humble greatness that all generations would call her blessed, but she also recognized that this greatness was only because "The Mighty One had done great things for her." (Luke 1:48-49.) One of those "great things", as we shall now see, was her conception.

6

Woman and Serpent, Take 2

The Immaculate Conception

Dwight: I expect the Catholic doctrine that is most objectionable to Evangelicals is Mary's Immaculate Conception. However, since our aim is to approach our differences directly, I'll state it right up front: Catholics believe that Mary was sinless from the moment of her conception through to the end of her earthly life. Or, as the doctrine was officially defined:

> the most Blessed Virgin Mary was, from the first moment of her conception, by the singular grace and privilege of almighty God and in view of the merits of Jesus Christ the Savior of the human race, preserved immune from all stain of original sin....[70]

We admit that this doctrine is not stated explicitly in the Scriptures. Does that fact end the matter for Evangelicals?

David: Well, we're a little more nuanced than *that*. It's true that our first question is always, "What does the Bible say?" Cardinal Newman himself acknowledged that "No one can add to revelation. That was given once for all."[71] (Evidently he alludes to Jude 3—"the faith that was *once for all* entrusted to the saints".) If a supposed doctrine is not actually within the sacred "deposit" entrusted by the Apostles to the Church (1 Tim. 6:20; 2 Tim. 1:14, 2:2), then it is not an authentic part of the Christian Faith.

However, we don't expect a Catholic to put on *Sola Scriptura*, Bible-only blinders. Instead, you'll make the point that even the oral teaching of the Apostles was authoritative (1 Thess. 2:13) and was handed down as such (2 Thess. 2:15); and if there's evidence that a doctrine was taught orally by the Apostles, you'll argue forcefully that such a doctrine commands our assent. Moreover, you'll argue that even truths *implicit* in the Apostles' teaching are a part of the Faith. (Cardinal Newman explained that, "as time goes on, what was given once for all is understood more and more clearly".) For example, neither the doctrine of the Trinity[72] nor the doctrine of Jesus Christ as true God and true Man[73] is explicitly taught in the New Testament, but each of these doctrines is a synthesis of what the Apostles certainly did teach. Thus, these theological and Christological truths do indeed command our assent.

In the same way, the case for the Mary's sinlessness could be pretty strong, even in the absence of direct Biblical support, if there is evidence that the first-century Church had received it orally from the Apostles, or if Mary's sinlessness is implicit in what the Apostles taught. So you will attempt to show how Mary's sinlessness is implicit in the Scriptures, right?

What it means to be perfect

Dwight: I want to consider what the Bible says, but I also want to explain how we actually think of Mary's perfection, and how it fits in with the whole plan of redemption. That way, even if our Evangelical readers still disagree with this doctrine, they will at least understand what it is they disagree with.

In previous chapters I've tried to show how the fact that Mary was a virgin indicates her character, and not just a lack of sexual experience. When the early Church taught that she was a virgin for her whole life, they were saying that Mary's special God-given purity included a wholeness that permeated Mary's whole being. By the end of the second century Mary was referred to as "all holy."[74] This does not mean that Mary was seen as some sort of goddess or superwoman. Instead, by God's grace, she was a completely fulfilled and whole human being.

So we believe Mary was perfect, but not in the same way Jesus was. His was the total perfection of God made flesh. Mary's perfection is the wholeness of humanity preserved in its original innocence by the redemption of Christ. We agree, don't we, that sin is a twist in our human nature? It is a lack in our lives. Because of sin, the glory of God's image is depleted in us. (Romans 3:23) Another way of saying this is that, in our sinful condition, we lack God's grace.

Full of amazing grace

Dwight: This was not so with Mary. Rather than lacking God's grace, Mary was "full of grace." (Luke 1:24.) Modern versions translate this phrase "highly favored one", but the Greek word is *kecharitomene*, a form of the verb *charitoo*. The root is *charis,* the word translated "grace" in the New Testament— and *kecharitomene*, which indicates a fullness or perfection of grace, can be paraphrased "completely, perfectly, enduringly endowed with grace."[75] If a person is completely, perfectly and enduringly endowed with grace, then sin, which is an emptiness or distortion in human nature, would be absent.

David: You infer quite a lot from "full of grace". The *Catholic Encyclopedia,* however, admits that "*kecharitomene* ... serves only as an illustration, not as a proof of" the Immaculate Conception. In fact, every forgiven sinner has received "the riches of God's grace", which God "has freely *given* us" and indeed has "lavished on us" (Eph. 1:6-8),[76] but this is no indication of sinlessness; rather, we receive grace precisely because we are sinners. If someone is said to be full of God's grace, this is not a description of *her* virtues. It is a comment on the graciousness of God, and not praise to the recipient.

Dwight: I agree. Mary's grace-full status glorifies God, not Mary. Mary says this too, when she sings, "The Mighty One has done great things for me." (Luke 1:49)

This particular form (*kecharitomene*) is used only once in the New Testament—in this reference to Mary. Furthermore, the grammatical construction of the angel's greeting means that *kecharitomene* is actually used as a name for Mary. This is similar to God giving Abram a new name meaning "Father of Nations" and Jesus calling Simon, "Peter the Rock." We know that when God gives people a new name he is emphasizing their character and the role they have to play in the drama of redemption.

It is vital to understand that this grace was in no way Mary's own merit. She shared in the curse of original sin (though not the "stain") and needed Christ's redemption. We believe in Mary's case Christ's redemption worked backwards through time as it did for the Old Testament men and women of faith.[77]

David: It's right that you distinguish grace and merit, but you fail to carry that distinction through: No matter how complete, perfect, and enduring was this grace that Mary received—make it as unique as you like—by its nature, that superlative grace was *grace*, and was therefore evidence of God's generosity (as indeed Mary saw it to be; see Luke 1:48-53) and not of Mary's being somehow special. In your view, though, because Mary was "full of grace", she had never had to repent of sin. Her recitations of the penitential Psalms would have been hypothetical. Any sacrifices and offerings for sin that she had made under the Law of Moses would have been superfluous. She never had to "mortify the flesh", and if she underwent sanctification, it would have been nothing like that process as we experience it. She was not one of us.

Dwight: Mary didn't receive grace because she was special; she was special because she received grace. Mary was most certainly "one of us". That's why we praise God when we see what he has done in her life. Mary was simply given the wholeness that is the destiny of all believers. We are all called to perfection. (Matt. 5:48, 19:21; 2 Cor. 7:1; James 1:4; I John 3:9) In fact, we were predestined in Christ to be "holy and blameless." (Eph.1:4) Mary is simply the first Christian to be brought to that total perfection in Christ Jesus. As the Protestant theologian John de Satge writes,

> The Immaculate Conception of Mary gives the clue to understanding her particular place among her son's people. She is "the first Christian, the first of the redeemed, the first of our flawed human race to have received the fullness of redemption. From first to last—in Catholic dogma, from Immaculate Conception to Assumption—she was a human being transformed by the grace of God into what, in the divine purpose, she was intended to be."[78]

This graced wholeness means that Mary was in a fulfilled creature-creator relationship with God. As such Mary was natural. From this perspective it is everybody else—twisted by original sin—who are distorted and un-natural. This is vital to understand: in her fully natural state, Mary was all that every woman was created to be. We say Mary was sinless, but that is really a negative definition. It is better to understand Mary's perfection as wholeness. Mary then, was not a goddess but a woman preserved in all her primal innocence, as fresh and natural as Eve. This is why the Christians of the first and second centuries taught that Mary was a perpetual virgin, and why the first Christian theologians—Justin Martyr and Irenaeus—referred to Mary as the "second Eve." Their teaching is based on the prophecy of Genesis 3:15, where the offspring of a woman will conquer the serpent, and Revelation 12, where that woman is revealed as Mary. They saw that, in Mary, God had given humanity a second chance.[79]

The second Eve?

David: A Mary with restored full humanity certainly feels less objectionable than a Mary who is a demi-goddess. However, this argument based on the Eve-Mary parallel implicates our prior discussions about poetry becoming dogma. First of all, why assume that Eve was a virgin when she was tempted and fell? On the very first day of Adam and Eve's existence, God told them to "be fruitful" (Gen. 1:28); and the Biblical teaching about man and wife becoming "one flesh" (Gen. 2:24) *precedes* the Fall. Thus, if the Mary-Eve parallel depends on their both being virgins, the parallel is problematic.

Dwight: You're going all literal on me again. We are simply saying that in her first created state Mary, like Eve, was innocent and pure in the widest definition of the term.

David: If linking Eve and Mary depends on their both being virgins, then for me it's in doubt. But even if they are both presumed to be virgins, inferring Mary's sinlessness from unfallen Eve's is still quite a stretch. It was a fallen angel who tempted Eve, but Mary's messenger Gabriel was unfallen, so the Eve-Mary comparison includes that unpoetical asymmetry. Poetically speaking, wouldn't it be more pleasing to have a symmetrical comparison (a *chiasmus*, perhaps?)—In Eden a fallen angel (Satan) leads an unfallen woman (Eve) from righteousness into disobedience, but in Nazareth an unfallen angel (Gabriel) leads a fallen woman (Mary) from unrighteousness into obedience. It's more symmetrical and better poetry that way, but of course I can't let my poetical judgments drive my doctrine. My point is simply that the Eve-Mary comparison is unreliable to teach us a doctrine (*e.g.*, Mary's supposed sinlessness); we have to know the doctrine already, and then see it (or not) in the comparison.

The Church's Understanding Matures

Dwight: This Biblically-based comparison isn't proof for the Immaculate Conception. It is part of the whole belief and practice of the early Church regarding Mary. As we've already seen the belief that Mary was sinless was formulated very early. As the Church came to a fuller understanding of the incarnation in the early fourth century, she also matured into a fuller understanding of the extent of Mary's grace-filled wholeness. As theologians reflected on the incarnation, they came to realize that if Jesus was free from sin, and if he *really* took Mary's humanity, then Mary had to have been preserved from the stain of original sin.[80] Saint Augustine sums up their view,

> [W]ith the exception of the holy Virgin Mary, in whose case, out of respect for the Lord, I do not wish there to be any further question as far as sin is concerned, since how can we know what great abundance of grace was conferred on her to conquer sin in every way, seeing that she merited to conceive and bear him who certainly had no sin at all.[81]

For logical reasons we believe that Mary was blessed with this fullness of grace from the first moment of her life. Some theologians in the Catholic and Orthodox churches have debated when this fullness of God's grace touched Mary's life, but none has denied that she enjoyed this wholeness. Mary's full and wholly graced humanity has been praised by the vast majority of Christians–Eastern and Western—down through the ages. Many Anglicans believe in the supernaturally graced humanity of Mary,[82] and Martin Luther wrote, "It is a sweet and pious belief that the infusion of Mary's soul was effected without original sin; so that in the very infusion of her soul she was also purified from original sin and adorned with God's gifts.... [T]hus from the first moment she began to live she was free from all sin."[83]

To be fair, the doctrine of the Immaculate Conception as defined in 1854 is not fully articulated in these passages. However, the early church texts as well as Luther's words, are in complete harmony with the more precise doctrine of the Immaculate Conception, on the other hand, the typical modern Evangelical view is totally out of synch with the predominant thrust of Christian doctrine in this matter.

David: You make two points to which I'd like to respond now: As for the early Church's consensus, the idea that Mary is sinless is admittedly an ancient and widely held belief, though not a *unanimously* held belief. Most notably, Origen (185-254) observed that if Mary had not sinned, then "Jesus did not die for her sins", which (he suggested) could not be "if 'all have sinned and fall short of the glory of God'" (quoting Rom. 3:23).[84]

Dwight: Even Origen referred to Mary as "all holy".[85] It's just that he considered her perfection to be something she grew into, rather than being granted at conception.

Avoiding Original Sin: the Sequel

David: As for the "logic" of the doctrine, I'll just say that it is not obvious to me. It was the Virgin Birth that assured the sinlessness of Jesus by sparing Him the transmission of sin from a human father,[86] and any further theories about how Mary's nature would have affected Jesus' nature are just that: theories.

Dwight: There are two matters that are logical here. Although Jesus was spared original sin because he was not generated in a natural way, he would still have been "infected" by original sin as he assumed Mary's human flesh. If he *really* took Mary's flesh as we both agree, then Mary needed to be preserved from original sin.

David: By your reasoning, Mary would have been "infected" by original sin as she assumed Anna's flesh, unless Anna had been preserved from original sin as well—and so on, through her ancestry.

Dwight: We could chase our tails on this one for a long time. Let me point out another logical reason why Mary needed to have been preserved from the stain of original sin. One of the effects of original sin is that our will is tainted. Original sin causes us to choose wrongly. In order for Mary's "yes" to God to have been valid it needed to be a totally free choice. So Mary had to be preserved from that stain of original sin that would have biased her choice.

David: I can see how sinlessness could have *facilitated* Mary's "Let it be", but even sinners with tainted wills can do God's will. As God said to Cain, "Sin is crouching at your door; ... but you must master it." (Gen. 4:6.) Jesus' lineage is full of sinners who said yes to God at crucial moments: Abraham heeded God's call (Gen. 12:1-4); Rahab the pagan harlot hid the Hebrew spies (Jos. 2); David the sometime adulterer was, in spite of his sin, a "man after God's own heart" (Acts 13:22); and so on.

Dwight: Of course sinners can choose to do God's will, but the underlying point is that Mary's will also needed to be totally free because it was the human will which Jesus was going to take to himself. For her will to be totally free Mary had to have been preserved from the stain of original sin. When did this fully graced condition begin? It could only have begun at the beginning of Mary's life. As we came to understand better just exactly when human life begins, it became clear that this "all holiness" began at her conception. But you make a fair point when you ask how far logic can take us. You ask, "how can we know?" You are right that we are helpless on our own to fathom such mysteries. Left to our own devices, we end up chasing our own hypothetical theories. To avoid such quicksand of private interpretation, we turn to the Church to understand the mysteries of redemption. So St Paul writes, "His [God's] intent is that now, through the Church, the manifold wisdom of God should be made known…" (Eph. 3:10)

Scripture and Tradition

David: Before asking what the Church finds *implicit* in the Scriptures, the Evangelical bumps into a few *explicit* things: If Mary was conceived without sin and if she thereafter unfailingly avoided actual sin, these were things that no one, not even Mary, could have known without supernatural revelation, so when and to whom was it revealed that Mary was sinless? The Apostles taught the generality that all humans have sinned (Rom. 3:9, 10, 23; Rom. 5:12, 18; 1 Cor. 15:22; Gal. 3:22; Eph. 2:3), and when they wanted to teach that someone—namely, Jesus Christ—is sinless, they knew how to do it; and we can line up their "Bible proof texts" for Jesus' sinlessness. (Matt. 27:4, 19; Luke 23:41, 47; John 8:46; 2 Cor. 5:21; Heb. 4:15; Heb. 7:26; 1 Pet. 2:22; 1 John 3:5.) The New Testament writers made no such case for Mary.

Someone who believes in Mary's sinlessness might take care to exempt her from blanket statements about human sin,[87] but Paul did not bother to do so, even when writing to her home town of Ephesus (*see* Eph. 2:3), and Mary's own adopted son John implied no exemption for her when he wrote, "If we claim to be without sin, we deceive ourselves and the truth is not in us…. If we claim we have not sinned, we make [God] out to be a liar and his word has no place in our lives." (1 John 1:8, 10.) Moreover, Paul said that "death came to all men, *because all sinned*" (Rom. 5:12), and Mary herself indicated that she was one of those who need a "Savior" (Luke 1:47). For the sake of argument, however, I'll concede that even a *non*-sinner might have been graciously *kept* from sin only in view of the Savior's merits; still, at least *in general* it's actual sinners who need a Savior. Thus, the Scriptures teach a generality of human sinfulness that tends against Mary's sinlessness. An exception would be possible, but I would expect that exception to be founded on at least some pretty strong implications. And as

I've already explained, the implications you find in Gabriel's "full of grace" and in the Eve-Mary parallel seem very weak to me.

Dwight: Why did Paul and the gospel writers not acknowledge Mary's sinlessness? Two reasons: First, the church rightly needed to discern who Jesus really was, and only after they refined his true status could they go on to reflect on the stature of Mary. Second, by the very nature of her perfection, Mary was humble and hidden. Like all really holy people, she didn't stand out. If she was totally natural, then she didn't stand out, because what is natural is not unusual. I believe that if we had met Mary, she would have seemed like just another Jewish matron—perhaps with a special indefinable sweetness, or an intense quality of love and interest in others.[88]

I accept your point that the implications of two Biblical references are not proof of a dogma. As you've observed at the beginning of the chapter, Catholics do not rely on Scripture alone for the development of doctrine. Jesus said he had many things to teach, but that he couldn't reveal them because the disciples couldn't cope with it all. Instead, the Holy Spirit would come and lead them into all Truth. (John 16:3, 12.) At Pentecost the Holy Spirit inspired the apostolic Church, and now the Church is the very pillar and foundation of truth. (I Timothy 3:15.) We therefore submit our own theories to the dynamic and living tradition of the Church. For two thousand years the best Christian minds have been reflecting, praying, and debating these issues, guided by the promised Holy Spirit. One might be able to formulate other theories, but we believe that the consensus of the Church in this matter is the right one.

David: It's not just *any* tradition to which Christians adhere; it's *Apostolic* tradition. Jesus particularly condemned teachers who confused mere human tradition with authentic, divine doctrine (Matt. 15:3-8 = Mark 7:6-13), and the Apostles made the same distinction (Col. 2:8; Titus 1:14; 1 Pet. 1:18). The Church is the "pillar and foundation of the truth" when it faithfully perpetuates what the Apostles taught (and, arguably, what the Apostles' teaching implies); the Church is *not* a perpetual revelation machine. The "faith that was once for all entrusted to the saints" (Jude 3) consists of what the Apostles wrote and taught. Other ideas—even if generations of Christians have thought those ideas fitting or sweet—are simply not part of what was "once for all entrusted". I think you agree with me, at least in principle, if not in application.

The Universal Faith

Dwight: We have a larger understanding of apostolicity than you do, but basically I agree with what you say. We agree that there can be no new revelation. But it is also true that the Church comes into a fuller and fuller understanding of the "faith once entrusted to the saints" over the course of time. (CCC, para.66.)

David: Then the question is whether a given doctrine that is not explicit in the Bible (here, the doctrine of Mary's Immaculate Conception) is a legitimate development in the understanding of the Apostolic "faith once entrusted" or is, instead, a novelty. This "development vs. novelty" distinction is implicated in much of the debate about Catholic and Protestant differences. In that debate, the greatest difficulty of the Protestant is, fittingly, catholicity: The opponent of Roman Catholicism has the most difficulty when he opposes doctrine that can be shown to be truly *catholic*–that is, world-wide or universal—doctrines that (in the famous fifth -century formula of St. Vincent of Lerins) have been believed "everywhere, always, by everyone". Only the most audacious Protestant can easily shrug off the fact that all recorded Christian opinion on a given issue goes against him until, say, the sixteenth century.

However, the doctrine of the Immaculate Conception makes the Protestant debater breathe easy, since it is probably the least "catholic" and most novel of the Catholic dogmas. Third century theologians like Origen and Tertullian considered Mary to be a sinner, so that even the doctrine of her mere sinlessness lacks catholicity.

Dwight: You mustn't confuse catholicity with unanimity. Vincent of Lerins's statement is excellent as a sound bite, but catholicity means consensus—not unanimous consent.

David: The particular doctrine of the Immaculate Conception—*i.e.*, that her sinlessness began at her very conception—is even more awkward. Against the Immaculate Conception *per se* we can line up great popes like Innocent III (d. 417), Leo I (d. 461), and Gregory I (d. 604), along with esteemed theologians no less than Anselm of Canterbury (d. 1109), Bernard of Clairvaux (d. 1153), and "the angelic doctor" Thomas Aquinas (d. 1274),[89] who all, while they thought Mary sinless, nonetheless affirmatively opposed the doctrine of her Immaculate Conception[90]—at least, as they understood it. The doctrine was clearly not known and affirmed by them.

Luther (himself admittedly a devotee of Mary) was unduly generous to call this un-catholic and un-Scriptural doctrine "a sweet and pious belief". However, if Luther was right, then the doctrine of the Immaculate Conception is at most a *permissible* opinion. It is quite another thing to say, as the Catholic Church says, that the Immaculate Conception is a cardinal Christian doctrine, so that (according to the Pope who defined the dogma) someone who denies the Immaculate Conception should know—

> that he is condemned by his own judgment; that he has suffered shipwreck in the faith; that he has separated from the unity of the Church; and that, furthermore, by his own action he incurs the penalties established by law if he should dare to express in words or writing or by any other outward means the errors he think in his heart.[91]

Even making allowances for Pope Pius IX's nineteenth-century rhetoric to be, well, more *emphatic* than we might employ in our more ecumenical era, this dogmatic assertion is all out of proportion. If even Thomas Aquinas, surely the preeminent Catholic theologian, could fail to see this doctrine at least implied in what the Apostles wrote or taught, then it is hard to see how this doctrine could be Biblical, or catholic, or Apostolic.

Dwight: It's a curious thing to find Pope Pius IX and Martin Luther on the same side, but I think you overstate the case of Thomas Aquinas. Due to Thomas's thirteenth-century understanding of human conception, he reasoned that Mary was sanctified not at her conception, but at the point that her soul was infused into her body. In fact Thomas believes not only that Mary was sinless, but also that her perfection began before her birth, and before she had personally committed any actual sin.[92] The same applies to the objections of other Catholic popes and theologians.

David: Not exactly. The objections of Bernard of Clairvaux were a bit different from Thomas Aquinas's. Bernard was very devoted to Mary, and thought that Mary was sinless at birth, but he nonetheless objected to the celebration of the newly introduced Feast of the Immaculate Conception on the grounds that it was, in his view,

> a false honor to the royal Virgin, which she does not need, and ... an unauthorized innovation, which was the mother of temerity, the sister of superstition, and the daughter of levity.... He rejected the opinion of the Immaculate Conception of Mary as contrary to tradition and derogatory to the dignity of Christ, the only sinless being, and asked the [proponents of the doctrine] ..., "Whence they discovered such a hidden fact? On the same ground they might appoint festivals of the conception of the parents, grandparents, and great-grandparents of Mary, and so on without end."[93]

Bernard's objections are similar to those of the Eastern Orthodox, most of whom reject the Immaculate Conception because "[t]hey feel it to be unnecessary; ... it seems to separate

Mary from the rest of the descendants of Adam, putting her in a completely different class from all the other righteous men and women of the Old Testament."[94]

Dwight: Of course it is possible to discover Catholic teachers who disagree about the fine points. It is through theological debate that the Church comes to understand, define and defend the truth. There may be disagreement on the details, but neither the Orthodox nor Bernard nor Thomas is disputing the essence of the doctrine, that is, Mary's sinlessness.

You may well find instances of Catholic leaders disputing this doctrine before it was dogmatically defined, but you won't find them or the Eastern Orthodox actually supporting the Evangelical view. From the wider perspective, therefore, we have to ask which is the later distortion of the historic faith—the dogma of the Immaculate Conception, which is totally congruent with the beliefs of the early church or the Evangelical view which denies Mary's perfection altogether.

David: I admit that from the fifth century on, my view is all but un-heard of, until after the Reformation. Your position would have more persuasive force for me, though, if the Church's dogma stopped where that consensus ends—*i.e.*, at Mary's sinlessness. But by defining as dogma a refinement of doctrine that some of the Church's own heroes resisted shows that this doctrinal development is regulated not by what is ancient and Apostolic, but by something else—a Marian fascination that is hard to understand because it is so alien to my own spirituality.

The possibility of perfection

Dwight: As a debater, you naturally gravitate to the point where you think your case is the strongest and mine is the weakest. But this discussion is not only a chance to air our disagreements, but an attempt to find some agreement too. Maybe you should return to what you think of as the less problematic and more nearly catholic idea of Mary's sinlessness, and consider for a moment why this *is* so alien to your spirituality. Does it reflect the influence of Protestant theology, which is pessimistic about any kind of graced human perfection in this life?

David: It is true that Evangelicals do not expect perfection in this life (nor think that anyone is entitled to claim it), but our confident hope of *ultimate* perfection in Christ (Rom. 8:29; 1 John 3:1-3) is the thing that keeps us going.

Dwight: Catholics cultivate the same hope, with the exception that we think perfection *is* possible in this life by God's grace. This is why the doctrine of the Immaculate Conception glorifies the Lord, because at the heart of our belief in Mary's sinlessness is the realization that the great grace she received was won by the death and resurrection of her Son. We praise God for what he has done in Mary's life and see in her the perfection that is promised to each one of us by God's amazing grace.

David: Making Mary a Christian "Everywoman" would neutralize most of our objections—but the Catholic view is that Mary is different: She "has *already* reached that perfection", whereas "the faithful still strive to conquer sin and increase in holiness. And so they turn their eyes to Mary".[95] In running the Christian race, however, we do not "turn [our] eyes to Mary" but, instead, "fix our eyes on Jesus" (Heb. 12:2). I think we deny Mary's sinlessness not from pessimism but because evidence is lacking, and because the example and means of perfection that God has expressly and unmistakably given to us is none other than His Son, Jesus Christ.

Dwight: We look to Mary not as the "author and perfecter of our faith" (Heb 12:2) but as the first Christian in whom that redemption has been completed. We look to her therefore as an example of the promise in store for each of us. This wonderful possibility of perfection is the result of our intimate *union* with Christ. And what human could be more united with Christ than his mother? It is precisely because Mary and Jesus shared the same human nature that Mary was the first of the redeemed to share in the human wholeness that Christ died to win for us. Therefore, in the early church writings a high view of Mary is always linked with a correct view of Christ.

Athanasius or Evangelicals?

Dwight: This is one of the things I find so inconsistent with the Evangelical position. You affirm the Christological doctrines defined and defended by the fourth century church, but you dispose of the Marian doctrines that were developed and defined at the same time. These doctrines about Mary were not snap-on extra attachments to the faith. They were understood to be integral to the all-important Christological definitions. Many examples can be given, but let's take one. I know you would hail Athanasius, who championed the deity of Christ at the Council of Nicea, as a hero and defender of orthodoxy, but do you really then disagree with that monumental theologian when he writes, "the life of Mary, Mother of God, suffice[s] as an ideal of perfection and the form of the heavenly life"?[96]

David: Ouch! No fair, putting Mary between me and Athanasius! He should certainly be a hero to anyone who confesses Jesus Christ as God the Son, and I have to acknowledge that I'm out of step with Athanasius when it comes to Mary. As I understand it, Athanasius is not known to have expressly taught Mary's sinlessness; but he did of course affirm the Virgin Birth and Mary's title *Theotokos*, and also—more problematic for me— taught Mary's perpetual virginity, compared and contrasted her to Eve, saw her as the "Ark" of the New Covenant, and acknowledged her to be greater than any other created being. About Mary, I'm plainly on a different wave-length from Athanasius and others like him, whom I'd otherwise like to count as kindred spirits.

In my defense, I'll simply say that I do give great deference to Athanasius as an expounder of the Scriptures, which abundantly support his theology and Christology. His Christological opponents may have believed he *mis*-interpreted the Bible, but it was quite clear that he *was* interpreting the Bible. Where I part company with him is where he seems to cease repeating and expounding the Apostolic message and to begin elaborating and extrapolating, and perpetuating human reflections.

Dwight: There is much more to be said on this topic of the development of doctrine, and I hope our Catholic readers will consider your very honest objections to what seems to you like Catholic high-handedness in this matter. For there to be any progress towards unity in the body of Christ, I believe Evangelicals will have to honestly strive to understand and accept certain Catholic dogmas, but Catholics will have to reconsider how they handle doctrine and struggle to re-formulate their beliefs in ways that non-Catholic Christians can understand and accept.

Your basic stumbling block seems to be the fact that the Catholic Church felt it necessary to define as essential dogma a belief that is not explicit in either Scripture or early Tradition. I actually have a lot of sympathy for your position. For some time, as an Anglican, I took your view. I regarded the Immaculate Conception as a pious opinion and wished the Catholic Church had left it that way. In fact, even after I accepted the dogma myself as a Catholic, I still wished the Church had left it in the realm of pious speculation.

However, the longer I am a Catholic, the more I come to understand how holistic Catholic doctrine is. Every element is interwoven with all the others to present a unified whole, and the doctrines of the faith are integrated into the devotional life of the Church. Pius IX's stern words indicate our belief that to deny one defined dogma is to begin unraveling the whole tapestry of orthodox faith. In other chapters I will explain further why I think this particular dogma has come to be seen as an essential part of the faith, but suffice it to say that a widespread awareness developed in the whole of the Catholic Church that the time was right for this doctrine to be defined. As an indicator of this consensus, before Pope Pius IX defined this dogma he consulted with all the worlds' bishops, who in turn consulted with all their priests and people. Only four out of more than 600 bishops worldwide thought the dogma should *not* be defined. You may think they were the right ones, but I doubt it, since all four then submitted to the mind of the church.

David: Only four bishops opposed it, it's true; but fifty-two bishops thought defining the doctrine to be *not* expedient or opportune.[97] Naturally I agree with that minority of Catholic bishops on that score, and with your former Anglican self. I appreciate your sympathy for the Evangelical critique, and I wish I could imagine a way forward. It's difficult, because the Catholic position is now set in concrete—defined as dogma by infallible papal decree—and it would appear that all of the sympathy, humility, and goodwill of Catholics can't change that. We can agree to disagree, but this leaves us in disunity. Apart from a total unraveling of Catholic notions of authority in the Church, the only way toward unity is for Evangelicals to accept the Catholic position. Should we consider doing so? I can't see it.

If the Apostles finished their ministries without teaching on Mary's sinlessness; if Origen, Tertullian, and the early Church got by without unanimity on Mary's sinlessness; if all of medieval Catholicism got by without a definition of the doctrine of the Immaculate Conception; and if Eastern Orthodoxy and Protestantism largely agree in resisting the definition of this doctrine—in view of all that, I have to hope against hope that the Roman Catholic Church will somehow find a way to un-define this dogma, and leave this issue up to private conscience.

The Immaculate Conception is only one of the *two* Marian dogmas defined in the modern era by papal decree, and the second one is our next subject.

7

The Rapture of Mary

The Glorious Assumption

David: Metastasized cancer disappeared from the body of a friend of mine after her pastor and deacons prayed and anointed her with oil (following James 5:1415). I think it was probably a miracle. Do you?

Dwight: I'm a Catholic, remember? We sign up for all sorts of miracles that you guys don't even consider. We're the folks with stigmatics, weeping statues, uncorrupt bodies of saints, miraculous apparitions and healing miracles at Lourdes. Of course it was a miracle! On the other hand, I think it's always common sense to look for a natural explanation first.

David: Exactly. This belief in the supernatural is one of the things that unite us. Catholics and Evangelicals both believe in supernatural things like the existence of God, the devil, Heaven, and Hell; the miracles recorded in the Bible; and most especially the Resurrection of Jesus Christ. I suppose non-Christian skeptics will dismiss as impossible *all* supernatural stories—those included in the Bible *and* those from other sources—and I don't exactly blame

107

them. Frankly, when I hear other Christians' stories about supposed miracles, I'm often skeptical. Nevertheless, we have to admit the *possibility* of extra-Biblical miracles. At the same time, we have to distinguish the plausible from the implausible, and be careful about how much credence we lend even to the ones we think plausible.

Dwight: The Catholic Church takes a similarly sensible view on the supernatural. We acknowledge that supernatural occurrences may happen, but when a miracle is alleged to have taken place, we step back and investigate the whole thing very thoroughly. We look for every other possible explanation, consider the theological implications, the fruit of the alleged supernatural event, and the sanctity of those involved. In other words, we suspend judgment until we ascertain all the facts. Then, in some cases, the Catholic Church will pronounce certain events to be miracles.

David: I respect the way your Church handles these investigations today. I've read news accounts of how alleged miraculous healings at the Marian shrine in Lourdes, or healings alleged as evidence for a saint's canonization, are subjected to strict scientific scrutiny by committees that even include non-believers, and only the truly unexplainable events are treated as possible miracles by the Catholic Church. I know of no Evangelical Church or denomination that has comparable procedures; we often instead just pass along unverified hearsay.

Miraculous legends about New Testament characters come to us in great numbers from the early centuries of the Christian Church. These legends vary in their plausibility—some mundane, and some elaborate and wildly improbable. For example, the Apostles Philip and Thomas both did battle with dragons— Philip, using a cross at the pagan temple of the Roman god Mars, and Thomas, invoking the name and authority of Jesus. Mary Magdalene spent the last 30 years of her life in a cave in France, and was miraculously transported just before her death to a chapel presided over by the man born blind, whom Jesus had healed (in John 9). Did these things really happen? To say the least, I've got my doubts.

Dwight: So do I. But Revelation 12 talks about the Virgin Mary and her son battling with a dragon. We accept it, but we do not interpret it literally. Perhaps the early Christian stories about Philip and Thomas used imaginative language to make a spiritual point. But basically, you're right to dismiss fantastic legends from apocryphal sources. But I thought this chapter was going to be about the Assumption.

David: I mention these stories because the Assumption of the Virgin Mary into heaven is, in my way of thinking, one of these Early Church-era legends, and we've got to evaluate its plausibility. I was therefore trying to get a feel for how similarly you and I approach questions about the miraculous.

The Earliest Accounts

David: The New Testament says nothing about Mary's Assumption—not even in Paul's discussion of resurrection in I Corinthians 15 (a passage that really should have mentioned the Assumption, if it really happened). Instead, the earliest written account of the end of Mary's life is an apocryphal treatise from the fourth or fifth century, and it reports that she was "assumed" bodily into heaven.[98] St. John of Damascus (b. 676), who is often cited in support of the Assumption, recounted the event this way:

> St. Juvenal, Bishop of Jerusalem, at the Council of Chalcedon (451), made known to the Emperor Marcian and Pulcheria, who wished to possess the body of the Mother of God, that Mary died in the presence of all the Apostles, but that her tomb, when opened, upon the request of St. Thomas, was found empty; wherefrom the Apostles concluded that the body was taken up to heaven.[99]

So actually two miracles are alleged—first, that the Apostles were miraculously assembled to witness this event,[100] and second, that Mary was assumed bodily into heaven. Attention has been focused especially on the second of these—the Assumption *per se*.

The Core Event and the Elaborations

Dwight: Tradition has focused on the second miracle not only because it is the core event, but also because there has been a fair amount of unreliable elaboration around this simple historical event. The apocryphal writings spin fantastic tales about the apostles being whisked from their far-flung missionary outposts to appear at the bedside of the Virgin Mary.

This may have happened, but I think the basic story is far simpler. The word "apostles" is often used in the early church not only for the twelve, but also for the elders of the local church. I think the apostles or church leaders who were present in Jerusalem gathered at Mary's deathbed. When they checked her tomb after her burial, the body was gone, and they concluded that God had taken her body into heaven. I presume that, as the oral tradition was passed on, and people heard that the "apostles" were present, they explained the fact with the stories about the actual twelve apostles being supernaturally transported to Jerusalem from their missionary postings. Bishop Juvenal's simple account doesn't demand any kind of supernatural, apostolic transportation and neither does the dogma as defined by our church.

Doctrinal History

David: I'll return later to your hypothesis of a simple and reliable "core" story with unreliable elaborations, but to summarize the doctrinal history—in the eighteenth century, Pope Benedict XIV taught that Mary's bodily assumption into heaven "is a probable opinion, which to deny were impious and blasphemous."[101] Then on November 1, 1950, Pope Pius XII completed the "development" of this doctrine and formally declared, as binding, infallible dogma, that—

> the Immaculate Mother of God, the ever Virgin Mary, having completed the course of her earthly life, was assumed body and soul into heavenly glory.[102]

Possible vs. Plausible

David: For the skeptic, of course, denying this doctrine is easy, even reflexive. ("It's supernatural; it couldn't have happened.") The Biblically literate Christian, however, recalls that a human's being received bodily into heaven is an event that has occurred, not only in the case of Jesus (Mark 16:19 = Luke 24:51; Acts 1:9), but also in the case of Enoch (Gen. 5:24) and, more clearly, Elijah in his fiery chariot (2 Kings 2:11). You want to disclaim the supernatural transportation of the Apostles, but if one believes in miracles, then one must admit that this, too, is *possible.*

In fact, just such a transportation is recorded in the case of Philip (Acts 8:39-40) and perhaps Ezekiel (3:14, 8:3) and Paul (2 Cor. 12:34). Consequently, we cannot say that the Apostles' being transported to Mary's deathbed and Mary's being assumed bodily into heaven are impossible. Instead, we ask (i) whether the evidence is credible, and (ii) whether the alleged events are plausible. Further, if Mary's assumption is taken to be a fact, we ask (iii) whether belief in her assumption is a part of the "faith once for all entrusted to the saints" (Jude 3), so that only a heretic will deny it.[103] My answers are: (i) probably not, (ii) probably not, and (iii) certainly not. Where am I going wrong?

Dwight: What counts against the evidence being credible is that Bishop Juvenal's account is removed from the alleged events by four hundred years, and John of Damascus' re-statement of Juvenal's account is removed by another two hundred years. If we put it in contemporary terms, this would be equivalent to a present-day writer quoting a conversation that occurred at the signing of the Declaration of Independence, which recounted an obscure event that had happened in Europe in the Middle Ages. If the originally obscure event had been momentous in its implications, then it's not impossible that a modified account passed down by oral tradition and recorded six hundred years later would be true in its essential elements.

David: It's difficult to imagine a medieval event with "momentous" implications for which no written record existed until today. If it really happened and really were momentous, it could be traced in the writings of the interested community.

Dwight: We have to take into account that the story in question took place in a time where fewer written records were kept and far fewer have survived the passage of time. My basic point is that the simple core of a story can survive for a long time. However, it's also true that the event was probably embroidered in later tellings. It would be up to the historians to try to sort through the elaboration to discover the essential core story beneath the accretions. This is what the church has done in her simple "bare bones" definition. Nevertheless, all Catholic scholars admit that the historical support for this event is sparse. In addition, there is no mention of the death of Mary in any of the writings of the earliest church fathers.

Fourth Century Uncertainty

David: This complete lack of an early Christian affirmation of the Assumption is remarkable. The earliest known writer on the subject of the death of Mary was Bishop Epiphanius of Salamis (d. 403). In his *Panarion*, Epiphanius observed that the Scriptures are silent on the question of Mary's death. He recalls the Revelation 12 passage in which an eagle rescues the woman from the dragon, and then says,

This could have happened in Mary's case. But I dare not affirm this with absolute certainty, nor do I say that she remained untouched by death, nor can I confirm whether she died.... If the holy Virgin is dead and has been buried, surely her dormition happened with great honor....[104]

If the Assumption happened, Epiphanius was unable to find out about it in the fourth century. This makes me doubt that there really was an oral tradition of the event, and makes me incline towards the conclusion that the event was a fabrication first set out in apocryphal writings.

Dwight: Despite his hesitance about the precise facts, Epiphanius affirms the Assumption. So he writes, "If the holy Virgin is dead and has been buried, surely her dormition happened with great honor; her end was most pure and crowned by virginity."[105] There are several other reasons why Mary's death was not known even to someone from the area. First, as I've mentioned in the previous chapter, Mary was naturally humble and hidden. Tradition says she died between three and fifteen years of the Ascension of Jesus. Within that time she probably lived with John or his relatives in almost total obscurity. Only after her death did the church begin to reflect on her important status, and the events of her death would therefore have been limited to scraps of information recalled perhaps long after the actual events.

We've seen with the development of the other Marian doctrines, that reflection on the true status of the Blessed Virgin came after the Christological controversies in the fourth century. Only after the Church had worked out who Jesus really was could they go on to meditate on Mary's true role.

David: But if that's true, then it makes highly unlikely the existence and maintenance of a reliable oral tradition about her death. If she succeeded well at being hidden, and if her significance was perceived only later, then the knowledge of her passing would have died out before the fourth century. Epiphanius's testimony shows that it *had* died out.

Down-to-earth and Matter-of-Fact

Dwight: It didn't die out completely. Scraps remained. But there is a further reason why the core tradition would have been downplayed. By the third and fourth centuries a strong devotion to Mary had developed, but at the same time there were various heretical groups around, like the Collyridians, who worshipped Mary. To exalt Mary too highly before Christ's true identity had been defined would be to nurture the heretics. In connection with this, it may be that the miraculous events surrounding the end of Mary's life were deliberately downplayed because of the prevalence of apocryphal gospels with their fantastic stories.

It is this factor that makes Bishop Juvenal's story, by comparison, most credible. First of all, his story did *not* arise within a heretical sect. Neither is the story first discovered in an apocryphal gospel. Instead we have a down-to-earth account of a leader of the Jerusalem church about what happened to Mary's body. Second, the simple story recounted by Bishop Juvenal does not sound fantastic and legendary. If the early Christians had wanted to glorify Mary with a wonderful legend about her going up into heaven, you would expect the story to be far more elaborate.

Later on there were dubious writings in circulation that *do* give rather florid accounts of Mary's death. Most of these documents are flawed and suspect, either theologically or historically or both. Juvenal's early story, on the other hand, has the simple ring of truth: The apostles gathered at her deathbed, and buried her, but when they opened the tomb she was gone. It has the same matter-of-fact tone as the verse in Genesis about Enoch, "he was no more, because God took him away." (Gen. 6:24.)

David: You prefer Juvenal (through John of Damascus) as the source for the story, and you find his supposed bare-bones version more defensible than the elaborate stories of the heretics or the apocryphal books; but there are several problems with this approach: First, while I wouldn't call Bishop Juvenal a heretic, Pope Leo the Great did chide him for flirting with Christological error.[106] He was no Athanasius. Second, while John of Damascus did cite Juvenal in the instance quoted above, I know of no evidence that even John of Damascus himself—much less the Church generally—actually regarded Juvenal, and not the apocryphal books, as the source for the Assumption.[107]

In an earlier chapter we saw, from the *Protoevangelium of James*, that early Christians were not averse to believing apocryphal stories. Third, John of Damascus is the *only* source I know of for Juvenal's account, but John's own recounting of the Assumption does not lack "throngs of angels".[108] The only historical "proof" for the Assumption would also just as well "prove" the fantastical details you disclaim. I don't think this bare-bones, "core" story existed anywhere in the early Church. Instead, the earliest account of the Assumption must have been the full-blown, technicolor extravaganza, full of angels and flying Apostles. I can see why Church leaders would never dogmatically define the whole epic, but I think that your simplified, less embarrassing story is the *later* version, and not the original.

Myths and Legends

Dwight: To simply dismiss the apocryphal writings as fantastic fables and then to dismiss the Christians of the fourth and fifth century for believing them is too simplistic. Remember, this is a time when there was still some uncertainty about the New Testament canon. The apocryphal writings were in circulation with many other Christian writings, and most of them claimed apostolic authorship. Some of them were heretical; some were merely non-apostolic. Some claimed apostolic authority and only later have we discovered that the claims were spurious.

One of the Assumption stories claimed to be a letter written by the Apostle John. Even to call these writings "spurious" is not the whole picture. Quite often the authors attributed the book to an apostle because they were gathering together teachings that were rooted in the oral tradition from that particular apostle or from the preaching of a particular church that had an apostolic foundation. The same problem of authorship surrounds books we do accept as canonical. For example, from the earliest days there is uncertainty about the apostolic authorship of the second epistle of Peter, the book of Jude and the Book of Hebrews. This is not to denigrate these books of the New Testament, nor is it to elevate apocryphal writings to the level of Scripture. It is simply to make the point that in the fourth and fifth century it was quite easy to believe that the apocryphal accounts of the Assumption were more solid than we now know them to be.

You don't like my theory that there was a core tradition that was later elaborated, but this is the simplest solution, and the obvious way that legends develop. Take the story of Johnny Appleseed for instance. There really was an eccentric fellow, John Chapman, who wandered around the American countryside planting apple trees. From that simple event a folk legend developed. In the same way, the Assumption stories are most likely to be later elaborations of a simple core story based in the oral traditions of the Jerusalem Church. We do not base the dogma on these apocryphal writings as anti-Catholic writers suggest. However we do use them to show that there was, in the early church, a widespread belief in the Assumption of the Blessed Virgin. By the seventh century this belief had become virtually universal, since the Feast Day of the Assumption was celebrated everywhere.

David: Yes, some legends do have a core of truth, but others are made of whole cloth. Take the well-known story of George Washington cutting down the cherry tree and then confessing his misdeed. ("I cannot tell a lie.") Washington was a real person, of course, and later generations recounted this story very credulously and patriotically, but we now know that Parson Weems's cherry tree story was a fabrication. Some widely told stories about famous historical figures just aren't true. The fact that many people believed a story on the basis of lousy evidence doesn't make the story true.

Dwight: Neither does it necessarily make the core story false. But finally, the context of the Assumption story shows that there were no relics for Mary. We know the early church venerated the bodies of saints. As both the core story and the dogma suggest, the fact that there is not, nor ever has been, a claim for Mary's relics is simple and strong support that her body disappeared in some extraordinary way.

David: Maybe the absence of Mary's relics simply proves a lack of Marian devotion in the first century—a lack consistent with the silence of the New Testament. After all, if the story of the Assumption is true, then Mary did have a tomb that first-century Christians could have venerated—and *would* have venerated, if they had any such inclination. The majority of the early witnesses say that Mary's final days were spent at Jerusalem, but it wasn't until the sixth century that Mary's supposed tomb was venerated in Jerusalem. It's just hard to explain how it could be true that an epochal event like the Assumption occurred, *and* that the story of it was reliably handed down by oral tradition, *but* that the locals had failed for five centuries to mark the site and the event.

Why *not* Believe?

Dwight: The fact is we simply don't know very much about the end of Mary's life. The core evidence comes down to a simple account told four hundred years after the event. Should we believe it? Many millions of Christians down through the centuries have done so with simple faith. Maybe instead of the skeptical "Why believe it?" we should ask, "Why *not* believe it?"

Belief in the Assumption of Mary doesn't contradict Scripture. It doesn't detract from the glory due to Jesus Christ—in fact such a belief glorifies him further because it shows what great power he has to lift up his mother from the grave as the first Christian. This is the same resurrection power by which he promises to raise some of us up bodily (I Thess. 4:17) and all of us at the last day (I Cor. 15:51-57). Maybe instead of nurturing such a skeptical, doubting attitude, you ought to embrace the Assumption of the Blessed Virgin as an opportunity for good old-fashioned trust. To affirm the Assumption is to take someone else's word for it, and to accept a truth, which is glorious and fine even though the scientist and historian in you shudders. But which is better, to go through life doubting and poking, or to go through life with a heart open to belief? At the last day I'd rather be blamed for believing too much than too little. Surely gullibility is less culpable than disbelief.

David: There's something to what you say. One of the most winning Christians I know is a Greek Orthodox man who spoke with me very frankly about Mary. He explained that "we believe" in the Assumption of Mary, and he described the event pretty much as John of Damascus did. This is a well-educated man—a debate coach, in fact, so he knows full well how to require proof for a controversial assertion. But he affirmed to me his belief in the Assumption pretty much as I would affirm to an unbeliever my belief in the Biblical miracles: aware how it must sound to the hearer, but completely solid in his faith. In my conversation with this man, I felt a bit ill at ease with my own skepticism, and I preferred his docility. If you ask me, the authentic Christian personality is more like him than me. I see that there could be silly vanity, or sinful pride, in my imagining that I, in the twenty-first century, can find out for myself what happened at the end of Mary's life nineteen centuries ago, rather than just accepting what Christians have taught. At least part of me would like to just shut up, surrender my critical faculties, and stop quibbling.

"Test the spirits"

David: However, docility is only *one* Christian virtue. Somehow, we are supposed to be both as "wise as serpents, *and* harmless as doves". (Matt.10:16.) It's quite true that we should be uncritically accepting of the Apostolic truth, but we must wisely discern what is that Apostolic truth, and what are the counterfeits and pious frauds. The Book of Proverbs says it is not a good man but a "*simple* man" who "believes anything; but a *prudent* man gives thought to his steps." (Prov. 14:15.)

Warning about the possibility of error creeping into the Church, the Apostle John said, "do not believe every spirit, but test the spirits to see whether they are from God". (1 John 4:1.) Or, as Paul put it, "Test everything. Hold on to the good." (1 Thess. 5:21.) The Berean Christians, who "examined the Scriptures every day to see if what Paul said was true", were not criticized for pride or vanity or skepticism but were said, rather, to be of "*noble* character". (Acts 17:11.) The Apostle Peter marked a clear distinction between, on the one hand, the facts of the Christian Gospel verified by "eyewitnesses" and, on the other hand, "cleverly invented stories". (2 Pet. 1:16.) It's a distinction that we are obliged to uphold.

Dwight: And that's why the simple account, and the dogma as defined by our Church avoids the fanciful stories of the apocryphal writings in favor of a simple account of what happened at the end of Mary's life.

You mentioned the New Testament admonitions to "test" all teaching. But remember these instructions were written to the churches, not first and foremost to individual Christians. It is the role of the apostolic Church to test everything, examine the Scriptures, and avoid cleverly invented stories. It is our job to "obey our leaders and submit to their authority" because "they keep watch over our souls". (Heb. 13:17.) That is the only way to avoid the private interpretation which Saint Peter warns about in 2 Peter 1:20. This brings us to what I consider to be the real issue here. As you've observed, your Greek Orthodox friend believes this story with the same simple and admirable faith with which you accept the story of Elijah's Assumption into heaven. What this indicates is that he (like Catholics) accepts universal Church teaching with the same trusting and faith-full attitude that you have to the Bible alone.

This exposes a deeper division between us. As Catholics we really do believe that God has granted the Holy Spirit to guide the Church into all truth. We believe that Christ has granted to his church a measure of Christ's infallibility (CCC, ¶ 889) and that this, in itself is a supernatural gift to the Church. Therefore the Church has the inspired power to sift through the evidence and come to a conclusion based on the historic belief of the faithful down through the ages. We believe she then has the authority to call us to assent to this belief as part of the fullness of faith.

Interpretation vs. Innovation

David: I can see that it's difficult to discuss the Assumption without expanding into a full-blown analysis of our disagreements on the infallibility of the Church's teaching authority and papal pronouncements in particular. I'll simply invoke again the distinction I made in the previous chapter: interpretation vs. innovation: You can make good arguments that the Church is an authoritative teacher, interpreter, and expounder of the Apostolic message. There is no serious argument, however, for the proposition that the Church has authority to announce "new truths" or new revelation.

Your Church decrees that the Assumption is an essential Christian belief, and you suggest that we accept it in simple faith. But the distinction between things that are worthy of our belief and things that aren't is one that the Catholic Church itself often honors. You said earlier that Catholics "step back and investigate the whole thing very thoroughly.... In other words, we suspend judgment until we ascertain all the facts." As I said before, I respect this; but as you've admitted, there is very poor evidence both for the fact of the Assumption and for early belief in the Assumption. You say that Catholics examine all the facts, but if the doctrine of the Assumption were really put through this rigorous Catholic investigation, it wouldn't stand up.

Dwight: The question then arises, "What are all the facts?" You want to consider only the historical and documentary evidence from two thousand years ago. The Catholic Church says that there are actually other kinds of facts to be considered as well. There is the theological fact of the early church's universally high view of Mary. You've charged us with a belief that is extra and separate to Scripture. But as I've shown in the last chapter, the idea that Mary was preserved from the stain of original sin is a natural development from Genesis 3:15 and Luke 1:38. From the God-given purity of Mary flows the fitting conclusion that God would deliver Mary's body from the corruption of the tomb. As the first one to be redeemed by Christ we see Mary's assumption as a pointer to the resurrection glory that will be shared by all the redeemed. (Rom. 6:5; Phil.3:10-11.) Mary's assumption is the first fulfillment of Jesus' promise that "where I am there you will be also." (John 14:3) This is linked with a full understanding of the intimate relationship between Jesus and his mother. As the definition of the dogma says, "It seems impossible that she who conceived Christ, bore him, fed him with her milk held him in her arms and pressed him to her bosom, should after this earthly life be separated from him in either body or soul."

Another fact which influenced the definition of this dogma (and that of the Immaculate Conception) are the events in the church from the end of the nineteenth through to the middle of the twentieth century. I will discuss the significance of these events in more detail in the next chapter, but beginning with the apparitions of the Virgin Mary to Catherine Laboure in Paris, there was an upsurge in real and undeniably supernatural events that helped to confirm Marian beliefs and consolidate the Catholic Church's pious opinions into clear beliefs.

Finally, the Church also considers the fact that belief in the Assumption of Mary has withstood the test of time. History shows us that formal heresies and schisms die out. The branch that is not part of the vine withers and dies. Cardinal Newman teaches that for a doctrine to develop validly one of the signs is that it will have "chronic vigor." [109] Instead of dying out, belief in the Assumption of the Blessed Virgin Mary became established in the church. By the seventh century it was a universal part of the Christian faith and has continued to be part of the fullness of the faith for all Christians in both the East and the Western Church. It was only at the Reformation that it began to be doubted, but even then Luther never denied the Assumption,[110] and leading Protestant Reformers taught the Assumption vigorously. [111]

David: Errors do tend to die out—but not on any schedule that we can rely on. Islam is a heresy[112] that arose around the time of the doctrine of the Assumption, and yet, like the Assumption, it has survived.

Protestant Acceptance of the Assumption

Dwight: The Assumption has not only survived, but it has done so universally. This belief is held not only by Catholics and Eastern Orthodox, but it was held by Lutherans at the Reformation and by many Lutherans today. It is also affirmed by the Anglican Church. The Scottish Anglican lectionary actually celebrates a feast of the Falling Asleep of Mary on 15 August just as the Orthodox and Catholics do. The new lectionary in the Church of England also institutes a Marian feast on the fifteenth of August in keeping with the tradition. Even your own Episcopal Church of the USA celebrates a Marian feast on the traditional date for the Feast of the Assumption. On that day Episcopalians pray, "O God, you have taken to yourself the Blessed Virgin Mary, …grant that we may share with her the glory of your eternal kingdom."[113]

I realize these are not full-blown Catholic dogmatic definitions.

These liturgical affirmations are vague in a typically Anglican way, but they do join with the historic church to celebrate the Feast of the Assumption. The Catholic Church has simply specified and defined as dogma a belief which has been held by the majority of Christians at all times and in all places down through history.

David: The Episcopalian prayer you cite is, as you say, vague. Sadly, the ECUSA often tends toward vagueness (or worse) on doctrinal matters, and I'd say the Episcopalian prayer is intended to be a reference to the Assumption for those who believe in it, and noncommittal for those who don't. It is at most a concession to those who believe in the Assumption, not an endorsement of the doctrine.

Dwight: I suspect we may have found a little precipice on which to stand together. I know you dislike the skeptical and suspicious attitude, so do I take it that you are willing for this belief to stand as a pious opinion, while you also devoutly wish the Catholic Church had not defined it as dogma?

David: That's about right.

Dwight: Well then, we have made a little bit of progress.

David: A little, perhaps. Aren't we left, though, with my tolerating your view as a permissible opinion, but your having to regard my view as a heretical denial of cardinal doctrine? That is, as you said, "a little precipice", and not the most comfortable place to stand together.

Dwight: I think our ledge may be a bit wider than you say. If you allow for the Assumption as a permissible pious opinion you've left the door open, and that isn't really "heretical denial". As I said in the last chapter, I have a good deal of sympathy with your view. It was my view for a long time. I had come to a more open-minded approach through a little aphorism I came across while in seminary. The saying is, "A person is most often right in what he affirms and wrong in what he denies." Therefore as an Evangelical, when confronted with these beliefs which were alien to my tradition, but clearly held by the majority of Christians, my attitude was to try to put the habit of denial on one side and to try to discover why this belief was a good thing. This led me to realize that sometimes belief and acceptance come before understanding. So Anselm of Canterbury wrote, "I yearn to understand some measure of your truth, which my heart believes and loves. For I do not understand in order to believe, but I believe in order to understand."[114] In affirming the Assumption as an ancient and glorious part of the Christian faith, the Catholic Church invites all Christians to move "further up and further in" to the fullness of historic Christianity. We encourage Christians who deny this belief to set their skepticism and doubt on one side and hear the words of the Lord to the doubting apostle, "Blessed are those who believe but have not seen."

David: I know you wouldn't say that a Christian would be "blessed", and his spiritual life would be enriched, if he would simply be docile and believe that Philip used a cross to defeat a dragon at the Temple of Mars. You wouldn't say that he should believe this in order to understand it, or that he's more likely to be wrong in denying this rather than affirming it. It's only in the safe context of Catholic dogma that you really counsel docility. So your encouragement to put aside skepticism really does presume—and completely depends on—the Church's power to teach authoritatively. This argument is at its strongest when the teaching at issue is a disputed interpretation of the Scriptures, or a well-attested early teaching that can plausibly be attributed to Apostolic oral preaching. I am sometimes inclined to admit, in such contexts, that the teaching voice of the historic Church is an important and necessary correction to the private judgment of us Evangelicals.

Here, however, the Roman Catholic Church teaches something that everyone admits was *not* part of what the Apostles proclaimed to the world, something that no one proclaimed until centuries later. For centuries, even those enthusiastically devoted to Mary, who praised her as Ever-Virgin, Mother of God, Second Eve, and sinless—even these found no occasion to mention that she had been assumed into heaven. Maybe I should surrender my skepticism when the Church says it is telling me what the Apostles taught, but not here.

What it Means to be "Apostolic"

Dwight: This reveals a different understanding of what it means to be an apostolic church. We believe that the apostolic deposit of faith is just that—a deposit or down payment. It is the essential core from which the full understanding of the faith may grow. It's true that the Assumption isn't taught by Jesus or the apostles, but then neither is the idea that there would one day be such a thing as a New Testament. That the apostles' teaching should be gathered into a fixed canon which was actually on the same level as the Old Testament was a valid development by the apostolic Church.

David: You have chosen a very illuminating point of comparison: the Assumption compared to the existence of an inspired New Testament canon. For the latter notion, we can cite: Jesus' promises that the Apostles would be supernaturally guided into the truth by the Holy Spirit (John 14:26, 16:12-13), the Apostles' claims to having received that promised Spirit (in passages too numerous to cite), the importance that the Apostles attached to their own writings (*see, e.g.,* Col. 4:16; 1 Thess. 5:27; 2 Thess. 2:15, 3:14; Rev. 22:7, 18-19) and Peter's express characterization of Paul's writings as "Scriptures" (2 Peter 3:16). One who interprets these passages (as we do) to indicate that Apostolic writings are divinely inspired Scriptures might conceivably be *wrongly* interpreting them, but he is definitely *interpreting* them. Which Apostolic teachings are being interpreted (rightly or wrongly) to yield the doctrine of the Assumption? None.

Dwight: On the contrary. The Assumption develops naturally from the apostolic teachings on the true nature of Jesus Christ the God-Man, the subsequent fullness of grace that his mother enjoyed, and her status as the second Eve. It also develops from the apostolic teachings on eschatology especially the "woman clothed with the sun, with the moon under her feet and a crown of twelve stars on her head" in Revelation 12. This queenly glory of Mary indicates the royal glory of Christ that is shared with all the redeemed. (Rom. 8:17; James 2:5)

Queen of Heaven

David: At the risk of multiplying our disagreements, I should probably pick up on your mention of Mary's "queenly glory." This is another aspect of the Assumption that Evangelicals often find troubling. Catholics call Mary "Queen of Heaven", but we think this has no real Scriptural support (since, as we've already discussed, we think that the woman in Revelation 12 is the Church), and we find it problematic because it exalts Mary very highly, apparently making her a co-regent with Christ the King, or perhaps with God the Father.

Dwight: Of course there is Scriptural support for Mary as Queen of Heaven. In Luke 1.31-32 the angel Gabriel says to Mary, "You will conceive and give birth to a son, and you are to call him Jesus. 32 He will be great and will be called the Son of the Most High. The Lord God will give him the throne of his father David." If Jesus inherits the throne of David, then Jesus is the king of his kingdom.

There is an interesting Old Testament type of the Queen in the Kingdom of Heaven. King Solomon, who is a type of Christ

(Matt. 12:42), rules with his Queen Mother. Since kings in Old Testament times had many wives it was their mother who often ruled with her son as Queen.[115] A verse in I Kings shows the honor that Solomon pays his mother. (I Kings 2:19.) He rises up to greet her, bows down to honor her, then places a throne for her on his right hand. If Jesus is the King of Heaven, then it follows from a Jewish understanding of kingship that his mother is the Queen of Heaven.

The fact that Solomon's mother Bathsheba features in Matthew's genealogy of Christ (Matt. 1:6), and that the mother of Jesus in Revelation is crowned with twelve stars, gives further symbolic support for our devotional term "Queen of Heaven".

David: Your account of Bathsheba (whom the Bible never calls "queen", by the way) leaves out a critical fact: King Solomon rejects the request that his mother brings to him, and he then executes the person on whose behalf she had appealed to him (1 Kings 2:22-25)—a most unhappy typology for Mary's intercession. Solomon most certainly did *not* "rule with" his mother. In any case, the phrase "Queen of Heaven" is rather unfortunate, since in the Bible this is a name for an idol.[116]

That terminology has invited some very harsh anti-Catholic commentary from Protestants who think this shows that Marian devotion is a pseudo-Christian manifestation of goddess worship. It's true that goddess worship does recur throughout human history. It's also true that, in some cultures, Christianity is a rather thin veneer over a persisting paganism; and for all I know, in those cultures the Catholic exaltation of Mary as Queen of Heaven is used as a means for preserving the indigenous goddess worship. I have to leave it to the missionaries and pastors there to judge that issue. My stauncher brethren may think me naive, but in our culture I don't see Mary's status as "Queen of Heaven" resonating with the worship of Isis or Demeter or Gaia. In our culture, there is no substantial indigenous goddess worship that might be transformed into Marian devotion; rather, it appears that the neo-pagan goddess worshipers are hijacking and distorting Mary as supposed precedent for their novelties.

I do have concerns about idolatry as a recurring threat to spiritual health, and I'll air those concerns in our chapter on the veneration of Mary. For now, I'll simply say that Mary's promotion to "Queen of Heaven" is an unfortunate corollary to the doctrine of the Assumption, for which I think there is no good authority.

A Trusting Attitude

Dwight: You're right that our belief in the Assumption brings us back to the question of authority, and this question has really been lurking behind our whole discussion. I once had a meal with a friendly Franciscan who was fond of fried chicken. Over the meal I was (as an Anglican) arguing with him about the Immaculate Conception. He ended the conversation by saying cheerfully, "We believe in the Immaculate Conception because the Pope tells us to. Pass the fried chicken." At the heart of authentic Catholicism is a trusting spirit—one that is willing to submit and receive this authority as children (Mark 10:15). We eschew that skeptical spirit that has to "protest", challenge and deny all the time. I guess we could end it by saying, "We believe in the Assumption because the Pope tells us to. Pass the fried chicken."

But we believe in the Glorious Assumption of the Virgin Mary not out of blind obedience, but because it has been believed by the vast majority of the faithful down through church history, and because it is part of our corporate experience today. One of the ways this doctrine radiates within the modern Catholic experience is within the recent astounding apparitions of the Virgin Mary throughout the world.

8

Revelation Woman

Apparitions of the Virgin Mary

Dwight: About fifteen years ago, while I was still an Anglican, I went with some friends to the village of Medjugorje in what was then Yugoslavia. I wasn't really interested, but some people from the parish twisted my arm and even paid my airfare. At this time in my life Mary, the mother of Our Lord had a small role to play in my own devotional life. I had started to use the rosary as a form of prayer, and was trying to understand and accept this aspect of the Christian faith.

Medjugorje was becoming famous because of the alleged appearances of Mary to four peasant children of the village. The apparitions were supposedly happening every evening at twenty to seven. As a result thousands were flocking to the village on pilgrimage. There were reports of miraculous healings and strange phenomena which many people witnessed. People reported that the metal chains of their rosaries turned a gold color when they returned from Medjugorje. Thousands reported seeing the sun "spin" at the time when the Virgin Mary was supposed to have appeared. I was skeptical, but went along for the ride.

On arrival we joined in with the traditions of the place. At six o'clock virtually everyone in the village stopped what they were doing for prayer. Together we prayed the rosary—that ancient form of meditation on the gospels. I was praying with a friend on the balcony of our guesthouse. At six o'clock I looked up at the sun. It was a blaze of light in the sky, and impossible to gaze at for more than a moment. I noticed on the hood of a car below that the sun was reflected as a splash of bright light. I closed my eyes and we prayed with the rosary for forty minutes.

Then at twenty to seven my friend nudged me in the ribs and pointed at the sky. I looked up to see that the sun hovered in the sky like a white disc of light. The disc seemed to be spinning first clockwise, then counter-clockwise, while beams of light radiated from it like a spinning firework. Of course I immediately thought my eyes were playing tricks on me, then I looked down onto the hood of the car where I had seen the sun reflected before and saw that the reflection of the sun on the car hood was also a spinning disc of white light.

This happened at the moment when the four visionaries were allegedly receiving their daily apparition of the Virgin Mary. My friend had also seen the sun spin at the same time, and that evening we spoke to many people who had witnessed the same phenomenon. This happened to me three times during our week-long visit, and it is has been reported by thousands of visitors to Medjugorje over the years. What do you make of it?

Evaluating Subjective Experience

David: First, I believe you. I know you are reporting faithfully what you experienced. However, neither you nor I know what actually happened. We don't have to have any doubts about your sanity or your seriousness to think that this event might have been some sort of a delusion or mini-hallucination. You had heard about the sun spinning, had looked at the sun yourself and had been dazzled, and had then prayed for forty minutes. Whether your subsequent experience was merely subjective or instead had an objective supernatural reality, we can't know. I hope it's not an offense for me to say that I doubt it.

Dwight: No offense taken. You can imagine that I am a little embarrassed to relate the story at all. However, several details of this experience made me think very hard about what happened. First of all, I really am not the sort who is given to visions and supernatural occurrences. I wasn't looking for this to happen. Second, not only did I see the sun spin in the sky, but the reflection of the sun was spinning on the hood of the car as well. Third, my friend and many other quite ordinary people in the village witnessed the same phenomenon that week as well as thousands of times over the years.

The experience raises a few questions. First of all, we know the sun itself was *not* physically spinning. Thousands of people *perceived* the sun spinning. Furthermore, what is far more impressive at a place like Medjugorje is the miracle of thousands of people fervently repenting of their sins and seeking the healing love of Jesus Christ. By anyone's standards, Medjugorje is a place of intense Christian renewal.

However, I'm also aware that Medjugorje is *not* one of the eight Marian apparitions that are formally approved by the Catholic Church. Indeed, such controversial details emerge from the whole Medjugorje phenomenon that one is right to remain suspicious. I relate the story not to praise Medjugorje as such, but to link in to the more general point that something strange has been going on. Apparitions of Mary have been reported from time to time from as early as the fourth century, [117] but over the last one hundred and fifty years they have increased in frequency. In various places around the world, ordinary people have been experiencing apparitions of a person who they claim, with good reason, to be the Virgin Mary. She has appeared with messages of both hope and warning. She has called for repentance and prayer and pointed people to her Son as the way of salvation.

So as a very basic question, do you think it is possible that the Virgin Mary has miraculously appeared to people?

Commerce with Devils and the Dead

David: Is it *possible*? That's a very narrow question, and the answer must be a careful yes. A very few Biblical instances come to mind in which the departed have appeared to the living—the prophet Samuel appearing to King Saul after Saul consulted the witch of Endor (1 Sam. 28:7-20), and Elijah and Moses appearing to the Disciples on the Mount of Transfiguration (Matt. 17:3 = Mark 9:4 = Luke 9:30), and of course the special case of the risen Jesus after His Ascension appearing to Stephen (Acts 7:56), to Paul (Acts 9:3-6, 18:9), and to John (Rev. 1:13 *et seq.*).

However, one of the odd things about our Biblical religion is the relative dearth of this sort of communication: Divination is strictly forbidden in the Bible,[118] and one of the clearest of those Biblical instances (Saul's calling up Samuel) is strongly criticized as evil occultism (1 Chr. 10:13). When revelation was to be given, it was given by God the Holy Spirit (1 Peter 1:21), and not by human messengers, though sometimes God evidently used angels (Acts 7:53; Gal. 3:19; Heb. 2:2).

Consequently, I think we have to say that it is *possible* that a departed saint would appear to a believer (in a vision, dream, or other manifestation), but that such an appearance is against the Biblical tendency, which tends instead to ask, "Why consult the dead on behalf of the living?" (Is. 8:19).

Dwight: Hold on a minute. There's a world of difference between a person who consults a medium in order to summon up the dead and the unsolicited appearance of a departed saint. Saul's shady consultation with a witch is nothing like the Transfiguration. In the apparitions of the Virgin Mary the visionaries are simple people—usually children—going about their ordinary business when a beautiful lady appears. They are not engaged in séances and occult practices. There is the danger that an apparition is caused by a demon. In virtually all the authentic apparition events this possibility is considered, but dismissed when the lady praises God, asks the children to pray, repent, turn to Jesus, and proclaim the message of repentance and faith to a wicked world.

I want to be extremely cautious in discussing these phenomena. There have been many alleged apparitions of the Blessed Virgin Mary in the last century along with other unusual paranormal phenomena. Many of these are inauthentic either because of some natural explanation, low-level fraud, mental illness, or even the work of the devil. I am not so gullible as to believe in every reported sighting of the Virgin Mary. However, I am also not so dogmatic as to dismiss them altogether.

David: You are right to acknowledge the possibility of demonic involvement, and I'd like to emphasize that possibility.[119] The first adjective the Bible uses to describe Satan is "crafty" (Gen. 3:1). He is a deceiver (Rev. 12:9). The Apostle Paul warned that "in later times some will abandon the faith and follow deceiving spirits and things taught by demons" (1 Tim. 4:1), and he warned that Satan's work would be "displayed in all kinds of counterfeit miracles, signs and wonders" (2 Thess. 2:9). I don't mean to be paranoid or sensationalistic, but we do have to keep in mind that we have a formidable enemy who, God has warned us, will lead many believers astray.

We can confidently assume that Satan will use the most effective means at his disposal to accomplish this deception. Sometimes his method will be gross sin or rebellion or apostasy—but sometimes not: When tempting Jesus, the Devil quoted the Bible (Matt. 4:6). The "lying spirit" (2 Kings 22:22) that sent King Ahab to his death in battle against Ramoth Gilead did not counsel obvious sin but, instead, said simply but falsely, "the Lord will give [Ramoth Gilead] into the king's hand" (v. 6). When Satan deceived Peter about the necessity of Jesus' impending sacrificial death (Matt. 16:23), Peter's error sounded not like sin but like love and loyalty for Jesus. ("Never, Lord! This shall never happen to you!")

If Satan's target is a devout Christian, then the deceiver will certainly use strategies and devices different from those he would use for a different sort of person. A pious believer who is disposed toward a visit from the Virgin Mary would probably not be misled by a patently evil parody of Mary who spouts obvious blasphemy, so maybe Satan would use instead a more subtle pseudo-Mary who pretends to counsel praise, repentance, and conversion— while "she" craftily accomplishes her deception, confusion, and distraction. It has been very common (for example, at Fatima) for relatives and pastors of Marian "seers" to assert that the apparitions were demonic, and I am not set at ease by the Church's eventual contrary conclusions.

Good fruit

Dwight: The whole business is extremely complex. Some of the dubious apparitions *do* indicate personal delusions or even diabolical deception. The genuine apparitions however, are marked by the clear fruit of repentance, charismatic gifts including exorcisms and healing, genuine conversions, and lives transformed by Christ. The apparitions are opposed by some members of the religious hierarchy, but that might be a sign of their authenticity. Remember the religious leaders attributed Jesus' ministry to the devil (Mark 3:22-26), and in this context Jesus observed that Satan does not cast out Satan. Elsewhere he teaches that we are to judge suspected false prophets by their fruit. (Matthew 7:16-20.) The good fruit of the genuine apparitions repudiates the diabolical explanation.

Amazing Apparitions

Dwight: One of the most amazing apparitions in this respect was in Guadalupe in Mexico, where an Indian peasant saw Mary in 1531. Her image was miraculously imprinted on his cloak, which can still be seen in the basilica at Guadalupe. From 1532-1538, eight million native Indians were baptized. It was recorded that in five days 14,500 presented themselves to be anointed and received into the Church.

Hearing about Christian marriage, over a thousand couples presented themselves to be married on one day.[120] The important modern apparitions are to St. Catherine Laboure, a young nun in Paris in the 1830s, to Bernadette Soubrirous, a shepherd girl at Lourdes in Southwest France in 1858, and to three Portugese children at Fatima in 1917. These, along with a handful of others, are the apparitions that the Catholic Church has formally approved. Others which are very impressive took place at Medjugorje, Kibeho (in Rwanda), Akita (in Japan), Cairo, and Damascus. In each case, the fruit of the apparitions is mass conversions, repentance, renewal, and increased devotion to the Lord.

It is worthwhile for any Christian to read about these events because what comes across in even the most objective and critical studies is the sense that these phenomena could not be invented by the people involved. Usually they are illiterate peasants—often children. In addition there are some truly astounding events associated with the apparitions. So for instance, it is completely well documented by secular sources that at Fatima 70,000 people witnessed the miracle of the sun "dancing." Quite apart from what you make of it all, it is inspiring to realize how real the miraculous is in the world today.

David: There is much to be said against these apparitions and their seers,[121] but I'll admit that the evidence is quite strong that something supernatural was going on in Fatima. However, I don't know whether that's "inspiring", or disquieting, or just puzzling. Remarkable, unexplainable phenomena are not restricted to Christianity. In 1995 there was a well-documented phenomenon among Hindus all around the world—attested to by non-Hindu journalists—of statues of the elephant god Ganesh seeming to "drink" milk offered to him by worshipers. Spoonfuls of milk disappeared as if sucked up by the statues. Devotees took it as evidence that something important was about to happen, but then the phenomenon seemed to subside. Did the milk-"drinking" happen? Probably. What did it mean? No one knows. Of course, as a Christian I have more interest in and respect for well-attested alleged events that pertain to our Lord's mother, but in the end they are just as difficult to process as the Hindu milk phenomenon.

Dwight: Not quite so difficult. You have at least some understanding and acceptance the Virgin Mary. Milk-drinking statues of elephant gods are quite outside your orbit. But I accept that apparently supernatural phenomena on their own do not prove anything and are not necessarily Christian at all. Speaking in tongues, for instance, happens in all sorts of religions. It's not always a sign of the presence of the Holy Spirit.

Cautious Approval

Dwight: That's why the Church looks askance at these phenomena and is extremely cautious. When the Church grants approval to an apparition she is not saying definitely that the Virgin Mary has appeared or that the "messages" are from heaven. Neither is she saying that we must believe in the apparitions in order to be good Catholics. She is simply saying that it is permissible for the faithful to go on formal pilgrimages to these places and to worship God there.

The Church is also clear that if there are "messages from heaven" that they must conform to the revelation already given through the Scriptures and Church teaching. Mary—if that is who the heavenly lady is—can bring no new doctrinal revelation. There is a whole set of rigorous conditions which the Church establishes to authenticate such occurrences.[122]

To summarize, the Catholic Church allows that supernatural events may occur, but she suspends judgment until all the facts are ascertained. When faced with inexplicable phenomena the human mind always wants to make sense of it and make it conform to logical patterns. It is very difficult to do this. Anyone who has tried to force the Book of Revelation into a neat theological or prophetic system will know how slippery dream language and visionary images are.

It is the same when trying to analyze paranormal phenomena in religion. The matter is extremely complex, and only the experts can hope to begin untangling it all. As an Evangelical Christian who believes in the possibility of miracles, how does all this hit you?

Trying to Untangle It

David: I guess I have two main responses. First, my mind does immediately try to form a grid for evaluating the apparitions. It seems obvious that there are four logical possibilities: (1) Maybe the alleged events are tricks or lies by people who want to promote Mary's glory or want to get fame or attention or something else for themselves. (2) Maybe the people involved are subjectively sincere, but the alleged events are the results of hallucinations or delusions or some other psychological phenomena,[123] and they didn't really happen. (3) Maybe the events really happened, but they are caused by natural phenomena that we just don't understand. Or (4) maybe the events really are objectively real and supernatural in origin. If the events really are supernatural, we still have to decide whether (a) they are demonic, or (b) they are heavenly, but they mean something other than the visionaries suppose, or (c) they are heavenly, and they mean what the Catholic Church has concluded. So many branches on this decision tree are spiritual dead ends (or worse) that I'm discouraged from attempting the analysis.

Dwight: Me, too. That's why I try to keep a cautiously open mind, allowing for all of the possibilities you've outlined including the simplest explanation—that this really is Mary and she really has come to give us messages from heaven.

Messages from heaven?

David: These alleged messages are what cause me further disquiet. I find myself inclined to try to evaluate the messages and assess their fidelity to revealed Truth. You've indicated that this is an important part of the process of evaluating an apparition, and I believe that's salutary. I've not spent much time on this effort, but the little I've spent has not been reassuring to me. One could chase down many a rabbit trail on this subject, since, for example, Mary's alleged appearances at Medjugorje have been like clockwork over an unprecedented period of time, and her supposed messages[124]—still not approved by the local bishops[125] or the Vatican[126]—have come with a volubility that has seemed to some almost garrulous. Medjugorje has strident critics even among Roman Catholics who are enthusiastic Marian devotees.

Dwight: All the same, you should take time to read some of the alleged messages from Mary at Medjugorje. No Christian could object to their content. They are a repeated call for Christians to turn to Jesus, repent of their sins, pray and read their Bibles.[127]

David: It seems to me more profitable to consider messages that the Catholic Church has approved, and I think it's fair to say that no Marian apparition has a higher standing in the Catholic Church today than Fatima.

You say that, in the approved apparitions like Fatima, Mary "has always pointed people to her Son as the way of salvation", but the Fatima messages[128] don't read that way to me. There is much in them that a Protestant finds alien and objectionable, but the most troubling is their treatment of the relationship between Jesus, Mary, and the believer: The child-seers were told to pray for conversion of souls "through the infinite merits of [Jesus'] most Sacred Heart *and the Immaculate Heart of Mary*", suggesting (to me at least) an equivalence or parallel between the two.[129] Mary tells one seer (Lucia), "Jesus wishes to use you to make *me* [Mary] better known and loved. He wishes to establish in the world devotion to *my* Immaculate Heart."[130] Here it is not Mary promoting Jesus, but Jesus promoting Mary.

Dwight: I accept that the messages of Fatima sound alien to Protestant ears, but if we can try to see the concepts in a fresh way

I don't think the content needs to be totally objectionable. So for example, what is the real problem with Jesus honoring his mother? It's one of the Ten Commandments to honor one's mother. You have picked out this troublesome detail, but the overwhelming emphasis of Mary's messages is to point to her Son. The prayer which Mary taught to the Fatima children, and which is recited by millions as part of the rosary is, "Oh my Jesus, forgive us our sins. Save us from the fire of Hell and lead all souls to Heaven, especially those who have most need of your mercy."

David: Readers will have to judge for themselves. To me, your Christ-centered reading of the message is wishful thinking. I'll settle for this Catholic assessment—that the Fatima message "comprise[s] two essential elements": (1) "the singular role of the Immaculate One [*i.e.,* Mary] in the economy of salvation, a dogmatic fact"; and (2) "the value of devotion to [Mary's] Immaculate Heart for the individual life and for the future of the human race"[131]. It's about Mary.

Jesus and Mary are Intertwined

Dwight: In Catholic thinking Jesus and Mary cannot be separated. If you believe in the Incarnation, then Jesus is half Mary. You object to the idea that Jesus' heart and Mary's are intertwined in suffering, but the idea that Mary shares in the suffering of Jesus is a Biblical principle. Simeon prophesies to Mary that "a sword shall pierce through your own soul also, that the thoughts of many hearts may be revealed." (Luke 2:35.) While I understand that talk about devotion to the suffering hearts of Jesus and Mary sounds alien to Protestant ears, it is not alien to the New Testament.

David: Sharing in Jesus' suffering is indeed a New Testament concept (*see, e.g.*, Matt. 5:11, Acts 5:41, 2 Cor. 1:5-7, Php. 3:10, Col. 1:24, 1 Peter 4:13, 5:1), though not a distinctively Marian concept, but what troubles me is Mary's virtual displacement of Jesus in the

Fatima message. Basically plagiarizing divine promises, the Lady says, "I will never forsake you. My Immaculate Heart will be your refuge and the way that will lead you to God." However, it is God Who will "never forsake" us (Heb. 13:5); it is the eternal God who is our refuge (see, e.g., Deut. 33:27 and at least 10 Psalms); it is Jesus who is "the Way" to the Father, the only way (John 14:6). The Lady of Fatima makes herself a Savior.

Dwight: I understand your point, and would like to answer it, but I think we're stepping into another problematic belief—Mary as co-redemptrix. Shall we leave it for the later chapter?

David: Okay. Then there is the question of the undue honor given to Mary. The Lady tells Lucia "to pray the Rosary every day *in honor of Our Lady of the Rosary*, in order to obtain peace for the world and the end of the war *for she alone can help*." She suggests, "I would like a chapel built here *in my honor*." The Lady predicts, "In the end *my Immaculate Heart will triumph*." It is hard to see the humble, hidden Mary of Nazareth in this Lady.

Dwight: Let me repeat what I said in an earlier chapter. We honor Mary because of her humility and hidden-ness. Think of Mother Teresa receiving a Nobel Peace prize. She is being honored not because she is a queen, an accomplished academic or a film star, but because of her outstanding humility and Christian service. Honor and humility are not contradictory. Heavenly honor is based on earthly humility. As C.S. Lewis points out in *The Great Divorce,* "fame in this country [heaven] and fame on Earth are two quite different things."[132]

David: A recurring theme in the Fatima messages is reparation—not just reparation for offenses against God but also "reparation for the offenses committed against the Immaculate Heart of Mary", as if it is of eschatological importance that Mary's dignity, and justice to her, be vindicated. Indeed, the Lady says,

"There are so many souls whom the Justice of God condemns for sins committed *against me.*" This Lady will have her due.

At the risk of giving offense, which I truly wish not to do, I have to say there seems to be an almost whining quality to the Lady's complaint to Lucia: "Look my daughter, at my Heart, surrounded with thorns with which ungrateful men pierce me at every moment by their blasphemies and ingratitude. You at least try to console me ...." I can't help wondering whether the young Lucia had a lonely grandmother or elderly neighbor who made wheedling complaints that we hear imitated in the Lady's supposed request that devotees "recite five decades of the Rosary, and keep me company for fifteen minutes while meditating on the fifteen mysteries of the Rosary, with the intention of making reparation to me."

Jesus the Judge

David: Very troubling is the Lady's warning that "Our Lady can no longer uphold the arm of her Divine Son which will strike the world." That is, Jesus' wrath threatens the world, but Mary's intervention saves us from divine wrath. Jesus is mean, but Mary is nice. This is a horrible distortion of the Good News, which is that we shall be "saved from God's wrath *through Him*"—that is, through Jesus. (Rom. 5:9.) While He will one day be the Judge of the whole human race, Jesus now says, "Come unto Me, all you who are weary and burdened, and I will give you rest.... I am gentle and humble in heart, and you will find rest for your souls." (Matt. 11:28-29.) We do not need Mary to protect us from Jesus. He is our Savior, our brother, and our friend, ready to accept any who will come to Him.

The Lady of Fatima is hurt, unhappy, and demanding. She calls me to spiritual projects devoted to her own honor and vindication. If this is what Marian apparitions are about, then I find them more harm than good.

Dwight: You have isolated certain messages that you find most offensive and disregarded the others. Nevertheless, I admit that the tone of the messages *is* difficult for a twentieth-first century educated Anglo-Saxon male to understand and accept. I find it difficult, too. But we have to remember that in each apparition Mary speaks the local language. At Fatima therefore she is not only speaking Portuguese, but she is using terminology and concepts that can be accepted and understood by Portuguese Catholic peasant children. No doubt if you or I received an apparition of the Virgin Mary, she would not only speak English, but would also use concepts and a tone which we would find acceptable.

Is Jesus our Savior, Brother and Friend? Yes, and this is not alien to Catholic devotion and doctrine, but the Scriptures are clear that Jesus is also the judge eternal. (I Tim. 4:1,8.) Jesus portrays himself as the judge (Matt. 25:31-46) and says that God has delivered all judgment to the Son. (John 5:22, 27.) Furthermore, Paul says we must all appear before the judgment seat of Christ to receive to receive good or evil according to what we have done in our body. (2 Cor. 5:10.) This is a fearful prospect even for believers, for the New Testament teaches not only that our actions will be taken into account, but that it is possible to fall under this fearful judgment if we turn away from the truth. (Heb. 10:26-27.)

Mary's Role

Dwight: The visions would indicate that Mary has a role to play in persuading her Son to with hold his chastisement from the world. This isn't so different from Abraham pleading with God to spare Sodom and Gomorrah (Gen. 18:20-33) or Moses pleading with the Lord not to punish the people (Exodus 32:30-32). I can see that Mary playing such a part is strange to Protestants, but it is not contradictory to Scripture, and does not negate the fact that Jesus, while being the fearful judge, is also our brother and the friend of sinners.

The alleged messages from Mary are easy to summarize. Albeit with a very Catholic vocabulary, she calls the human race to prayer, action based repentance, renewed faith in Christ, and greater commitment to the gospel. In addition, the modern apparitions comment on the two Marian dogmas we have discussed earlier. There is a curious link between the apparitions of Mary and the Assumption of Mary. I don't think it is a co-incidence that the only really clear example of apparitions in the New Testament (*i.e.*, the Transfiguration) features the two Old Testament saints whose bodies were assumed into heaven.

Elijah's assumption into heaven is clear, but there was also an ancient Jewish tradition that Moses' body was assumed into heaven. The Biblical evidence allows for this while not stating it (Deut.34:5-6; Jude 1:9). Is there some kind of link between earth and heaven which allows those whose bodies were assumed to appear to the living more readily? It's no proof, but it is a supposition that lends credence to the doctrine of the assumption.

Dogma, Apparations and Demonic Paranoia

Dwight: More significant is the timing of the apparitions with the definition of the Immaculate Conception. In 1830 St. Catherine Laboure, a simple nun in Paris, received apparitions in which she was given instructions for a special medal to be produced and distributed to prompt the prayers of the faithful. This medal, now known as "the miraculous medal" was first called the Immaculate Conception medal, because according to the instructions given by Mary, the words "Mary, conceived without sin" were inscribed around the edge.[133] In an extraordinary way the medal became immensely popular by the middle of the nineteenth century and helped to prepare the way for the formal definition of the doctrine in 1854.

Then in 1858 the peasant girl Bernadette Soubirous received very convincing apparitions in Lourdes. The interesting thing about these apparitions is that when Bernadette asked who the lady was, the Lady replied, "I am the Immaculate Conception."[134] Although this dogma had recently been defined it was not understood or accepted by the masses of ordinary Catholics. Certainly a semi-illiterate shepherd girl in a rural backwater would not have known anything about it. The theologians therefore found the apparition's announcement that she was "the Immaculate Conception" to be totally astounding. Was this a sign not only of the apparition's authenticity, but also a confirmation of the dogma from heaven itself? I should add that the continued good fruit of Lourdes as a pilgrimage site and the subsequent sanctity of Bernadette's life are vivid testimony to the authenticity of these events.

David: Bernadette *said* that she had never heard of the Immaculate Conception before, and I assume she was sincere, but in fact the Feast of the Immaculate Conception had long been celebrated in France, so it's possible that all the pieces of the event were there in her subconscious mind. When I think of the possibility that, instead, Bernadette really did see a spirit "Lady" who called herself the Immaculate Conception, it makes me shudder. There's something very disturbing about the fact that both the "Lady" at Lourdes and the "Lady" at Fatima declined to identify themselves with the name "Mary", and that the seers seem not to have known for certain who she was.

Dwight: The lady was not seen as a ghostly spirit as you imply. The visionaries reported that they saw her with the same clarity and solidity as a real physical person. I find it curious that you worry that the visionaries are uncertain about her identity, yet you praise it when they are wary of her lest she be an evil spirit. They can't be both wary *and* certain can they?

I've said we need to be cautious about accepting the apparitions, but we also need to be cautious about assigning them to the devil don't we? After all, the one sin which Jesus says is unforgivable is to assign the work of the Holy Spirit to Satan (Matthew 12:28-33). In the same passage he again says that one can only judge by the fruit of an action (v.33). If you see good fruit, and assign it to the devil, then your reasoning backfires, because who then is the source of the good fruit in your own religion? (Luke 11:19) Assigning good fruit to the devil becomes very slippery, and if we're not careful we end up like the paranoid conspiracy theorist: "If the fruit is *really* good, why that just goes to show how very clever the devil really is!"

Finally, not only is the fruit impressive, but the overall emphasis of the Marian apparitions is to call people to repent and turn to Jesus as incarnate Lord, and it is only by the Holy Spirit that anyone is able to do this. (I Cor. 12:3; I John 4:2.) Furthermore, to banish all doubt that the lady comes from heaven not hell, at both Fatima and Lourdes the children are led to worship the Holy Trinity, adore Jesus Christ and pray for sinners. [135] Hardly the priorities of a demon.

The Danger of Distraction

David: Unless that demon was *very* crafty. But now I'm letting loose my imagination, so let me leave that line of thinking and return to something a bit more solid: Even if there were nothing fraudulent and nothing sinister about the approved Marian apparitions, and even if the messages were non-objectionable, the grave danger that remains is distraction. This Protestant concern has its Catholic counterpart: An article by a Catholic author, obviously devoted to Mary, makes the point that the recent multiplication of supposed Marian apparitions (including Medjugorje, whose good "fruit" he acknowledges) poses a danger of diverting or distracting the faithful—*from Fatima*.[136] Some Catholics may not realize how ironic this warning is in our ears: Beware Marian excess, lest it distract from Mary. The real risk, we think, is that fascination with Marian apparitions (and these supernatural visitations *are* fascinating) may distract the faithful from single-minded devotion to Jesus Christ.

Dwight: I admit that there is some excessive devotion to Mary among Catholics and that interest in the apparitions may feed that excess. I also accept that Catholics have sometimes seen Jesus as too much the Fearsome Judge and not enough the Merciful Master. I will discuss the reasons and remedies for this when we talk about the veneration of Mary in the next chapter.

I'm also aware of how weird all this is to the average Evangelical Christian. This average Evangelical believes in miracles, but *this* type of miracle makes him wince. Part of me wishes there were no apparitions because it would make dialogue with Evangelicals much easier. However, the phenomena are there, and its something we have to consider carefully. It does no good to dismiss them just because they upset our particular way of seeing the world.

The tendency for excessive fascination with the apparitions to the neglect of true worship worries me. Furthermore, the Marian apparitions with their apocalyptic warnings, prophecies and supernatural phenomena encourage a certain type of religious kook. People get distracted from the gospel and get caught up in a sort of Christian fortune-telling which involves a fantasy world of end time prophecies, conspiracy theories and an ugly self-righteous paranoia. However, this religious mania is not peculiar to Catholic Marian devotees. My memory of American Evangelicalism echoes with odd "dispensationalist" views that distort sound Biblical interpretation. With this went a similar fascination for prophecy, and conspiracy theories. In both cases this kind of religion leads to division in the church and a distraction from the redemptive mercy of Christ.

The simple Catholic view on Marian apparitions is that we take note that the Lord's mother may have been sent to earth with urgent warnings for mankind to repent and turn to Christ. We rejoice at the undeniably remarkable and great graces that have flowed from the authentic apparitions. We believe they confirm the Catholic view of Jesus and Mary and encourage those who believe in miracles to examine the fascinating evidence with an open mind.

David: If Paul could rejoice when the Gospel was preached, even for bad motives by people who wanted to hurt him (Php. 1:15-19), then I can rejoice when good fruit results from alleged Marian apparitions. I sometimes see eccentric Protestant worship and preaching that make me cringe, but I really do believe that God uses it. All human worship is imperfect in some way, tainted perhaps with error, bad motives, distraction, or some other flaw; but God seems to graciously accept it, redeem it, and use it. This grace shouldn't make us careless, but it should keep us from despair. If my worst fears about Marian apparitions are correct, and Satan is orchestrating some of these events to distract from Christ, I can still hope that God will use these events nonetheless to bring glory to Mary's Son and to bless His Church.

In each chapter so far, we've touched on the topic of the how high a view we ought to have of Mary. Fatima raises her to new heights, so let me now pick up the topic of the veneration of Mary and what her proper role is.

9

How Do You Solve
A Problem Like Maria?

The Veneration of Mary

David: When I look out my office window in Washington, D.C., a prominent feature on the skyline a couple miles north is the National Shrine of the Immaculate Conception, a huge basilica commemorating the Immaculate Conception of Mary. About five miles away is its Episcopalian counterpart, the Washington National Cathedral. I prefer the "National Cathedral" architecturally, but in terms of its unspoken message I've actually come to like it *less* than the Roman Catholic "National Shrine".

The Episcopal cathedral is an almost secular building (for example, it includes deist Thomas Jefferson in its stained glass); it is aggressively ecumenical, in that lifeless strain of ecumenism that seeks not unity based on the truth but instead some sort of truce based on a lowest common denominator of unbelief. The Catholic basilica, on the other hand, is decisively doctrinal, starkly confronting the visitor with the Christian proposition that God truly became a man, was born to an actual mother, in the flesh-and-blood person of Jesus of Nazareth. One might therefore suppose that in this place an Evangelical would feel like he was on his home turf.

149

However, visiting this Marian shrine is instead an exotic and disturbing experience for an Evangelical, since the building embodies and reflects the Marian doctrine that is, so far, the high-water mark of exalting Mary, the doctrine of the Immaculate Conception. We've already discussed that doctrine itself, but I thought the National Shrine might be a fitting place to go (so to speak) to discuss Roman Catholic veneration of Mary.

I don't really object to a church being dedicated to Mary; after all, Evangelical churches are sometimes named after Biblical characters, or even after churchmen like Wesley or Calvin, and Luther lent his name to an entire denomination.

Honoring a good person by naming a building after him or observing a "Founder's Day" or celebrating a birthday is the sort of thing that anyone might do; so in principle I don't mind that the National Shrine honors Mary, who is certainly worthy of honor. My objection is to the nature and proportion of the honor it pays her. The Shrine is filled with images of Mary, memorials of events in her life, and inscriptions related to her and to doctrines about her.[137] In my recollection, the most common images of Jesus in this place are as a child in the lap of His mother. The biggest image of Jesus is a huge mosaic ("Christ in Majesty") presenting him as the Judge, with a fearsome countenance. Mary, on the other hand, often appears, predictably, as the gentle, non-threatening, and inviting mother.

Dwight: Let me explain a little about Catholic culture. Since the very earliest times, we have dedicated our church buildings to particular saints and martyrs. It is natural that a church dedicated to a particular saint honors that saint with imagery of his or her life. So, if you visit the Basilica in Lisieux in France dedicated to St. Thérèse you will find mosaics representing scenes from her life. At the head of the apse, as the focus for the whole building, you will find a similar scene of Christ enthroned in glory surrounded by the saints. The National Shrine devotes a lot of space to depictions of Mary because of that particular church's dedication. However, all the images of Mary are subordinated and point to the immense and predominant image of the risen, ascended, and glorified Lord Jesus.

David: Of course, that's the key—whether images of (and honor to) any creature ultimately point to and glorify the Creator. Some Evangelicals may think I'm conceding too much by allowing sacred images at all. Some Presbyterians, for example, think that the Commandment against "graven images" establishes an absolute prohibition of sacred art, and I guess they would avoid even Sunday School materials with pictures of Jesus, or an unadorned cross on their steeples. But most of us conclude that the Mosaic Law actually allowed some sacred images (*see* Ex. 25:18-20; Ex. 26:31; Num. 21:8-9), and we think the real issue is whether we "bow down to them or worship them" (Ex. 20:5; Deut. 4:19, 5:9). So, again, the question about the National Shrine is the proportion, nature, and use of the Marian images there.

Dwight: When analyzing the church's architecture and decorations, be sure not to miss the forest for the trees. The whole building is built on a cruciform plan, and central to it all is a crucifix next to the altar. Even more important is what the church is used for: A Catholic Church is not a museum or gallery, or even mainly a shrine to a particular saint. Our worship is not about the decoration on the walls, but the worship of the Lord Jesus Christ. Every Catholic Church is the temple of the Lord, the upper room where we gather to worship the Lord and commemorate his death and resurrection through the celebration of the Eucharist as he told us to. (Luke 22:19.) In this way, through the building and our worship we constantly proclaim his death until he comes again. (I Cor. 11:26.) The decorations are filigree compared to this.

Wyszinski's "act of consecration"

David: I understand this, and don't have a problem with the theory. It is the degree of honor to Mary that is alarming. So let's continue our "tour" of the National Shrine: The main seating area of the church (the "nave") is lined on both sides by smaller chapels honoring Mary in various traditions. One chapel features the Miraculous Medal. A Mexican chapel features "Our Lady of Guadalupe". A Polish chapel features "Our Lady of Czestochowa". In that chapel is posted a prayer to Mary ("An Act of Consecration to the Mother of God") by the heroic Polish Cardinal, Stephan Wyszynski. His prayer caught my attention—it made me sad, actually—and impressed itself on my memory:

O *Mother* of God, Immaculate *Mary*! To Thee do I dedicate my body and soul, all my prayers and deeds, my joys and sufferings, all that I am and all that I have. With a joyful heart I surrender myself to Thy bondage of love. To Thee will I devote my service of my own free will for the salvation of mankind, and for the help of the Holy Church whose *Mother* Thou art. From now on my only desire is to do all things with Thee, through Thee, and for Thee. I know I can accomplish nothing with my own strength, whereas Thou canst do everything that is the will of Thy Son, and Thou art always victorious. Grant, therefore, O Helper of the faithful, that my family, my parish, and my homeland might become in truth the Kingdom where Thou reignest with Thy *Son*. Amen.

For life in the maternal bondage of *Mary* for the Holy Church,

My blessing,

Stefan Cardinal Wyszynski

If Cardinal Wyszynski's references to Mary and Jesus were replaced by references to Jesus and the Father, this prayer would be uncontroversially Christian. As it is, I cannot understand how a Christian minister can commend this prayer. To whom does the Christian properly dedicate himself, body and soul? (Php. 3:7-14.) Whom does the Christian want to serve, be with, work through and for? (Matt. 10:37; Col. 3:24.) Through whom can the Christian do all things? (Php. 4:13.) Who reigns in the Christian's kingdom? (1 Cor. 15:25.) My little citations to proof texts are ridiculous. Even the most careless reading of the New Testament admits only one answer to all these questions: Jesus Christ.

Can I hope that Cardinal Wyszynski's "Act of Consecration", addressed instead to Jesus' mother Mary, is an aberration, and that in reality Catholics are not encouraged to devote themselves to Mary in this extravagant way?

"To Jesus Through Mary"

Dwight: This is certainly the most lavish dedication to Mary I have come across, and I understand why you find it incomprehensible and offensive. To put it in context, though, this sort of "consecration to Mary" developed in the Catholic Church during the seventeenth century when Jansenism plagued the church.[138] This heresy portrayed Jesus as the harsh judge whom it was impossible to please.[139]

In the wake of Jansenism, Marian devotion blossomed because, as you've implied, Mary was seen as the merciful Mother. Part of this florid Marian devotion was "consecration to Mary" as developed by an admirable missionary priest named St. Louis de Montfort. He wanted his people, who were burdened by Jansenism, to experience the loving mercy of the Lord, and this seemed more accessible to them through Mary. This consecration spoke in terms of being the "loving slave of Mary", and Cardinal Wyszynski's prayer is part of this tradition. To be precise, the consecration is always "to Jesus through Mary"[140] but this subtle point is lost on its critics. I hasten to add that this kind of consecration to Mary is an optional private devotion. Cardinal Wyszynski is not stating church dogma. Such consecration is not demanded of all Catholics, nor is it either particularly popular or widespread.

David: Indeed, St. Louis de Montfort's extravagant Marian devotion has even sometimes been criticized,[141] but consecration to Mary is hardly an oddity or an aberration. St. Maximillian Kolbe, the Nazi-era priest and martyr we spoke of earlier, popularized a consecration to the Immaculate that I hear about from time to time.[142] Within the Roman Catholic Church, Consecration to Mary is a mainline, approved form of devotion.

Dwight: It is approved, but it's hardly "mainline". It's an extra. It certainly isn't demanded or expected of anyone. You expressed justifiable concern at Cardinal Wyszynski's prayer, but let me offer a critique of your critique. The problem with your analysis is the little word "instead". From your perspective, this paean of devotion and praise to Mary is something that must be offered in place of devotion and praise to Jesus. But even the most Marian of Catholics would be bewildered to hear you draw that conclusion.

The good Cardinal would splutter, "But, the consecration is always *to Jesus* through Mary! Of course my love of Mary is not in place of her Son. Don't you see? In the Eucharist my life revolves around the daily commemoration of his death. My whole year pivots on Holy Week when we celebrate his glorious resurrection. He is my Savior, my Lord and my God. My devotion to Mary is not something that takes the place of Jesus; it is intertwined with Jesus. The two go together. This has always been the Church's teaching.[143] By loving Mary and devoting myself to her I am entering ever more deeply into my love for her Son."

David: I like your explanation, but I still object to his actual words. You suppose he would say that the consecration "is always *to Jesus* through Mary", but that's not what it says: In his prayer, he tells Mary, "*To Thee* I dedicate my body and soul…." It's just not the same.

Mary Worship or Bible Worship?

Dwight: The problem with your analysis is the "either-or" mentality. You assume Marian devotion must take the place of proper devotion to the Lord.

Let me use an analogy to show you how strange this charge seems to Catholics. Try to imagine what it would be like if you discovered that another Christian group thought Evangelicals were in grave error because of your emphasis on the Bible. These fictional Christians say rather aggressively, "You evangelicals stress the Bible to the neglect of Jesus. You call your churches 'Bible' churches and have 'Bible' colleges instead of 'Christian' churches and colleges. Inside your church you don't have pictures of Jesus, you don't have any crucifixes; and you don't have the Stations of the Cross. Instead, all you have is a big central pulpit to preach the Bible. The New Testament says that the early Christians "devoted themselves … to the breaking of the bread" (Acts 2:42) and that the way to remember Jesus and proclaim his death is through the Eucharist (1 Cor. 11:24-26); yet you Evangelicals have the Lord's Supper once a month, or even less often, and the main feature of your church service is a long Bible sermon. You have removed the cross of Christ and replaced it with the Bible."

"You even have a formal doctrine named *sola Scriptura*. This man-made dogma is a later distortion and addition to the Christian faith— something that is unheard of both in the Scriptures themselves and in the early church. This dogma (which you treat as infallible) states that the Bible and not Jesus is the only source of Truth. You teach your children to memorize Bible verses instead of receiving Jesus in communion. You teach them to sing, 'The B-I-B-L-E, / Yes that's the book for me. / I stand alone on the word of God….' Notice how they are not to stand alone on the sure foundation of Jesus Christ (1 Cor. 3:11), but on the Bible instead! Evangelical preachers say that there is no way anyone can come to God without believing the Bible. They declare their undying love for the Bible instead of Jesus. They say how their lives are totally dedicated to preaching the Bible instead of the cross of Christ."

If someone were to make this charge a good Evangelical might well snort with dismay and bewilderment. How could someone so misunderstand his position? Surely they are doing it on purpose! The good Evangelical would patiently explain to his critic, "You have misunderstood completely. *Sola Scriptura* doesn't set the Bible in opposition to Jesus. It does exactly the opposite: it helps us to glorify Jesus. Don't you see that we love the Bible because it gives us access to our Savior? It's true that we believe people need to know the Bible, but that's because the written Word and the incarnate Word are inextricably intertwined. You can't have one without the other. It is really Jesus we worship and proclaim through the Bible. If you just look at our whole practice and teaching with an open mind you would see how misguided and mistaken you really are."

To your dismay your critic dismisses your explanations. "No, no," he says as he sadly shakes his head. "That all sounds very plausible, but you will never convince me. I just know that you worship the Bible instead of Jesus, and all your clever word play just goes to show how blind you really are."

Now perhaps you understand how Catholics feel when Evangelicals say similar things about their Catholic understanding of Mary. We reply, "Are you serious? How can you possibly make such a fundamental and basic mistake about what we believe? We don't venerate Mary on her own, but because she has given us our Savior and because she constantly leads us to him. If you took time to study our whole teaching and practice you will see how this is true. We admit that some Catholics may over-emphasize Mary, just like some Evangelicals may take extreme views on the Bible, but when you see the full picture you can't make such a terrible mistake."

Pius IX's *Ubi Primum*

David: I understand your point, and will address it in a moment, but before I enter that conversation, I want to give one more example, to round out my complaint of distorted honor to Mary:

In an earlier chapter, we discussed Pope Pius IX's 1854 definition of the Immaculate Conception, the doctrine that gave its name to

Washington's National Shrine. Five years earlier, in 1849, Pius IX had asked the Catholic bishops of the world about their desire that the doctrine be defined as official church dogma. His encyclical letter, *Ubi Primum*,[144] included this high praise for Mary:

> From our earliest years nothing has ever been closer to Our heart than devotion—filial, profound, and wholehearted—to the most blessed *Virgin Mary*. Always have We endeavored to do everything that would redound to the greater glory of *the Blessed Virgin*, promote *her* honor, and encourage devotion to *her*.... Great indeed is Our trust in *Mary*. The resplendent glory of *her* merits, far exceeding all the choirs of angels, elevates *her* to the very steps of the throne of God. *Her* foot has crushed the head of Satan. Set up between Christ and His Church, *Mary*, ever lovable and full of grace, always has delivered the Christian people from their greatest calamities and from the snares and assaults of all their enemies, ever rescuing them from ruin.... The foundation of all Our confidence, as you know well, Venerable Brethren, is found in the Blessed *Virgin Mary*. For, God has committed to *Mary* the treasury of all good things, in order that everyone may know that through *her* are obtained every hope, every grace, and all salvation. For this is His will, that we obtain everything through *Mary*.

Again, if Pius IX's references to Mary were replaced by references to Jesus Christ, this excerpt would be uncontroversially Christian. As it is, however, it says things of Mary that should be said only of God: *Nothing* was "closer to [his] heart" than devotion to *Mary*? "The *foundation* of *all* [his] confidence" is *Mary*?

Not every papal statement is regarded by Catholics as an *ex cathedra*, infallible pronouncement. Can we therefore take this as a personal lapse by Pius IX and say that it's not representative of Catholic Marian devotion, which should be Christ-centered? Or would that be an intellectually dishonest dodge?

Dwight: You've uncovered another genuine show-stopper! At first reading it takes your breath away. Pius IX's praise of Mary *is* high, but granting Mary high praise has been part of the fullness of Christian worship from the earliest ages of the church. While we're slinging long quotations back and forth, allow me one:

> O noble Virgin, truly you are greater than any other greatness. For who is your equal in greatness, O dwelling place of God the Word? To whom among all creatures shall I compare you, O Virgin? You are greater than them all. O [Ark of the New] Covenant, clothed with purity instead of gold! You are the Ark in which is found the golden vessel containing the true manna, that is, the flesh in which divinity resides. Should I compare you to the fertile earth and its fruits? You surpass them…If I say that heaven is exalted, yet it does not equal you…If we say that the cherubim are great, you are greater than they, for the cherubim carry the throne of God while you hold God in your hands.[145]

This quotation is from St. Athanasius in the fourth century. Which is closer in feeling and sentiment to Athanasius—the quotation of Pius IX or your own position?

Bible analogy, Part II

Dwight: Pius IX thus seems to be in good company, but let me take your complaint seriously. As a former Evangelical I understand how Pius IX's statement sounds excessive. It sounds that way to me too. I understand what he's saying, but I wish he hadn't put it that way. So is Pius IX's statement just a personal lapse? Yes and no. We have to remember two things. It is not a lapse into heresy, but it *is* a personal expression. Pius IX is stating his own personal devotion to Mary. He is not making a definitive statement of dogma.

Second, this is part of a document about Mary. It is therefore an explication of a detail, not our whole belief system. You have to read it closely[146] and place this within the context of the whole history, teaching and practice of the Catholic Church. I'm not exactly comfortable with the way Pius IX expressed himself, but I think I would feel just as awkward trying to defend the following passage from an evangelical textbook that praises the Bible:

> The Bible ... has produced the highest results in all walks of life. It has led to the highest type of creations in the fields of art, architecture, literature, and music.... [Y]ou will find everywhere the higher influence of the Bible. ... William E. Gladstone said, "If I am asked to name the one comfort in sorrow, the sole rule of conduct, the true guide of life, I must point to what in the words of a popular hymn is called 'the old, old story,' told in *an old, old Book, which is God's best and richest gift to mankind.*" [147]

Does Mr. Gladstone really believe that not Jesus but *the Bible* is his "one comfort", his "true guide", "God's best and richest gift to mankind"? I don't think so, and it would be unfair to use this purple passage as "proof" that Evangelicals really do worship the Bible instead of Jesus. You have to look at the whole picture to understand the parts.

David: Indeed you do. But I'll allow it's fair to scrutinize even the "parts", whether Catholic or Evangelical. And I do find the "part" you quoted there to be distorted. Without passing judgment on Mr. Gladstone personally, I'll say that his statement is unfortunate. The Bible is indeed a real comfort, a reliable guide, and a wonderful gift from God; and it is true that the Bible enthusiast can quote the Psalmist saying to the Lord, "You have exalted *above all things* your name and *your word*" (Ps. 138:2)—a statement, by the way, that the Scriptures do not make about Mary. But "*one* comfort", "*true guide*", and "*best and richest* gift" sound to me like attributes of Christ Himself, and talking about the Bible this way is out of balance. To Evangelicals I would say: Let's make sure this is not representative of our teaching. The Bible is a means to an end, and the end is God Himself.

You imagined that the Evangelical who heard your hypothetical criticism of his supposed distorted emphasis on the Bible—can we call it "Bibliolatry"?—would "snort with dismay and bewilderment", and deny the very possibility. On the contrary, I hope that would not be the response, and for many thoughtful Evangelicals, I think it would not. There is in fact a very good point lurking there in your pugnacity:

From time to time throughout my Christian life, I have heard wise preachers and teachers warn that one's study of the Bible *could* lose its focus and become a substitute for personal communion with God.[148] I've been cautioned that Bible knowledge could indeed be a counterfeit for true piety. Knowing and affirming Biblical doctrine, they said, isn't necessarily the same thing as real saving faith in Jesus Christ. Evangelicalism, with its admitted and commendable emphasis on the Bible, does carry with it the risk of "Bibliolatry", and it is the job of our pastors to sound this warning. When our critics point out this risk, our response should be *not* denial and defensiveness but a resolve to avoid this danger that is so nearby. If in fact we do instead tend to be defensive to our Catholic critics, and to insist that we're immune from this risk, then may God make us wiser and more humble.

That would be my prayer, too, for any Catholic who sees the extravagant language of Pius IX or Cardinal Wyszynski, and hears a warning about giving to Mary honor that is due only to God, but insists that "Mariolatry does not exist in Catholic piety."[149]. As I know human nature from my own different but equivalent experience, such distortion *could indeed* happen. I fear it does happen.

Of course, if Evangelicals have been rude and accusatory, then Catholics have to be excused for being defensive—and I do apologize for the times we have been rude. But as one Christian to another, asking God to please help me see my own sins and faults before I try to counsel others, can I get to a place where my Catholic friends can hear me speak frankly about this?— Mary, who should be a blessing and a help, could become a distraction and a hindrance.

Dwight: This is a fair point. Some Evangelical attacks on Catholicism are rude and ignorant in the extreme, and it is natural when one's belief is attacked in an aggressive way to respond with vinegar, not honey. My earlier analogy was intentionally extreme to illustrate how some Evangelical criticisms of our devotion to Mary sound to our ears.

David: I get your point.

Dwight: I think we do hear your concerns. We admit that Marian devotion can be excessive and distorted at times. As your good Evangelical leaders warn of Bibliolatry, so our Catholic leaders have warned of exaggerated Marian devotions. Pope John XXIII warned, "The Madonna is not pleased when she is put above her Son." [150] In *Marialis Cultus* Pope Paul VI warned against the tendency to separate devotion to the Blessed Virgin from Jesus Christ.[151] The Second Vatican Council did the same. In the document *Lumen Gentium,* which dedicates five chapters to expound the correct understanding of the Blessed Virgin Mary; chapter four addresses your objection specifically:

> [The council] strongly urges theologians and preachers of the word of God to be careful to refrain...from all false exaggeration in considering the special dignity of the Mother of God....[L]et them rightly illustrate the duties and privileges of the Blessed Virgin which always refer to Christ....[L]et them carefully refrain from whatever might, by word or deed, lead the separated brethren or any others whatsoever into error about the true doctrine of the Church."[152]

Our Catechism gives complete and sound teaching (487-511, 721-726, 963-975), which begins by sounding the theme of Christ-centeredness—

What the Catholic faith believes about Mary is based on what it believes about Christ, and what it teaches about Mary illumines in turn its faith in Christ [¶ 487]

—and includes the warning that the "very special devotion [given to Mary] ... differs essentially from the adoration which is given to the incarnate Word and equally to the Father and the Holy Spirit." (971).

St. Louis de Montfort, who teaches the most exalted devotion to the Virgin Mary, is quite clear about her subordinate relationship to God. The first sentence of his *Treatise on the True Devotion to the Blessed Virgin Mary* affirms, "I hold, with the entire Church, that, in comparison with the infinite majesty of the most High God, Mary is no more than a mere creature formed by his hand; that, in the light of such a comparison, she is less than an atom—nay more, that she is nothing, since only He Who Is has existence as of Himself."[153] Even the present (most Marian) of Popes has carefully ensured that we have the correct teaching about Mary in his encyclicals. In his most recent Marian teaching about the Rosary (which we'll discuss at length later), the Pope says clearly, "The Rosary, though clearly Marian in character, is at heart a Christocentric prayer."[154] He also reminds us, "the Rosary clearly belongs to the kind of veneration of the Mother of God described by the Council: [i.e. the Second Vatican Council] a devotion directed to the Christological centre of the Christian faith."[155]

David: Giving "the correct teaching" isn't the same thing as confronting and correcting the errors. By Catholic lights, "the correct teaching" is that Mary is sinless, the Mother of God and the Church, the Queen of Heaven, the highest created being. One doesn't effectively address the concerns of excessive veneration by repeating this "correct teaching".

Latria, Dulia, and *Hyperdulia*

Dwight: Error is most often a misunderstanding or a distortion, so giving the correct teaching is actually the best way to confront and correct error isn't it? I agree that part of correct teaching is to warn of exaggeration and distortion—which we do, as I've illustrated. You worry that we give honor to Mary that is due to God alone, but Catholic theology has been careful about this from the beginning.[156] In chapter two I outlined the theological definitions which help us distinguish the worship we render God and the honor we ascribe to the saints. The technical terms are *latria* for the worship of God, *dulia* for the honor given to saints, and *hyperdulia* for the special honor reserved to Mary.

David: I understand the theoretical distinctions, but what I don't understand is the practical difference. Some people lack a refined religious sensibility and have to be taught and encouraged and reminded to reverence even God Himself. Low-grade veneration may be the highest spiritual plane they ever achieve, even when they intend to worship God. If *dulia* is the best that they personally have to offer, then when they offer *dulia* to Mary, they are giving her the best they have to offer, and they are saving nothing special for God.

On the other end of the human spectrum—say, a very religious Marian devotee—is this person's Marian *hyperdulia* really subjectively different, in his actual experience, from the *latria* he offers God? Maybe the different labels immunize his conscience against a charge of idolatry, but in fact his Marian enthusiasm brings him to the point where Mary takes a place in his heart that really should be reserved for God. I know how inadequate labels are to identify and distinguish my various subjective feelings, and how often I am unable to determine what's really going on in my own heart; I have to assume that people who pray to Mary are subject to the same sort of confusion.

Dwight: Ordinary Catholics may not be familiar with the technical terms, but the distinction between Marian veneration and divine worship is lived out in a practical way because they worship within the confines of Catholic liturgical life.

A Catholic worships God and adores his Son primarily, and without any confusion, in the Eucharist. All Catholics are obligated to attend Mass every Sunday. The Mass is the burning heart of all Catholic worship. Remembering and proclaiming Christ's death through the breaking of the bread is the center of our whole worshipping life. No one offers the Eucharist to Mary, and when a heretical sect called the Collyridians did so in the fourth century, St. Epiphanius quashed them sternly by insisting that adoration in the Eucharist was reserved to God alone.[157] All forms of Marian devotion are, by their very nature, subordinated to the Eucharist. It is this focus that keeps ordinary Catholics on target and focused on the gospel, and on the death and resurrection of our Lord Jesus Christ. It is this utter centrality of the Mass that is the surest and most practical prevention of excessive or distorted Marian devotion. So we are naturally bewildered when outsiders suspect that our worship is anything *but* Christ-centered.

The "I" Word

David: I hope that's true for all Catholics. I raise the issue of idolatry with some unease, because I know the term has been flung around in a most unhelpful way. "Idolatry" is not a spiritual cuss-word that we reserve for attacks on Marian devotion; it is instead a recurring problem of the spiritual life. My father introduced me to a hymn that prays,

> Do not I love thee, O my Lord?
> Behold my heart and see;
> And turn each cursed idol out
> That dares to rival thee.

The Apostles were repetitive and emphatic in denouncing idolatry and warning against it,[158] because idolatry is something into which fallen human nature tends to lapse. "Idolatry" can comprehend not just the conscious worshipping of statues, but any instance of looking to a creature to take the place of God, or to fill the role of God, or to meet a need that only God can rightly meet.[159] For example, *greed* is a form of idolatry (Eph. 5:5; Col. 3:5). Excessive or distorted patriotism can constitute idolatry.[160] Our teachers warn us against idolizing objects of even the most wholesome sorts of affection, such as wife and children.

Of course it's true that God commands me to love my wife (Eph. 5:25), and it's true that my love for God is bound up with my love for my brother (1 John 4:20-21); but these loves for humans are not interchangeable with love for God. To make the point emphatically, Jesus said that these other affections, good though they be, must in effect be hatred compared to our love for Him, which always claims a distinct priority. (Luke 14:26.) This demanding statement requires rigorous self-examination. If a husband were to say, "I am commanded to love my wife, so it is impossible that my love for my wife could ever become disordered and idolatrous," that husband would be ignoring Jesus' requirement of self-examination.

Idolatry is possible even in the context of ostensible Christian worship. C.S. Lewis's fictional demon Screwtape, expert in distracting Christians from effectual prayer, explained:

> I have known cases where what the patient [the human] called his "God" was actually *located*—up and to the left at the corner of the bedroom ceiling, or inside his own head, or in a crucifix on the wall.[161]

While receiving his apocalyptic vision, John twice fell down to worship angels, who had to correct him and remind him to "Worship God!" (Rev. 19:10, 22:8-9.) On the Mount of the Transfiguration, Peter had to be diverted from his plan to honor

Moses and Elijah. (Matt. 17:4-5.) The Apostles sometimes had to deflect undue veneration offered to themselves. (Acts 3:12, 10:26, 14:11-15.) Answering critics who found fault with worship in the Church, Augustine said, "I know that there are many worshippers of tombs and pictures ... [but] ... the Church herself condemns [them], seeking daily to correct them as wicked children."[162] Rather than denying the problem, he resolved to correct it.

Dwight: Isn't there a problem here? You say we are denying the problem of idolatry, yet you quote from numerous Catholic authorities who condemn idolatry. You quote Augustine who says the Church seeks daily to correct them. We still do.

David: Augustine is not exactly an up-to-date source; his information is about a millennium-and-a-half old. I don't have the impression that nowadays these potential abuses are the subject of "daily" correction. Yes, the Catholic Church does condemn idolatry, but my concern, obviously, is whether this condemnation reaches the Marian sphere.

Dwight: Pope Paul VI addressed this exact problem when he warned against "any tendency (as has happened at times in certain forms of popular piety) to separate devotion to the Blessed Virgin from its necessary point of reference—Christ."[163]

David: I'm glad he recognized this risk, and warned against it. If devotion to Mary is capable of strengthening one's love for God, such devotion is also capable of undermining one's love for God. Someone who looks to Mary for comfort, hope, security, consolation, heavenly grace, answers to prayer, and salvation has to ask himself, "Am I putting Mary in a place in my heart where only God should be? Is Jesus still first and foremost?" I don't presume to answer that question for someone else, but I do feel bold to say that the question should be asked. If someone says, "Devotion to Mary is good, so it is impossible that my devotion to Mary could ever be idolatrous", then he is on a different wavelength from the Apostles.

Dwight: I share your suspicion of any Christian who denies totally that abuse is possible. I also admit that at various times and in places there has been a distortion of Marian devotion. But to use my Bible analogy again, one who misunderstands Evangelicalism might hear Evangelicals say that they look to the Bible for "comfort, hope, security, consolation, heavenly grace, answers to prayer and salvation." To then say that Evangelicals look to the Bible *instead* of God and Jesus is a total misunderstanding. It's the same with us and Mary. She, like the Bible, is not the ultimate source of these blessings. Instead she is one of the channels for these blessings to flow to us.

Distortion by Neglect

Dwight: In a restrained way you have presented us with a strong challenge in this chapter. I'm grateful for your diplomatic tone, and I challenge our Catholic readers to listen to your concerns carefully. May I now challenge you back? Catholics are accused of an extreme and dangerous devotion to Mary. We are accused of exaggerated devotions that distort the historic faith. But which is more likely to be a distortion—our veneration of the Blessed Virgin, which is shared by the vast majority of Christians and can be shown to stretch back to the early second century, or the modern Evangelicals' almost total neglect of Mary?

You hold up a mirror and suggest that we may be guilty of distortion and idolatry, but may we not hold a mirror up to you and suggest that you follow a dangerously sectarian opinion? Doesn't your view represent an attenuated Christian faith— one that has diminished the glorious fullness of our religion by denial and skepticism? Might not this distorted and diminished opinion undermine the doctrine of the Incarnation of Our Lord by neglecting to honor the one whose flesh he took? By neglecting Mary and disparaging devotion to the Mother of God, might you not be in danger of falling under Epiphanius' stern words that "who dishonors the holy vessel [Mary] also dishonors his Master"?[164]

The Scriptures tell us that the angel Gabriel honored Mary, (Luke 1:28) Elizabeth honored Mary, (Luke 1:42) the unborn John the Baptist honored Mary, (Luke 1:41) the Holy Spirit honored Mary through Elizabeth (Luke 1:41-42) and Mary prophesied that all generations would call her blessed. (Luke 1:48) Jesus gives Mary to us as Mother (John 19:6) and John affirms that she is the mother of all Christians (Rev. 12:17) From the earliest times Catholics have rejoiced to honor Mary their mother and through their devotions to call her "blessed". The vast majority of Christian believers in all ages and in all places have honored the Blessed Virgin. But we are to believe that suddenly a relatively small group of Protestants in their neglect of Mary have got it right and everyone else was wrong?

We understand and accept your proper concerns, but we find it difficult to understand why Evangelicals (who are usually so admirably fervent in their faith) have such a hard and frosty heart when it comes to this matter.

David: I hope there's not really a widespread problem of Evangelical *dis*honor of Mary. I doubt that there is. The "lowest" possible view of Mary that is true to Scripture still acknowledges her as a remarkable and admirable woman of God, and as "the mother of my Lord" (Luke 1:43). Those of us who use the Apostles' Creed or the Nicene Creed in our Sunday worship affirm every week that Jesus was born "of the Virgin Mary". And virtually all Evangelicals make a very big deal of celebrating Christmas, when Mary is featured favorably and prominently in our remembrance of our Lord's nativity—in our Bible readings, our carols, our crèches, our Christmas cards, and our Christmas pageants. And of course every Good Friday we see Mary at the Cross, with the beloved disciple John.

It's probably true that we don't often go out of our way to consciously and affirmatively honor Mary (or any other saint).

The Bible passages you cite prove that people in Mary's presence treated her with respect and courtesy—and I, too, would hope to show courtesy, even elaborate courtesy, if I came face to face with Mary (or with any of the patriarchs, prophets, or Apostles, for that matter). I hope it's no disrespect to Mary that I reserve that courtesy until that face-to-face moment arrives.

When Mary said that "all generations will call [her] blessed" (Luke 1:48), it was a prophecy (as you noted), and *not* a command or a law. The secular equivalent might be for a woman to say, "I'm the luckiest woman in the world"; it's a comment not on her qualities or entitlements but on the good fortune she has received. Mary's statement—in one sense probably hyperbole, in another sense literally true—described not an obligation of future generations but the happy state in which she found herself.

That they would call her "blessed" wasn't a paying of honor to *her* but an acknowledgement that grace had been shown to her by *God*. In the same way, the prophet Malachi said that if Israel would be faithful to God in tithing, then God would "open the floodgates of heaven" upon Israel, and "all the nations will call you blessed" (3:10-12). It's not that they *should* call Israel "blessed", or that Israel deserved honor (quite the opposite), or that the nations would insult Israel if they failed to call it "blessed"; the point, rather, is that those whom God blesses extravagantly will be widely acknowledged as having been divinely blessed. And Mary was indeed so blessed—extravagantly, indescribably.

Dwight: You have done a good job describing the Evangelical response to Mary in positive terms, but we have to set this against the historic "anti-Mary" attitudes of many Protestants. Not least of these were the wholesale destruction of Marian shrines, the total abolition of Marian devotion at the Reformation, and a strong and steady stream of virulently anti-Mary propaganda. These attitudes die hard, and I'm afraid my memories of the Evangelical response to Mary is not really the gently positive version you offer. Let's be honest. In Evangelical circles the attitude to Mary was, and is very suspicious and negative. At best she is ignored, at worst she is denounced.

Nevertheless, I think we have made some progress. I hope I have been able to lay some of your fears to rest, while acknowledging your rightful concern. While I am sticking up for Catholic practice and teaching about veneration of Mary, it is not because I want to "win" the debate or score points, but because I genuinely wish for my fellow Christians to share in that closer connection with Jesus that I have experienced since I opened up to the ancient and beautiful tradition of venerating Mary the Mother of Jesus.

The way I first realized that devotion to Mary was part of the fullness of the Christian faith was when I first started to use the rosary as a form of prayer. I know most Evangelicals are suspicious of the rosary, but it is a Scriptural prayer. It is one of the simplest ways that Evangelicals could open up their prayer lives to a Marian dimension without taking on board the more extreme Marian devotions which you've accented in this chapter. Let me explain it to you and tell you how I got started.

10

Worry Beads

The Rosary

Dwight: Our discussion has revealed certain facts about the early church and the tradition of Christians down through the ages. Despite our particular disagreements, we have agreed in general terms that Mary, the mother of Our Lord, has been greatly honored by the Christian faithful from the very earliest days of the faith. We've seen that she was honored as "perpetual virgin" from the early second century, and prayers asking for Mary's protection and intercession are recorded from the early third century.[165] Then in the early fourth century the title "Mother of God" was recognized as a suitable title for Mary.

I believe if one wishes to have a Christian faith that is in continuity with the worship, practice, and teaching of the early church, then proper veneration of the Blessed Virgin Mary should play a part. We've discussed what the proper role of that veneration ought to be. You've expressed your view that Catholics venerate Mary too highly, while I've suggested that Evangelicals neglect Mary. I think we agree that veneration of Mary is proper in some sense. We also agree that this veneration should assume its proper level in respect to the worship we offer

171

God alone. If we do agree in these general terms, do you think we might also agree on a devotional practice that helps us to venerate Mary on the one hand, while safeguarding the proper relationship between her and Christ's unique, once-for-all redemptive work?

David: I think there may be some ambiguity in the word "veneration". It's probably true that, as you say, we "agree that veneration of Mary is proper in *some* sense", but the sense in which I would "venerate" Mary is quite different from the sense in which you would do so. I agree that Mary is a Christian hero who should be admired and emulated; I also agree that her inclusion in the Gospel story reveals the nature of God's Incarnation as "true Man"; I agree that Bible stories are given to us not for entertainment but for edification (Rom. 15:4), and that we should therefore meditate on them; and I agree that meditation on the life of Jesus Christ will include reflection on His mother. I would "venerate" her in that sense; I would (in the words of Webster's dictionary) "regard [her] with reverential respect".

However, talking to her (*i.e.*, praying to her) is another matter. In this chapter we're talking about the Rosary, and the recurring feature of the Rosary is, of course, a prayer to Mary—the "Hail Mary" (in Latin, *Ave Maria*), a prayer that evolved in the Middle Ages.[166] It begins with quotations from the Gospel according to Luke: "Hail, [Mary,] full of grace, the Lord is with thee [1:28]; blessed art thou among women [1:28, 42], and blessed is the fruit if thy womb [1:42], [Jesus]." It concludes, "Holy Mary, Mother of God, pray for us sinners now and at the hour of our death. Amen"—words that were added by custom, over time, in various places until they became conventional within the last few centuries. I guess it's good that the first half of the prayer is Biblical, but not every salutation quoted in the Bible ought to be taken up by Christians as a prayer. (See, e.g., Neh. 2:3; Dan. 2:4, 3:9, 5:10, 6:21.)

Dwight: So here we are, millions of Catholics not only memorizing Bible verses, but using them daily in prayer and praise and you're still not happy!

"Pray for Us"

David: My point is that *respecting* Mary doesn't, by itself, prompt *prayer* to Mary. We honor the memories of many whom we believe are in heaven—relatives, leaders, and heroes—but we do not pray to them. It is undoubtedly proper for me to ask other Christians to pray for me. (1 Thess. 5:25.), and "the prayer of a righteous man is powerful and effective" (James 5:16). I can admit that believers in Heaven, or at least some of them, are able to "witness" our lives here on earth (Heb. 12:1), and that they seem to pray about earthly matters (2 Peter 1:15; Rev. 6:9-11).

However, this Scriptural pastiche, while it keeps me from criticizing an occasional request to a saint to pray for us, doesn't justify a major, time-consuming program of prayer to saints. I would of course be grateful to learn that any of the believers in heaven had prayed specifically for me and my concerns, but I'm not counting on it. The Bible says quite a bit about prayer, but nothing about prayer to saints; the Bible urges us to pray much, but plainly assumes that our prayers are addressed to God. For this reason, few Evangelicals would take on any regular routine of prayer to any saint. We don't think it's warranted.[167]

Prayer Partners in Heaven

Dwight: I don't really understand the objection to this Catholic practice. As you've shown, Scripture teaches us that the faithful dead are alive in Christ, and are praying. We ask fellow Christians on earth to pray for us, why shouldn't we ask those who are in heaven to pray for us, too? The "Hail Mary" is our way of asking Mary to pray with us as a senior prayer partner.

You mustn't imagine that we are praying to Mary and the saints instead of God. We are asking them to pray for us, and with us as prayer partners. If you had a prayer partner named Richard and you sent him an e-mail asking him to pray for your father who has had an operation, we wouldn't say you are praying to Richard instead of to God. Asking the saints to pray for us is one aspect of our prayer life, but we are also praying *with* them. This is an essential element to the fullest understanding of the communion of the saints. Praying with the saints is expressed most beautifully in that passage from Hebrews where our faith is joined with the faith of those who have gone before us. (Heb. 11:39-12:1.)

You've referred to the Biblical evidence, but not to the evidence of Jewish and Christian tradition down through the ages. Asking saints in heaven to help was part of the ancient Hebrew tradition. The parable of Lazarus and the rich man indicates that Jesus accepted the idea that people in heaven could intercede for those on earth (Luke 16:22-28) and the Jews thought Elijah could pray for them.[168] That's why the Pharisees misunderstood Jesus' words from the cross, "Eli, Eli lama sabacthani." (Matt. 27: 46-49.) Furthermore, asking the saints to pray for us continues from the Hebrew tradition seamlessly into the tradition of the early church. Engraved on the catacombs in Rome we find requests for the departed loved ones to pray for those left behind.[169] Origen (in agreement with several early fathers) writes, "But not the high priest [Christ] alone prays for those who pray sincerely, but also the angels . . . as also the souls of the saints who have already fallen asleep".[170] The earliest recorded request for Mary's prayers comes from around the year 200, and reads, "Under your mercy we take refuge, O Mother of God. Do not reject our supplications in necessity, but deliver us from danger."[171]. And hymns and prayers to Mary abound in the writings of the first five centuries of the church.

Once again, I have to ask whose prayer practice is more in keeping with that of the ancient church? Catholics who pray, "Holy Mary, Mother of God, pray for us sinners now and at the hour of our death." Or Evangelicals who don't?

Minoring on the Minor

David: I think we have to assume that the overwhelming practice of prayer by the early Christians was heavily Biblical, employing the Psalms as well as the words of the Apostles' teaching and, to that extent, would have been devoid of prayers to saints. The invocation of saints must have been at most a minor aspect of their prayer lives.

Dwight: Of course. And it is the same with Catholic worship today. One of the problems here is that many Evangelicals are unaware of the full devotional and worship life of the Catholic Church. If you study our forms of morning and evening prayer, the liturgy of the Eucharist and our various traditions of spirituality it will reveal that our worship is predominantly Biblical, and focused on the life of Christ. In comparison the Rosary is an important, but small part of our devotional life. It is a side chapel in a vast cathedral. You mustn't assume our devotion to Mary is higher than it actually is.

David: How long does it take to pray five decades of the Rosary—ten or fifteen minutes? That's a very sizable chunk of many people's daily prayer time—more than my own some days, I confess, depending on what you count. The very idea that I would spend fifteen minutes of my devotional time asking Mary to pray for me, rather than simply praying to God, seems way off base. By way of analogy, I have seen many Evangelical "prayer meetings" devolve into spiritualized group therapy, where "prayer requests" become extended discussions about self, and little time is left for actual prayer. As prayer, the Rosary strikes me in something of the same way—there's too little prayer going on at that long prayer meeting.

Dwight: It must be that Catholics pray more than Evangelicals! Seriously, you should remember that the rosary is not the only prayer Catholics use. It is one part of a vast treasury of prayer and worship.

I should also point out that the Rosary is not required for Catholics. Many Catholics don't find it a helpful form or prayer at all.

Meditation or Vain Repetition?

Dwight: I'm sorry we got side-tracked. You imply that the "Hail Mary" is simply a repetitious prayer to Mary. I realize that the prayer reads that way, but the Rosary is essentially a form of meditation, not just a parroted prayer to Mary or even a form of intercessory prayer. This fact illustrates a crucial aspect to the Catholic tradition of prayer. We do pray for certain specific needs, but for us prayer is also a form of worship. Meditation is the link between intercessory prayer and worship.

When I use the word meditation, I am not referring to the practice of Eastern religions where the devotee seeks to empty his mind completely. A similar type of prayer is present in the Christian tradition, but we use the term contemplation, and we don't so much empty our mind as clear it to focus on God alone. Christian meditation is a form of mental prayer in which we dwell on a Scriptural event or a Scriptural truth not in an analytical way, but with a heart of love. The vital part of the rosary is not so much the prayer to Mary, but our meditation on fifteen or twenty different events associated with our redemption.

David: So the words that you say with the Rosary are just background noise?

Dwight: The words occupy one channel of the mind and free other parts to engage in meditation more deeply. So in a way it is like background music, but with the difference that the words are meaningful and true, not meaningless like static or shallow like muzak.

David: My disagreements about praying the Rosary don't end my interest in the Rosary. Although you may find me rather dismissive (by your lights) of its value as prayer, I am more interested in its value as meditation. Why don't you describe the nuts-and-bolts procedure for using the Rosary?

Praying with the Rosary

Dwight: When a Catholic uses the rosary for prayer, he or she holds a necklace-like chain consisting of about fifty beads. The fifty beads are divided into five "decades" of ten beads each. These "decades" are associated with a different event from the life of Christ. We call these events "mysteries".

Each decade is separated from the next decade by a single bead. As we hold a bead between our fingers we repeat a Scriptural prayer. So we begin a decade with the single bead and say the Lord's Prayer. Then for each of the ten following beads we repeat the "Hail Mary". At the next single bead we praise God with "Glory be to the Father, and to the Son and to the Holy Spirit, As it was in the beginning, is now, and ever shall be, world without end, Amen." Then we pause to reflect on the event from the gospel associated with that decade.

To say the full rosary we used go three times around the chain of beads, for a total of fifteen decades. This would take us through fifteen different gospel events called "mysteries". [172] However, in his recent encyclical on the rosary Pope John Paul II introduced a new set of five mysteries called the "Luminous Mysteries" or "The Mysteries of Light."

The first set of five are about Jesus' conception, birth and childhood. These "Joyful Mysteries" are:
1. The Annunciation by the angel Gabriel to Mary,
2. The Visitation of Mary to Elizabeth,
3. The Nativity of Jesus,
4. The Presentation of Christ in the Temple
5. The Finding of the Boy Jesus in the Temple.

The new set of mysteries focuses on the public ministry of Jesus. They are:

Jesus' Baptism
Jesus' First Miracle at Cana
Jesus' Teaching on the Kingdom and Repentance
The Transfiguration
The Institution of the Eucharist

The third set is "The Sorrowful Mysteries", which are:
1. Jesus' Agony in the Garden of Gethsemane,
2. The Scourging of Jesus at the Pillar,
3. The Crowning of Jesus with the Crown of Thorns
4. Jesus' Carrying of the Cross, and
5. The Crucifixion and Death of Jesus.

The "Glorious Mysteries" comprise the fourth set. They are:
1. The Resurrection of Christ,
2. The Ascension of Christ,
3. The Coming of the Holy Spirit at Pentecost,
4. The Assumption of Mary into Heaven, and
5. The Coronation of Mary and the Glory of All the Saints.

This may make the whole thing sound rather arcane, formal, and complicated. It's not.

Those who use the rosary daily would only say one set of five mysteries daily, not the whole lot. Many don't pray the rosary daily, but only once a week. Some would only say one decade daily and meditate with their family on one gospel story at a time.

Non-"vain" Repetitions

David: Is this where I'm supposed to complain about "vain repetitions"? Our Lord did warn us that in our prayers we should not use "vain repetitions, as the heathen do" (Matt. 6:7, KJV)—or, as the NIV puts it, "Do not keep on babbling like pagans, for they think they will be heard because of their many words." However, it was not *all* repetitions but "vain" repetitions that He criticized. Certainly Christian worship includes "repetitions": Examples we can't criticize include Psalm 136, which says "His love endures forever" twenty-six times, and many of our own worship songs.[173] To my sensibilities, a daily routine of fifty-three Hail Marys (in five decades of the Rosary), or two hundred and three (if one says the entire Rosary, as John Paul II has revised it) could quickly devolve into "vain repetition"; but obviously I'm not competent to judge another's heart.

Dwight: When Jesus condemned "vain repetition" he was referring to pagan prayer practices which linked an automatic spiritual benefit to the repetition of a certain number of prayers. These prayers were often in an esoteric language, and had to be repeated a set number of times in a prescribed way. They were more like incantations or magical spells. There is a danger of the repetition being vain, and at its worst the rosary can be a semi-pagan meaningless or superstitious chant. But then non-Catholics can also be blamed for lapsing into mindless drivel or superstition in their attitude to prayer. I think most Catholics use the rosary in an intelligent and alert way. There is a sense in which the repetition works a little bit like the *mantra* of Eastern religions, but the motive is different. Those who use a *mantra* use repetition to empty their minds. We use the repetition of the rosary prayers to take us beyond words so that our minds can be filled with the redemptive work of Christ.

Walking Through the Gospel

Dwight: The best way I can describe how the rosary works is to say that through the repetition your mind and heart are prepared for the action of meditation. Then in the meditation you are not so much thinking about the events of Jesus' life, but you are taken into an intimate identification with them. It's fitting to call these events "mysteries", because through praying with the rosary we are mysteriously taken into these events in a way too deep for words. It should go without saying, that in doing this we are also entering deeply into Scripture. Pope John Paul's recent letter on the rosary emphasizes again how the rosary is a Bible-based prayer. He instructs us, "In order to supply a Biblical foundation and greater depth to our meditation, it is helpful to follow the announcement of the mystery with *the proclamation of a related Biblical passage*, long or short, depending on the circumstances."[174]

David: Again, entering deeply into the Gospel events is an unimpeachable spiritual goal, but the obvious difficulties that an Evangelical would have with the Rosary are its strong Marian emphasis and its inclusion of Mary's Assumption and Coronation. Evangelicals couldn't accept this aspect of the Rosary.

Dwight: I understand the objection to the Marian emphasis, but Pope John Paul II says, "One thing is clear: although the repeated *Hail Mary* is addressed directly to Mary, it is to Jesus that the act of love is ultimately directed, with her and through her."[175] But if you are troubled by the last two mysteries, exchange them for others. So for example, when I was still an Anglican I began using the rosary, but I thought the final two mysteries were too Marian, so I put the Transfiguration in as the first glorious mystery, and substituted the Second Coming of Christ for the last one.

Remember, the Rosary is an optional extra—even for Catholics. Although there is a traditional form for praying with the Rosary, it is also flexible and open-ended. I believe the Rosary is just the right way for non-Catholic Christians to integrate a Marian dimension to their worship and prayer life in a non-threatening way.

The Rosary without Mary?

David: The Rosary will always seem too Marian as long as its main feature is the "Hail Mary". But imagining the Rosary without the "Hail Mary" sounds like toast without bread, or cotton candy without sugar—you've taken out the main ingredient.

Dwight: Using the "Hail Mary" prayer is a centuries-old tradition, but the rosary beads and the basic form of prayer can be adapted. One could substitute other prayers for the "Hail Mary." Some people use words from the psalms like "Lord you are my refuge and strength." Or "Lord make haste to help me."

The roots of repetitious prayer as a medium for meditation probably lie in a very ancient practice of prayer from the Eastern Orthodox tradition called the "Jesus Prayer". It is beyond our subject here, but, to be brief, it consists of a meditative repetition of the words, "Lord Jesus Christ, Son of God, have mercy on me, a sinner." By repeating the words over and over again, this prayer eventually occupies the mind and turns the heart to the Lord throughout the day.[176]

Many people use this Jesus Prayer with the Rosary; or indeed, one could use any short repetitious form of prayer. But in saying this, I don't want to downplay the "Hail Mary" too much. The Marian dimension to this meditative practice is important. It is important because Mary, by virtue of her intimate link with Jesus, was closer to the events of our redemption than any other human being. She pondered the Gospel events in her heart (Luke 2:19, 51), and through the rosary we follow her example and meditate with her on the wonders of our salvation. By using the "Hail Mary" it is as if Mary herself leads us into a more concrete and personal experience of the mysteries of our Redemption. Other prayers may help us do the same thing, but hundreds of years of Christian tradition show us that the "Hail Mary" has done pretty good service. Why fix it if it ain't broke?

Neglecting the Gospels

David: That's the issue, isn't it?—whether it's broken. As

I have thought about the Rosary from time to time over the past few years, and have tried to imagine how, from my point of view, it could be "fixed", it has occurred to me how little, and how irregularly, I truly meditate on the life of Jesus. I have also noticed that Evangelical churches that do not follow a lectionary, and that do not pay much attention to the Church calendar, tend to neglect the Gospels in their Sunday Scripture readings and their expository preaching.

I think we're very good about teaching the life of Christ to our children in Sunday School, but I fear it then falls far down on our adult agenda. Of course, I can't prove that this is generally true. I have only my own anecdotal impression, and others will have their own judgments. But I now tend to credit a criticism I have read of Evangelicals: In our reading and teaching, we emphasize Paul's epistles at the expense of the Gospels. Our salvation theology concentrates on the forensic aspects of the atonement, and therefore emphasizes Jesus' death and Resurrection—events truly worthy of emphasis—but, if I'm right, we tend to neglect the other events of His life. I shared this thought with a few friends, who reminded me that we do meditate on Jesus' life in some of our hymns and songs,[177] and in some of our devotional reading. And of course at Christmas we reflect intensely on His infancy. While this is true, my own judgment is that our meditation on the life of our Savior is very deficient.

We should, however, be *immersed* in the events of Jesus' life. We should appreciate more and more, with specificity, Jesus' solidarity with us in the mundane realities of human life. Our forms of worship should lead us into meditation on Jesus conceived in Mary's womb, nursing at her breast, learning to walk in Egypt, engaging the elders in the Temple, working in the carpenter shop, entering the Jordan for Baptism, sitting in the synagogue to read, and so on. And I don't mean to suggest that the problem is just institutional, in our churches; it's personal to me. When I think about my own devotional life, it seems that it is too much directed toward supplication (asking God for things) and not enough toward adoration; it's too much about me, and not enough about Him. It would be very wholesome for me to have some routine or discipline in prayer that kept me focused outward, on Jesus Christ.

Who really Neglects Jesus?

Dwight: There is something in what you say. I hesitate to remove a splinter from my brother's eye, but I attended a conservative Evangelical church with my parents some time ago, and I was surprised how very *little* Jesus was even mentioned. The sermon was from the Psalms. In the whole service there was only one brief reference to Jesus and the Gospels.

Another example is the very popular form of systematic Bible teaching called Dispensationalism. Some forms of this Evangelical school of thought actually teach that we are in the "church age" and that the teaching in the Gospels is not for our time. The pastor of the church in which I was brought up was influenced by this unusual strand of thought. I can remember very few sermons from the Gospels. Instead there was a heavy emphasis on St. Paul's epistles, and the Old Testament prophets. There was also a habit of interpreting the Bible in terms of current events with a strong emphasis on Dispensationalist views regarding the end times.

In comparison, the Rosary (as well as the Catholic Mass with its focus on the gospel and the saving events of Calvary) is absolutely Christ-centered.

David: "Absolutely Christ-centered"? Alas, that's the issue, and your comment inspires my disagreement.

Dwight: But you speak from outside the Catholic experience. This is the problem we keep coming back to. You can't see that our devotion to Mary is integrally linked with our love for her Son. Mary magnifies the Lord. (Luke 1:46.) She reflects his glory as the moon does the sun.

David: Well said: I "can't see" it. However, while I find it easy to *criticize* the Rosary, for the reasons I've already said, I find it difficult to *replace* the Rosary—that is, to come up with a routine or mechanism that avoids the Rosary's faults (as I see them) but that approaches its success in workability and durability. If I'm right about the Rosary, then millions of Catholics are meditating on the life of Jesus rather imperfectly—but they *are* meditating on the life of Jesus.

If somehow I could miraculously persuade them all to immediately stop using the Rosary, but if I had nothing to suggest that they put in its place, would I have accomplished any good? I doubt it. People are probably not brought nearer to God merely by *not* praying the Rosary. Luther once observed that when his followers diminished their saying of rosaries to Mary, they unfortunately did not increase their prayer to Christ:

> Once we said so many rosaries to Mary; now we are so sleepy in prayer to Christ that we do not pray even once in a whole year. God will surely punish this indifference to the Savior. Is it not a shame once to have elevated the Mother so highly and now completely to forget the Son?[178]

The statement is surely a bit of hyperbole (so typical of Luther), but he makes a good point. Tearing something down (in this case, the Rosary) is so much easier than building something up. I'd like to see a simple method for prompting daily, disciplined meditation on Jesus Christ.

Dwight: Luther's observation is fascinating, and I wonder if it could be generalized. We have already observed that there is an unfortunate element of Evangelicalism that focuses on the cross of Christ for our redemption, but seems to sideline the life and teaching of Jesus in favor of other parts of the Bible. If this is true, then doesn't it support the Catholic insistence that neglect of Mary ultimately leads to neglect of her Son? If so, then a very powerful ironic point is being made. Throughout our discussion you worry that veneration of Mary distracts from Jesus. We, on the other hand, insist that proper veneration of Mary exalts the Lord, and keeps him before our eyes. We think that not venerating Mary actually leads to the very problem you worry about: neglect and marginalization of Jesus. Protestant experience, from Luther down to you and me, seems to support this theory.

David: I can believe that for some at least, Marian devotion really is a vehicle for greater devotion to Jesus. However, I've seen a fair amount of apparent evidence that Marian devotion has a contrary effect for others, and I've heard more than a few complaints by former and current Catholics that Marian devotion tends to crowd Jesus out. For that reason, I can't believe that, if Jesus is being ignored, the best solution is usually to pay attention to Mary.

The Rosary Challenge

Dwight: Wrong devotion to Mary will not focus on Jesus, but correct devotion to Mary may well help to correct the fault you've pointed out. So I would recommend non-Catholics to use the rosary. Plenty of Anglicans use the rosary. One of the classic books on the rosary was written by a Methodist minister.[179] There is no good reason why Evangelicals shouldn't pick up a rosary and explore this ancient and beautiful aspect of prayer. Okay. It is Catholic with a big 'C'. But if you were to put that prejudice on one side, you would find it very helpful as a way to meditate on the mysteries of your salvation in Christ, and this tendency to neglect the life and teaching of Christ may be amended.

But most of all, I recommend the Rosary because it helps the non-Catholic to really understand our devotion to the Virgin Mary. What we believe and how we pray are linked, and I can say from experience, that I never really "got it" about Mary until I prayed the rosary. Likewise, I keep repeating that our veneration of Mary is intimately linked with our love for the Lord, and I'm not getting through. If you were to use the Rosary in prayer, what I'm repeating like a broken record would start to sink in.

This is not to recommend that people jump into Marian devotion blindly. However, most things cannot really be known unless they are experienced. So for example, we might have all the right theory about marriage. We might respect the married state and uphold Christian marriage, but until we are married and stay married for some time, we cannot *really* understand marriage. It is the same with the Marian dimension to our faith. The rosary helps people understand more fully where Mary fits in. It does so, not through theory, discussion and debate, but through experience.

I can guarantee you that "opening up to Mary" through the rosary takes you into a closer and more intimate appreciation of the incarnation. It really puts you in touch with Jesus and what he has done for you. Catholics are sometimes blamed for not having "a personal relationship with Jesus." I'm sure there are many Catholics who don't have that personal relationship, but it has been my experience that the rosary is one of Catholic devotions through which individual Catholics have a very personal and profoundly intimate relationship with Jesus Christ. Certainly since becoming a Catholic the life and work of Jesus has been almost alarmingly real in my life—and believe me, it has not always been a comfortable experience!

David: I'm a little more interested in your earlier suggestion of a modified quasi-Rosary in which the Marian element is minimized —perhaps using Bible verses or a prayer other than the Hail Mary, and featuring exclusively Biblical events solely about Jesus Himself. Your current suggestion that one address these Marian issues by experimentation is a little disquieting to me, and I couldn't recommend that approach. I think you'd agree, at least in the abstract, that experimenting with something that one believes improper, in order to see whether it might be okay after all, would be illicit. Here you counsel us to try Marian devotion because *you* are sure that it is wholesome and good; but for the person still concerned that Marian devotion is or may be improper, your approach would be question-begging. He must first address his concerns and then engage in Marian devotion only if his concerns have been satisfied.

Dwight: Distanced analysis and intellectual dissection of a problem can only take you so far. I'm not suggesting that you discard analysis, only that you get to the point where you are sufficiently satisfied to give it a try. This is what happened to me. A friend gave me a rosary, and when I thought about it, I didn't really see anything wrong with the proper use of the rosary. Furthermore, I asked myself who was more likely to be right, the fraction of Christians who are Evangelical Protestants, or the millions of Catholics (as well as Lutherans, Anglicans, Methodists) who accept the rosary, and use it as a simple way to focus their love of Christ. I simply thought it was worth a try, and once I did, I began to understand the proper role of Mary in Christian worship and tradition.

David: One thing that especially disinclines me to Marian experimentation is the feeling that one might be persuaded to take a little taste, and then a little more, and a little more after that, and pretty soon it's a steady Marian diet. Perhaps that sounds silly to you, but this does concern me, because I see that Marian doctrine and devotion really do grow—and are growing in our own time. In our next chapter we look at Marian doctrines that some are now urging be newly defined as Catholic dogma—the doctrines of Mary as "Co-Redemptrix, Mediatrix, and Advocate".

11

There is a Redeemer

Co-Redeemer, Mediatrix, and Advocate?

David: Memorizing Bible verses is a staple of Evangelical spirituality. In our personal devotions, in Sunday School, at Bible camp, in Bible and religion classes at Christian high school and college—in all these contexts we "hide God's Word in our heart" (Ps. 119:11). One of the verses many of us have committed to memory is 1 Timothy 2:5: "For there is one God, and one Mediator between God and men, the man Christ Jesus." In a German conversation class at my Christian college, we were required to memorize a dozen Bible verses in German, and this was one of them. It has been drilled into my head that there is "one Mediator"—in German, "*ein Mittler*"—and He is Jesus Christ.

And, yes, I'm sure there was a partisan Protestant motive behind the selection of that verse: We saw the Catholic priest as purporting to stand between the believer and God in the Confessional, and we saw the Church generally purporting to stand between the believer and God in its administration of the sacraments, so this verse equipped us to insist that the believer has direct access to God through Christ, and the believer can have an immediate relationship with Jesus Christ. Jesus is my Priest (Heb.

2:17), and I need no other. I say this not to draw you into a debate about the priesthood, but to remind you of the context in which we thought "mediation" was the controversial issue.

It came as a genuine surprise to me to learn, as an adult, that Catholics call Mary "Mediatrix".[180] One's first thought is that this must be a parody of Catholic Marianism; surely someone is exaggerating the Catholic position and depicting it with deliberately inflammatory terminology. We know that if there's *one* title that Jesus possesses uniquely, and that Mary could never share with him, it's "Mediator". Paul said "there is … one Mediator". You can look it up! What (one wonders) can they possibly be thinking?

Dwight: I remember the first time I came across the Catholic idea that Mary is a co-redeemer and mediator (Mediatrix) with Christ. I was a student at an Evangelical Anglican seminary in England, and I had gone to visit a Catholic Benedictine monastery. While I was there I told one of the monks that during a time of contemplative prayer I had sensed God's presence in a very real, but feminine way. The femininity disturbed me because I knew God isn't feminine, but at the time the Virgin Mary had no part to play in my devotional life. The monk smiled and said, "Don't worry. That's not God. It's the Virgin Mary. She is the Mediatrix. She wants to help you with your prayers and help bring you closer to God."

Of course I was shocked. As a good Evangelical boy, I, too, had learned 1 Timothy 2:5. This incident seemed to confirm my prejudice that Catholics really did believe things that were in clear contradiction to the Bible. To my mind it also confirmed my suspicion that Catholics gave Mary an equal status with Jesus. As a result I put this teaching firmly on one side and didn't really consider it again until after I had already come into the Catholic Church. I should explain that this postponement was possible because Mary's role as co-redeemer and Mediatrix of grace is not a formally defined dogma of the Catholic Church. It remains a pious opinion—a useful devotional and theological way of meditating on Mary.

Pious Opinion, not Formal Doctrine

Dwight: I have taken the time to understand this teaching, and I accept it on those terms—*i.e.*, as a devotional and theological opinion, and not a formal doctrine. In fact, I believe there are some very important insights into the gospel that are unlocked by this belief. But it is controversial even amongst Catholics. There are some ardent devotees of Mary who want the Church to define this role for Mary as a "final Marian dogma." Their campaign for this dogma is linked with a sincere desire to "complete" the picture on Mary.

At the same time, there are other Catholics who see the difficulties this would cause ecumenically. They think Mary has been honored enough. They worry that these terms encroach on the unique redemptive role of Christ, and hope the church does not define this extra dogma. I am on the side of those who are cautious. However, I don't think the proclamation of truth should be totally dependent on ecumenical sensitivities. If something is true, sometimes it must be spoken in a prophetic way—even if we know others will disagree with it. So, for example, the Catholic Church has come out against the ordination of women, even though the majority of non-Catholic Churches have now made this change. If Mary really is co-Redeemer, Mediatrix and Advocate, we need to take the ecumenical problem into consideration, but we also need to examine the belief on its own terms.

David: You mentioned the desire of some to define these titles as "the *final* Marian dogma". Is there any reason to think that that this would be "final"? What would halt the further development of Marian doctrine and devotion?[181]

Dwight: The proponents of this Marian dogma say it rounds out the Church's view of Mary. Protestant opponents worry that Mary might one day be elevated to Godhead itself.[182] I don't think this is a problem. Even the most extreme Marian devotees know that Mary is not God.[183]

David: Surely that must be true, but to suggest that Co-Redemptrix-Mediatrix-Advocate is the end of Marian doctrine sounds to me like a failure of imagination. When Pius XII defined the Assumption, he called it "the supreme culmination of [Mary's] privileges". If one had inferred from that superlative that the Assumption was the culmination of Marian *doctrine*, one would apparently have been short-sighted—at least from the vantage point of those who now clamor for her status as Co-Redemptrix, Mediatrix, and Advocate. I'd say that Marian doctrinal development might be lively after this "final dogma".

Dwight: With respect, you speak as a non-Catholic who admits to having no element of Marian devotion in your religious practice. I can understand your fears, but think they are unfounded.

Christ is Sufficient

Dwight: But rather than scrapping so soon, let's begin this discussion with the primary truth we both agree on. Catholic teaching has always proclaimed the truth that Christ's death is sufficient, and we need no other sacrifice.[184] This is a truth even the most ardent Marian affirms. So a leaflet from the office campaigning for this "final" dogma begins with these words: "The salvation of humanity was accomplished by God's only begotten Son, Jesus Christ. The Passion and Death of Christ, our sole Redeemer, was not only sufficient but 'superabundant' satisfaction for human guilt and the consequent debt of punishment."[185]

David: That *is* a good place to begin, and I'm sincerely glad they affirm this truth. Our Lord Jesus Christ is the Priest who "offered for all time one sacrifice for sins" (Heb. 10:12), who "died for sins once for all" (1 Pet. 3:18). The perfection and finality of His sacrifice is a truth we must not compromise.

Dwight: The authors of this leaflet would agree, but they go on to say, "But God willed that this work of salvation be accomplished through the collaboration of a woman, while respecting her free will." (Gal. 4:4.) While all Christians would agree that God willed to use the Virgin Mary to accomplish the incarnation, this does begin to expose a significant chasm between the Catholic and the Protestant mentality.

Much of Protestantism, at its very roots, is resistant to any sort of co-operation between human beings and God in salvation. The proper emphasis on "grace alone" has often led to an improper exclusion of even the possibility of human co-operation with God's grace. On the other hand, Catholics believe that while Christ's work on the cross is totally unique and sufficient, human free will can also be empowered by the grace of that redemption to co-operate with God to complete the work of salvation.[186] I realize this is a generalization, but I believe it does color our approach to this question.

Human co-operation with God's grace is a Scriptural principle. So, for example, you mentioned Jesus' role as High Priest but while the New Testament shows him to be the great High Priest, it also calls us to share in that priesthood. (Rev. 1:5-6; I Peter 2:5,9.) We do this by sharing in his sufferings. (Mt. 16:24; I Pt. 4:13.) Paul calls himself a "co-worker with Christ" (I Cor. 3:9) and says part of this is that he shares in Christ's sufferings (2 Cor. 1:5; Php. 3:10). Paul goes on to teach that this sharing in Christ's sufferings is actually effective. It completes "what is still lacking in Christ's afflictions" on behalf of the church. (Col. 1:24.)

Paul is not saying that the all-sufficient sacrifice of Christ is somehow inadequate. Instead he is teaching that the sufficient sacrifice has to be completed by being preached, accepted, and embraced by our co-operation, and that our suffering plays a mysterious part in this action. In that way the redemption of Christ is applied and brought alive in the present moment by our own co-operation in that one, full, final sacrifice. No one says we are equal to Christ, instead, by grace, our co-operation becomes a *part* of Christ's all sufficient sacrifice. So it is true, isn't it, that we "complete" Christ's redemptive work in this way?

David: I have to answer no if I am to give the word "redemption" its real meaning. I think your discussion of our sharing in Christ's sufferings mistakes the believer's priestly role for the role of the Redeemer. If it is correct to say that we "cooperate" with Christ's redemptive work when we appropriate it for our own salvation, it would *not* be correct to call the believer his own Co-Redeemer. That would be like calling the saved drowning victim a Co-Rescuer because he grabbed the lifeline that was thrown to him. If the term Co-Redeemer refers to anything, it must therefore refer to a believer's supposed role in joining with Christ to save others. But that usage of the term, too, is very problematic:

It's true that all believers form a "priesthood". What is our priestly function?— A priest teaches about God (Deut. 33:10), and Christians too perform this function (1 Pet. 2:9). A priest intercedes in prayer on behalf of God's people (Joel 2:17), and Christians obviously have this prayer role, too. We Christian believers also perform the critical priestly function of sacrifice, but in our case the sacrifice we offer to God is not the propitiatory sacrifice—which was in fact offered once for all on Calvary (Heb. 10:10-12; 1 Pet. 3:18.)—but rather thank offerings of ourselves (Rom. 12:1, Php. 2:17, 2 Tim. 4:6), our praise (Heb. 13:15, 1 Pet. 2:9), our good deeds (Heb. 13:16, Php. 4:18), and our converts (Rom. 15:16, Is. 66:20).

Even in a priestly system, however, it is always and only God who is the Redeemer. In the Old Testament, only God is given this title, never the priest. Jesus is called our Redeemer not simply because He is the Priest who offers the Sacrifice but because He Himself is also the sacrificial Victim who is offered *and* the God who accepts the Sacrifice. Jesus does it all. Any Christian who would call himself a "Co-Redeemer" because he possesses the believer's priesthood and takes his little part in sharing Christ's sufferings would be roundly criticized, if he were taken at all seriously. Not even the Church as a whole is Co-Redeemer; she is, rather, the one who is redeemed. Mary called God her "Savior" (Luke 1:47); so surely she counted herself as one of the *saved* and not as a Co-*Savior*. I am just as sure that she must have counted herself among the *redeemed*, and not as a Co-*Redeemer*, not Christ's *partner* in redemption.

Mary's Participation

Dwight: Of course Mary is one of the redeemed, and our doctrine makes that clear.[187] But part of the fruit of that redemption is that Mary is called in a unique way to participate in the redeeming action. This does not mean she is equal with Christ. We are simply recognizing that Mary, as the first Christian, was the first one to co-operate with God in the drama of salvation.

When the theologians of the early church called her the second Eve they understood that her "yes" to God was a crucial part of the whole plan of redemption. In the Latin translation of Genesis 3:15 it is a female seed of Eve who tramples the serpents' head[188], and in Revelation 12 Mary is active in the battle against the great dragon. Just as a man and a woman shared in the fall, so a man and a woman share in the plan of redemption. St. Paul echoes this truth when he stresses the total interdependence of man and woman. (I Cor. 11:8-12.) This interdependence, however, does not indicate total equality in the plan of redemption. Adam was held responsible for the fall, and Jesus, as the second Adam, is solely responsible for our restoration.

However, in both cases God saw fit to involve women in the overall plan. Mary co-operated with the redemption in a unique way with her total "yes" to God at the Annunciation. In agreeing to be the God-bearer she actively co-operated with God in bringing the redeemer into the world. As such she also epitomizes the role of the Church,[189] for the people of God are also called to join their will with God's will (Mt. 6:10) and bear the redeemer to a dying world. (Mk. 16:15.) John Saward sums it up like this,

To describe the beauty of Our Lady's co-operation with her Son's saving work, some of the Popes of our century have called Our Blessed Lady "Co-Redemptrix". It is a long and daunting Latin word, but its meaning is summed up in one syllable of Anglo-Saxon—the word that is the true heart of Mary: *Yes*. No word is lovelier when uttered to God's glory.... Saying 'yes' to God is co-redemptive."[190]

David: "Co-Redemptrix" or "Co-Redeemer" is not that long a word, and not at all daunting. Its meaning is obvious, but in order to remove the obvious offense of the word, your source dilutes the term to near meaninglessness. Anyone who says yes to God is "co-redemptive"? Then why define *Mary* as Co-Redemptrix?

Dwight: So the term is offensive, but then when we explain the term we are "diluting" it. The implication here is that our explanation is intellectually dishonest. Could it be that you have misunderstood the term and our "diluted" form is actually an honest explanation of what we think it means?

David: The authentic meaning of these Marian titles must be the meaning intended by those who enthusiastically champion the titles, not the meaning defended by those who want to suppress, resist, or minimize the titles.

Dwight: Why must the extremist view be the authentic one, while the sensible view I put forward *must* be the inauthentic? Is there anything but your (understandable) prejudice which demands that this is true?

David: It feels to me like the process works this way: A Marian title, defensible in a *minimalist* sense, is accepted as a *permissible* pious opinion, and the title gets a foot in the door; eventually, though, the title is defined as *binding* dogma, and it *develops* well beyond its minimal sense (which comes to be seen as rather narrow and crabbed). So, yes, I am rather jaded about explanations that explain away the clear sense of the words. Those minimalist explanations will fade when the champions have achieved their goal. The energy for defining these proposed new dogmas is *not* coming from folks who think everybody's a Co-Redeemer; that energy comes instead from people who evidently have a longing—which I do not understand— to see Mary promoted to ever-higher glories.

Dwight: Remembering my "bibliolatry" analogy, how would it be if I took that extremist view of Evangeliclaism as the norm? It would be unjustified. Nevertheless, I understand your point, and agree that Mary's "yes" to God has wider implications, but that doesn't mean one has to take the extremist view. Mary's total co-operation with God's will enabled her to enter fully into her redemption. In doing so she reminds us that Christ "stands at the door and knocks" (Rev. 3:20) and that we too can co-operate with the redemption that has been won for us by opening the door. The fullness of her co-operation is what gives her a unique status amongst humanity, and enables her to be our example of co-operation with God's grace.

David: In His sovereign accomplishment of our salvation, God did graciously use the "yes" of Noah, Abraham, Joseph, David, and a long line of obedient believers, among whom Mary is enormously important; but the Savior Himself—the Redeemer—is unique, incomparable, and distinct from them all, including Mary. No less than Cardinal Newman put it this way:

> [H]ow can we any longer prove our Lord's divinity from Scripture, if those cardinal passages which invest him with divine prerogatives, after all invest him with nothing beyond what his mother shares with him? And how, again, is there anything of incommunicable greatness in his death and passion, if he who was alone in the garden, alone upon the Cross, alone in the Resurrection, after all is not alone, but shared his solitary work with his blessed mother.[191]

I affirm with Cardinal Newman, and with some Catholics today who oppose the "Co-Redemptrix" title,[192] that Jesus Christ's redemption was a "solitary work" that he performed "alone" in His passion, death, and resurrection, which work he did *not* "share[] ... with his blessed mother." Even Pope Benedict XVI, as Cardinal Ratzinger, Prefect of the Vatican's Sacred Congregation for the Doctrine of the Faith, has criticized "Co-Redemptrix" as "giv[ing] rise to misunderstandings" precisely because it seems to emphasize Mary's cooperation at the expense of Christ's priority.[193]

Dwight: This is a valid point, and this is where I, as an individual Catholic, am on your side. In fact, I'm encouraged by Ratzinger's clarification and his pessimism about this belief becoming a new Marian dogma. But notice that Ratzinger does not dismiss the idea totally. His main point is that the terminology leads to confusion. With the actual terms being used it is difficult to get around the idea that co-Redeemer must mean "equal partner in redemption." But that is not what Catholics mean by the term. So let's use the word "partner" instead. I can see that Mary is a partner with her Redeemer inasmuch as her "yes" to God allowed her to participate in the plan of redemption in a unique way and reverse Eve's "no".

David: I think your clarification doesn't satisfy Evangelical concerns. We're not content just so long as Mary remains no more than a junior partner of the Redeemer; we think He had *no* partners in redemption; like Newman said, He was alone. He accomplished not just 95% of our redemption, not just 99%, but all of it.

Dwight: Paul himself said he "completes what is lacking in the cross of Christ" (Col. 1:24) so there must be some aspect of our sharing in the redemptive work. Likewise, I think, in some sense, we must admit Mary as a partner in the whole plan of redemption. Furthermore, there was at least a natural human aspect to her sharing in Christ's suffering on the cross. Surely as Jesus' Mother, Mary identified with his passion and resurrection with a unique kind of sorrow and joy. (After all, who can understand a Mother's grief and joy when her only child dies and is returned to her?) I also appreciate that this unique suffering of Mary is a fulfillment of Simeon's prophecy about a sword piercing Mary's heart. (Luke 2:35.) Furthermore, I think one might see this suffering as Mary being "crucified with Christ" in the sense that St. Paul speaks of it. (Gal. 2:20.) However, I do not agree with some Catholic teachers when they seem to make this natural suffering of Mary into an equal share in the suffering of the crucifixion. So I can agree with *Lumen Gentium* when it says she, "lovingly consented to the immolation of this Victim which she herself had brought forth."[194] But I don't agree with those who try to turn Mary into a key player in the actual act of redemption. So I find it difficult to accept the words of Pope John Paul II's words that Mary is "crucified spiritually with her crucified son…she united herself with the sacrifice of her Son."[195]

At this point, like Newman, I draw back. If Mary is a bridge, this is a bridge too far. And if the Church *does* one day define Mary as Co-Redeemer, I hope that definition will be limited to the Scriptural and minimalist understanding which I have explained above, and as I've explained it above, I don't really see why any Christian ought to have a problem with it.

Participating in Mediation

Dwight: What about Mary as Mediatrix? A similar continuum of belief can be drawn here. So while we affirm that Jesus is *The* Mediator, can't we agree that all Christians are called to participate in that mediation by proclaiming the gospel, and living out the life of Christ in the world? Jesus accomplished our reconciliation with God, but we are said to have a "ministry of reconciliation" as we bring others to Him (2 Cor. 5:18-19).

David: One *could* use the word "mediation" in that broad way, but that is not the way the Scriptures use that word—instead assigning it uniquely to Christ as the "one Mediator". Moreover, that broad application is not really consistent with the way the word is used in Mary's proposed title of "Mediatrix". This is not a title she is proposed to share with all believers but is instead a title and role special to herself. Pope Leo XIII put Mary's mediation (and her "advocacy", too) in its true, unique light:

> Thus as no man goeth to the Father but by the Son, so no man goeth to Christ but by His Mother. ... We believe in the infinite goodness of the Most High, and we rejoice in it; we believe also in His justice and we fear it. We adore the beloved Savior, lavish of His blood and of His life; we dread the inexorable Judge. Thus do those whose actions have disturbed their consciences [*i.e.*, sinners] need an intercessor mighty in favor with God, merciful enough not to reject the cause of the desperate, merciful enough to lift up again towards hope in the divine mercy the afflicted and the broken down. Mary is this glorious *intermediary*; she is the mighty Mother of the Almighty; but—what is still sweeter—she is gentle, extreme in tenderness, of a limitless loving-kindness.[196]

Pope Leo XIII thus said, of Mary the Mediatrix, things that could *not* be said of Christians generally. If "mediator" were really a title befitting *all* Christians, then there would be little reason to urge that it be defined as a *Marian* dogma. If the title means anything, it ascribes to Mary a unique role in the Church.

In fact, the things Leo XIII said about Mary should be said emphatically and uniquely of Jesus Christ: Jesus is the "one Mediator" precisely because it is *Jesus* who is gentle, tender, and of a limitless loving-kindness. (Matt. 11:28, 12:20, 19:14; Is. 40:11; John 10:14-17, 13:1; Eph. 5:25-26; 1 John 4:19.) It is *Jesus* who is precisely that combination of the Almighty and the compassionate that God ordained for our need. (Heb. 4:14-16.) I'll bet that the hymn-singing of your childhood included Charles Wesley's hymn—

Jesus, lover of my soul, let me to Thy bosom fly,
While the nearer waters roll, while the tempest still is high:
Hide me, O my Saviour, hide, till the storm of life is past;
Safe into the haven guide; O receive my soul at last.

Other refuge have I none; hangs my helpless soul on Thee;
Leave, ah! leave me not alone, still support and comfort me.
All my trust on Thee is stayed, all my help from Thee I bring;
Cover my defenseless head with the shadow of Thy wing.[197]

I suspect that these sentiments are not at all strange to Catholic sensibilities. I do not understand why someone should be deprived for an instant of this true picture of Jesus as our haven, our refuge, our comfort, and should be routed instead through Mary. The invention of Mary's role as Mediatrix seems to have been founded on a sad misunderstanding of Jesus Christ as a threat, when in fact He is the lover of our souls. Do we have the Jansenists to thank for the Mediatrix doctrine?

Dwight: I can smell the influence of Jansenism pretty strongly. At the same time, Pope Leo *does* give us a salutary reminder that Jesus is the stern judge as well as the merciful master. Furthermore, the pope is in good company. St. Cyril of Alexandria in the fourth century writes,

Hail Mary Mother of God, venerable treasure of the whole world...it is you through whom the Holy Trinity is glorified and adored...through whom the tempter, the devil is cast down from heaven, through whom the fallen creature is raised up to heaven, through whom all creation, once imprisoned by idolatry, has reached knowledge of the truth, through whom nations are brought to repentance.[198]

I accept that Leo XIII's language is alien and disagreeable to Evangelicals, but then they must also find themselves in disagreement with the fathers of the fourth century, whose theology otherwise they would wish to embrace. Nevertheless, I also I find Leo XIII's nineteenth-century florid style disagreeable. But as with your other extreme papal quotations, a close reading won't reveal any heresy. Underneath all the hype, I sense that you are content with Mary as "a" Mediatrix, inasmuch as all Christians "mediate" the gospel. But you're right that Catholics take it further than that, and I think one *can* profitably go a little further, without necessarily jumping on Leo XIII's bandwagon.

Inasmuch as Jesus came into the world through Mary we have to admit that the grace of Jesus Christ came through Mary. We can see that Mary mediates at the wedding of Cana in Galilee. (John 2:1-5.) John calls this miracle a "sign" (2:11). In other words, we are to take every detail as significant. As my quotation from Cyril shows, this role of Mediatrix was taught from the early fourth century in the Church.[199] While it isn't a formally defined doctrine, this teaching has gone on to become an established part of the fullness of the faith. I know you won't go this far with me, but I accept that Mary, by virtue of her unique relationship with Jesus, is the Mediator of His grace to the world. Notice that she is not the source of that grace. She is merely a vehicle for it. This, it seems to me, is a corollary of a fully orthodox view of the incarnation. Isn't it possible to accept this theological insight without signing up to the lavish nineteenth century devotional language of Leo XIII?

Continuing Roles for Mary?

David: No doubt there are many possible stops on the road between Leo XIII and Marian minimalism, but I don't see any good reason to transmute Mary's one-time role as the mother of Jesus into a role of her being His eternal agent. The rhetorical method that is used to justify the Co-Redemptrix and Mediatrix titles for Mary shows the problem: With each of these two titles, two almost contradictory arguments are asserted:

First, the title is defended as valid because it simply acknowledges Mary's one-time child-bearing role as the Mother of Jesus. (*I.e.*, "Jesus accomplished redemption, and she cooperated by bearing Him; Jesus is Grace personified, and she was the channel of that of that grace when she bore Him.") Second, the title is defended as valid because it simply describes a function that Mary shares with all believers. (*I.e.*, "All Christians participate in Christ's redemptive work and are thus 'co-redeemers', and all 'mediate' the Gospel to the world.") These two arguments obviously pull in two different directions. The arguments based on her unique child-bearing don't justify a *continuing* role. The arguments of a continuing role based on the function of believers generally don't justify *unique* titles for Mary.

Either she was a Mediatrix in the unique sense that was completed during her life as Jesus' earthly mother (in which sense the role is not continuing), or else she is a Mediatrix in a continuing sense that she shares with all the Church (in which sense the role is not unique). There is thus no basis for granting Mary a role as Mediatrix that is continuing *and* that is unique to herself.

Dwight: I'm sorry, but I don't see the contradiction. To my mind the two aspects complement one another. As Mary conceived Jesus, she began to co-operate with the work of redemption. (Luke 1:38.) She continued to do so as she bore him (Luke 2:7), and continued to do so as she attended to him at the cross. (John 19:25.) As the first Christian, she continued to co-operate with grace by being present at the founding of the Church at Pentecost. (Acts 1:14.) She continues in this role as our mother in heaven today. (Rev. 12: 17.) She is given a unique title because her relationship to Christ *is* unique. He did not take his human flesh from anyone else but her.

Mary as Advocate

Dwight: Mary can be seen as an advocate as well. We affirm fully that Jesus is *The* Advocate (1 John 2:1; Rom. 8:34; Heb. 7:25, 9:24), but it is also true that any believer may advocate or intercede with God on behalf of others (*see* 1 Thess. 5:25; James 5:16), as Abraham did for Sodom and as Moses did for Israel. What is the harm, at this level, in calling Mary an Advocate?

David: If she were merely "an" Advocate, then I think the proposal wouldn't feel the way it does. But, again, this is a title proposed uniquely for Mary, yet it happens to be, as you've noted, a title that the Bible expressly assigns to Jesus: "If anyone sins, we have an Advocate[200] with the Father, Jesus Christ the righteous" (I John 2:1 (NASV)). One *could* use the word "advocate" in a less restrictive, more broadly applicable way; but, again, that would be a departure from Scripture, and that is not what is proposed in the Marian title of "Advocate".

Dwight: You're right. Catholics don't limit the term to the minimalist description I've given above, and I don't mean to suggest that we do. I'm simply trying to find some basic ground for agreement. Even so, I don't know what you find so objectionable. I can see that the word "advocate" may be disagreeable. Why not call her "prayer partner" instead, because when we say that Mary is "advocate" we are simply saying that we believe Mary prays for us.

This tradition goes right back to the end of the second century when we find a prayer that says, "Under your mercy we take refuge, O Mother of God. Do not reject our supplications in necessity, but deliver us from danger, [O you] alone pure and alone blessed."[201] St. Ephraem called Mary, "the friendly advocate of sinners,"[202] and most important, St. Irenaeus as early as the second century calls Mary the "advocate of Eve."[203] This early evidence indicates that regarding the Mother of God as an intercessor and friend of sinners in participation with her Son is a most venerable and ancient part of the tradition. I have tried to show how this works, and how her prayers take us more intimately into the gospel events in my explanation of the Rosary.

David: We could never object to something that "take[s] us more intimately into the gospel events", if that means into intimacy with Jesus. But for Leo XIII, at least, Mary's role as Advocate arose from us sinners' "need [for] an intercessor mighty in favor with God, merciful enough not to reject the cause of the desperate, merciful enough to lift up again towards hope in the divine mercy the afflicted and the broken down"—i.e., not Jesus but Mary. In fact it is none other than Jesus who is this intercessor.[204] Since childhood, one of my favorite hymns (another by Charles Wesley) has been—

> Arise, my soul, arise, shake off thy guilty fears:
> The bleeding Sacrifice in my behalf appears:
> Before the Throne my Surety stands,
> My name is written on his hands.

> He ever lives above, for me to intercede,
> His all-redeeming love, His precious blood to plead;
> His blood atoned for all our race,
> And sprinkles now the throne of grace.

> Five bleeding wounds he bears, received on Calvary;
> They pour effectual prayers, they strongly plead for me;
> Forgive him, O forgive, they cry,
> Nor let that ransomed sinner die!…

I'm confident that this view of Jesus is not a Wesleyan eccentricity but is, rather, shared by all Christians. Jesus is our Advocate with the Father. To borrow Leo's phrases about Mary, it is in fact *Jesus* who is indeed "mighty in favor with God", yet "merciful enough" to lift up the dirtiest of sinners. I admit that, with regard to heavenly Advocacy, I am jealous on behalf of Jesus. I want everyone to know that they may, they *must* call on Him, and that He assures, "the one who comes to Me I will certainly not cast out." (John 6:37.)

Dwight: We are back to the question of whether Jesus is our Divine Judge, as Scripture says,[205] or whether he is the interceding Advocate. He is both, but maybe Catholicism has emphasized his role as Eternal Judge (thus seeming to require another advocate) while Protestantism has emphasized his role as advocate (while neglecting the fact that he is also the stern judge).

But in answer to your charge, I can only repeat that when we claim Mary as advocate we do not see this as separate from Christ's advocacy. The two always go hand in hand. Mary's advocacy is empowered by Christ's advocacy. It is a subsidiary part of his greater work.

What Next?

David: "Advocate" is probably the least troublesome of these three Marian titles, but I think part of my abiding misgiving about granting Mary even this title results from my inability to imagine the end of this process. The Marian movement evidently takes Biblical titles of Jesus and finds senses in which they can arguably be ascribed to Mary. How far can this process go before the Catholic Church will object and say, "No more"?

Jesus is *Immanuel,* "God with us" (Matt. 1:23). Could we say that, *in a sense,* Mary is *Immanuel* because she was the literal embodiment and means of God being "with us" in the Incarnation of Jesus Christ? Jesus is the *Logos,* the Word (John 1:1). Could we say that, in a sense, Mary is the Word both because she spoke the word—her *fiat,* "let it be"—that inaugurated the Incarnation, and because she pondered God's word (Luke 2:19) and believed God's word (Luke 1:45)? Jesus is "the Alpha and the Omega, the First and the Last, the Beginning and the End" (Rev. 22:13). Could we say that, *in a sense,* Mary is Alpha and Omega because she was the first to believe in Jesus as the Messiah and she, in her sinlessness and her glorification, is the "end" to which all the redeemed are destined? Yes, people could talk that way, and could use those words in those senses, and "explain away" the difficulties, but they would in fact be diluting, distorting, and doing violence to the *real* sense of those words as they have been revealed to us.

Dwight: This is a little far-fetched isn't it?

David: Again, that may just be a failure of imagination on your part. I once would have said that Catholics would never call Mary "Co-Redeemer" or "Mediator". Those titles still seem surprising to me.

Dwight: I have agreed with you that these titles are potentially misleading. "Co-Redemptrix" is especially easy to misunderstand. I think the devotional language surrounding these terms is often excessive. I've also expressed my own reservations about the full-blown exposition of these titles for Mary. I'm glad no less an authority than Cardinal Ratzinger has also expressed his reserve on this matter.

On the other hand, I've tried to use these titles for Mary in a proper way. I have tried to share with you how they unlock part of the mystery of the church. Understood in the proper sense, I believe these titles show how Mary's total co-operation with God points the way to our own intimate union with Christ (John 17:21) and shows how that union enables us to be "co-workers" with Him. (I Cor. 3:9.) While I accept (and share) your concerns here, I don't feel you've really tried to understand how these titles might be helpful at all.

David: I guess you're right, and I'm sorry to be a disappointing dialogue partner on this particular subject. But I have to pause at the very threshold of this issue and, in effect, question the whole reason for this particular discussion. As much as I want to open my mind to new ways of looking at things, and as much as I want to find common ground with Catholic Christians, we reach with these doctrines—Mary as Mediatrix, Co-Redeemer, and

Advocate—a point where I feel I simply have to say no. From time to time in the history of the Church, orthodox Catholicism has had to suppress a Marian enthusiasm that went too far, and I believe this is one of those times. I urgently hope that sober and responsible Catholics will insist that these titles go too far.

I am sure that the proponents of these doctrines mean well; and for all I know, they subjectively have a healthier and more Christ-honoring spirituality than I do. But by their objective terms these doctrines ascribe to Mary titles that, in the Scriptures, are uniquely ascribed to Christ. I have to believe they are the kinds of excessive Marian assertions that Cardinal Newman had in mind when he wrote of "statements which can only be explained, by being explained away ...."[206] I am grateful that, so far at least, the Roman Catholic Church has declined to define these Marian doctrines as binding dogma. I pray this restraint will persist, and that attention will be directed toward Jesus' loving readiness and ability to be our Mediator, Redeemer, and Advocate.

Dwight: I'm also grateful that the Catholic Church hasn't taken this step. On the other hand, a dogmatic definition of these terms might actually help. A proper, minimalist definition could be just the thing that puts the whole issue in its proper perspective, quells extreme speculation, and inhibits further Marian extravagance. A proper definition of these terms could actually settle the question and point us (as Mary always should do) towards the one full, and complete mediation of her Son. A definition therefore might actually suit you by coming down more on your side!

Time will tell. I do believe that, despite some excesses, the Catholic Church finally gets these things sorted out. It is hugely significant that the fathers of the Second Vatican Council chose to discuss Mary within the context of the Church. I believe this was prophetic, and that as the whole Christian Church moves towards a closer reconciliation and integration, Mary will quite naturally assume her proper place—neither overemphasized nor neglected. I am optimistic about the future, and in our final chapter I hope we will find some real grounds to share that optimism as we summarize and conclude.

12

Our Lady or Your Lady?

Summary and Conclusion

Dwight: When I first became a Catholic I came across a whole genre of books and websites I had never encountered before. They come under the category, "Catholic Apologetics." I learned a lot from their content, but I wasn't impressed by their style. The authors were defending the Catholic Church from attacks by Protestants. I understand that often the Protestant attacks were shabby, extreme and intellectually weak. Sometimes they were tainted with a kind of bitter paranoia against the Catholic Church. But the Catholic apologists were often not much better.

I don't think apologetics is about winning arguments or scoring points. You might win an argument, but lose a friend, and if that friend is a Christian brother you've actually stepped backward. But if I doubt the value of theological polemics, I'm also suspicious of that kind of sentimental ecumenical dialogue that doesn't believe there is really a problem. This sort of discussion cuts corners, ignores flash points, and "re-interprets" the faith to find grounds of agreement where there is none. I think the right way cuts between these two approaches. It requires real listening on both sides, some tough talking on both sides, and most of all a real passion for both the unity of Christ's Church and the spiritual growth of the disputants. Our conversations should be driven by a real evangelical spirit. Rather than just winning arguments or making converts we should have something on our side which we really think is wonderful, and which we want to share with our fellow Christians.

Sharing the treasure

Dwight: I am normally a somewhat cynical and self-centered person. By some gift of grace, however, I seem to have been given a little measure of this joyful spirit. What I have discovered in the Catholic faith is really so invigorating, true, and life-changing, that I have been surprised to find that I genuinely want to share it with others for their own sake—not just because I want to win a debate or convince people to join my church. Becoming a Catholic has meant entering into a wide and deep stream of Christian tradition, worship and teaching whose source is in the apostolic church. Despite its human failures, it is a tradition that remains orthodox, and yet alive, dynamic, and growing today. The wealth of Christianity is there to be explored and treasured, and a lifetime will not be long enough to take it all in.

So when I discuss the Blessed Virgin Mary with non-Catholic Christians, it really is because I wish to share this treasure of the Catholic tradition with them. Sometimes the discussions turn into debates. At times I have ended up being on the defensive, at other times I've felt it necessary to challenge the non-Catholic position. But beneath these postures I hope I have communicated the fact that devotion to the Blessed Virgin Mary is a positive tradition, in which Catholics rejoice. We love Mary because she bore our Savior into the world. We delight to have her as our mother, and consider devotion to her in the church to be as natural, beautiful, and wholesome as it is for any family to honor and love their mother.

As I said at the beginning of this book, my discussions about the Mother of God are not intended simply to convince you, or to win an argument. Instead I have tried to win you over—to help you understand and be more open to this ancient, beautiful, and Christ-honoring aspect of the Christian faith. If this has been my goal, have I made any progress?

David: Hmm. Well, I have to begin my answer by admitting my bad habits—as if they weren't obvious. I'm a trial lawyer by trade, and my natural orientation is toward controversy, argument, and *winning*. I have to resist this tendency, or I'll never really learn anything. In this dialogue of ours I've tried to be open and honest, oriented not towards winning but towards discerning what's really true; but it's hard to know your own motives, and to be really honest with yourself. As to whether I've been open enough to allow you to "make any progress"—

Out of Step with the Saints and Martyrs?

David: I'd say that there's one thing I've learned that has made the issue of Mary more of an open question for me, intellectually at least, and that is the antiquity of Marian devotion, a theme you've sounded throughout our discussion. Not all Evangelicals feel the way I do about this, but some of us feel very keenly our connection to the historic Church. We resolve to be brothers in Christ with the Apostles, the Martyrs, and the Fathers of the Church. Like we sing in the hymn "Onward Christian Soldiers", "Brothers, we are treading where the saints have trod."

However, I'm sorry to say that your arguments about antiquity haven't carried the day for me. Whenever you point out that such-and-such an instance of Marian devotion can be traced all the way back to the Third Century, my reflexive response is that you're a couple centuries short. As I've surely made tediously clear, my primary determination is to know what the Apostles taught and did in the First Century. Two hundred years is a long time. Customs and opinions in my country (for example) have changed quite a bit in a hundred years; and the way we think and behave today would be poor evidence for the way they thought and behaved at the beginning of the nineteenth century. The analogy is imperfect, but still the Church's practice two hundred years *after* the Apostles is inconclusive evidence for what the Apostles did.

Dwight: I hear you, but I should repeat that we Catholics acknowledge the development of apostolic teaching. We understand that it was not all there in its full flowering during the time of the apostles. How could it have been? But we do claim that what the church taught about Mary in the third and fourth centuries is a valid exposition of the kernel of apostolic teaching. What we now teach is consistent with, and in direct continuity with, the teachings of the great fathers of the Church in those crucial centuries.

Furthermore, you do the same do you not? The foundation of the Evangelical religion is the doctrine of *sola Scriptura*—a doctrine which is not found explicitly in either the Scriptures or the first centuries of the church. How could it have been when there there was no agreed New Testament canon until the fourth century? You believe this crucial doctrine was there in the Bible in kernel form.

Full-blooded doctrine of the Incarnation

David: I won't repeat my disputes on that score, but will simply admit that to be out of step with Athanasius, Augustine, or Irenaeus is a most unhappy feeling for someone who is trying to adhere to "the Faith once for all delivered to the saints". The witness of these Christian heroes about the role of Mary speaks to me, and I'm not finished hearing them.

I may not have answered your real question, though, since I've responded only intellectually. I sense that you want to know if not in my head but in my heart I've caught a glimmer of your joy at the role of Mary in your life. Honestly, I have not. To understate it only slightly, she remains for me an important historical figure; and the idea of her becoming emotionally or spiritually important to a Christian still makes me uneasy.

Maybe, though, you will take some satisfaction from this: As you and I have discussed our Lord's mother over the past months, the thought has grown in me that my heart and mind are both deficient in understanding Jesus' *humanity*. I was raised in the Fundamentalism that fought—and still fights—our era's battle in the Church's perennial war with Arianism, the heresy that denies Jesus Christ's deity. I'm grateful that I was taught to affirm, insist on, and do spiritual battle for the truth that Jesus is God. I think that fight is needful, and those who wage it are doing God's business and deserve the thanks of other Christians; but since they are called to emphasize the truth that Jesus is *God*, there's a risk they'll de-emphasize the truth that Jesus is *Man*. I've always known that Jesus is Man, but have I really *known* it?

A thoroughly Protestant friend of mine, who is an Episcopalian minister, wrote something interesting when he learned that you and I were engaging in this dialogue: He said in an e-mail, "I hope for a renewed worship of the sacred humanity of our Savior, Jesus, in the veneration of our Godbearer and his Mother, Mary." It's an unusual statement for a Protestant to make, and it struck me. The first part of his sentence resonates for me. One way of describing my defect is to say, with his phrase, that I fail to "worship the sacred humanity of our Savior, Jesus"; maybe I worship Him as the eternal Word but fail to worship Him as my brother, the baby in the cradle, the Man on the cross, and the King on the throne. The second part of my friend's sentence—asserting in effect that the veneration of Mary might be part of the cure—doesn't resonate in the same way, but it's thought-provoking: It's true that historically, corporately, and scripturally, the Church has affirmed Jesus' humanity by recalling His birth to Mary; maybe recalling Mary is also the personal way, practically speaking, to the same affirmation. I need to think about this some more.

Dwight: I think the most important battle for the faith today is to re-affirm a full-blooded doctrine of the Incarnation. What we think about Jesus ultimately affects everything, because in him we solve the whole problem of the clash between earth and heaven, the physical and spiritual, the natural and supernatural worlds. A full-blooded doctrine of the incarnation must also include the reality of miracles, Jesus' bodily resurrection, and His ascension into heaven. The current, unhealthy trend is to "spiritualize" these events and therefore to deny the reality of the incarnation itself. In both Catholicism and Protestantism there is a strong trend in this direction, and it ultimately leads to a religion in which Jesus is simply a good teacher, and our redemption is a theory. The result of this is that Christianity becomes just another religion of interesting ideas and religious rituals.

In my own experience, these trends towards the hyper-"spiritualization" of the faith simply do not exist where there is a strong devotion to the Blessed Virgin Mary. Somehow she really *is* the guarantee of an orthodox Christology. This is not to say that those without a strong Marian devotion will necessarily have a faulty Christology—only to say that where there is a strong devotion to the Mother of Jesus, there is always (in my experience) a strong and conscious affirmation of the full-blooded doctrine of the Incarnation.

This is the main reason why I pray the rosary and encourage others to do the same: because in our devotion to Mary the incarnation is most powerfully brought into focus. Through devotion to her and through her meditation of the mysteries of our redemption, we are locked into the wonder of the Incarnation of Our Lord Jesus Christ—true God and true Man.

The Preeminent Christ

David: Clearly, that's the positive side of a Marian focus—affirming that Jesus was "born of a woman" (Gal. 4:4), with all the mundane, earthy, human reality that that birth entails. It seems clear to me that God revealed Mary to us in the Gospel story precisely to communicate that reality to us, and I think Evangelicals will benefit from a greater appreciation of Mary's place in the Incarnation.

I wonder, though, if I have "made any progress" with you. The non-Catholic's wariness about Marian devotion springs from a desire to see Jesus Christ put in His rightful role—both exalted as the preeminent One, and adored as the loving and merciful Savior. We think both these aspects of the believer's relationship to Christ are implicated by, and are potentially at risk in, devotion to Mary. My heart must turn out anything that rivals Jesus Christ. From our own sins and failings, we Evangelicals know quite definitely that the fallen human heart—even the devout Christian heart—can twist even good things and make them harmful. Even our spouses, our children, our Bibles, or our Christian ministries can, if we're not careful, become distractions and idols, unless they are subordinated and oriented to God and His ends. The same could be true for Mary. Moreover, Jesus calls us to an immediate relationship with God in and through Himself, and one can't let his fears or feelings of unworthiness make him despair of that immediacy and settle instead for an indirect relationship for which Mary is the broker. Have our concerns have gotten through?

Dwight: I accept your concerns, and I share them. You have found some genuinely astounding overstatements of Marian devotion from popes and cardinals in the church. I think some Marian devotees have gone too far. Certainly their zeal for Mary looks to the outsider like it overshadows Jesus himself. However, these things need to be put in the context of the whole Catholic faith and practice. While admitting excesses, it would be dishonest for me to downplay devotion to Mary too much. An exalted view of Mary has been part of Christian teaching from the earliest centuries. The proper thing is not to reject Marian devotion, but to correct it. You are also right to point out the danger of idolatry. I think there are some weird examples of Marian devotion that look very much like idolatry, and some where the border line between idolatry and proper devotion is probably blurred. However, from my daily experience as a Catholic, I'm not convinced that these abuses are as prevalent as you seem to fear.

You are absolutely right to keep Christ central, and I'm grateful for your insistence on this point. But the problem in our discussion is my inability to get across how proper Marian devotion actually helps keep Christ central. This is always the problem with such a dialogue. We talk and talk, but aren't really sure if the other guy has really seen our point.

Have you managed to shake my Catholic convictions about Mary? Not really. Certainly going into detail has made me scrutinize our Marian beliefs and devotions, and that has been a healthy process and a kind of progress. You presented a strong argument on the perpetual virginity of Mary, and I was disappointed to find that there is so little historical evidence for the Assumption of the Virgin Mary in the earliest centuries. In addition, your careful analysis of Marian apparitions helped me pick my way through that minefield. If part of the aim of this book was to clear up misconceptions and misunderstandings, then our study has helped clear up some of my own skewed thinking.

Barking at the passing train

David: It's gracious of you to say so. However, we've bumped up against one of the problems with Catholic-Evangelical dialogue. When the matter is not Catholic dogma, Catholic individuals have the liberty of expressing their own doubts more freely, or even making personal concessions. But when the questions are about defined Catholic dogma, there isn't really much to discuss, is there? You simply have to follow your Church's teaching. I'm not complaining; I'm just observing what "dogma" means. In these circumstances, maybe I'm like the dog barking at the passing train. The train is not going to stop.

Dwight: I know. Catholics aren't going to say, "Oh well, I guess you're right about the Assumption of Mary into heaven. We've got it wrong for the last fifteen hundred years." In that respect Catholics can't concede much, and the Evangelical isn't going to make much "progress" with his dialogue. On the other hand, a dialogue like this *does* do a lot of good. It helps clear away some misunderstandings about the Catholic faith for Protestants, and it helps Catholics understand the very real objections that non-Catholics have. It's good for Catholics to realize that not all Protestant objections proceed from bias, prejudice, ignorance, or hostility to Mary. We may (and do) disagree with your objections, but we can certainly appreciate (for example) your determination to keep Jesus in His preeminent place. That has to be progress because we'll come out of it understanding one another better even if we still don't agree.

This will lead to two trends in the future. First, I believe Protestants really will start to come closer to the historic church on the issue of Mary. The position you have expressed in our discussion is quite different from the reflexive anti-Catholic, anti-Marian disposition that characterizes much of Evangelicalism. I hope you're not offended if I hope this is anecdotal evidence of such a shift. Second, I think Catholics really will temper their Marian devotion in a direction that you might think of as more Protestant. Remember those words from *Lumen Gentium*, where—

[The council] strongly urges theologians and preachers of the word of God to be careful to refrain...from all false exaggeration in considering the special dignity of the Mother of God.... [L]et them rightly illustrate the duties and privileges of the Blessed Virgin which always refer to Christ.... [L]et them carefully refrain from whatever might, by word or deed, lead the separated brethren or any others whatsoever into error about the true doctrine of the Church.[207]

Part of this movement is not only the result of ecumenical discussions, but the more natural result of the second Vatican Council. As a result of the council, Catholic faith and practice is simpler and more obviously Bible-based than before. This trend must alter our devotion to Mary; taking it in a simpler and more Scriptural direction.On a wider level, I wonder if you think discussions like ours might help things along on the wider scene. In the Vatican II document, *Lumen Gentium,* Mary's role is integrated with the mission of the Church, and no matter how incredible it may seem, Catholics believe that she can actually be a focus for unity. I really believe that proper, Christ-centered devotion to Mary is one of the things that will bring Christians of different traditions closer together.[208] This doesn't mean that everyone must hop on the next train to Rome. It simply means that as people draw closer to Jesus Christ—through devotion to his mother, among other things—they will be drawing closer to one another. For many reasons Catholic and non-Catholic Christians cannot share together in the fullness of Eucharistic communion, but a shared devotion to Mary is one way we could be drawn closer together. Do you think it is too much for me to hope that this may eventually start to happen?

Bridge or barrier?

David: It's hard for me to picture that. It may well be that Marian devotion will be an ecumenical bridge between Roman Catholicism and Eastern Orthodoxy, and Pope John Paul II was probably reasonable to hope for that in his encyclical *Redemptoris Mater.* I suppose that Marian devotion might also be a bridge between Catholics and the small numbers of Lutherans, Anglicans, and Methodists who profess a devotion to Mary, or who seem at least to be more open to such devotion. However, a Marian devotee would be extremely rare in the Evangelical wing of any of these denominations. As for fellowship between Evangelicals and Catholics, I can't help thinking that Marian devotion is more likely to continue to be an impediment, rather than a help.

Dwight: But all sorts of interesting things might develop. This devotion doesn't have to be totally Catholic in its form. It may take forms we have not seen before which are more Anglican or Charismatic or Evangelical. It may come about through hymns, sermons, Bible studies, and retreats. Little things move us forward. So, for example, look how many Evangelicals are quite happy to attend churches where they light candles, keep the Christian year, use liturgy, and have a nativity scene with statues of Mary and Joseph at Christmas. These are all "Catholic" customs which would have been considered anathema by our Puritan or Anabaptist great-grandparents, and even some of our Evangelical grandparents. You might not be one of them, but there are many non-Catholic Christians who are discovering the important role Mary has to play in their day-to-day faith in ways that are consistent with their own tradition.

Stumbling Block or Stepping Stone?

David: We'll see. So far, though, isn't it true that almost *none* of the Evangelicals who have converted to Catholicism say they were drawn there by Marian devotion? Most of them (like you) say that, on the contrary, Mary was problematic and was one of the last issues they resolved. Mary made their conversion more difficult, not less. Most of us Evangelicals who are interested in Catholicism and respectful of it, but who have no thought of converting, are even more averse to Marian devotion.

Dwight: Maybe Catholic devotion to Mary is *supposed* to be difficult. In other words, where these converts were most off-track it was most difficult to come on track. Our blind spot is just the place where it is most difficult for us to see. So for example, a person who has trouble becoming a Christian because he has to believe Jesus is God is *right* to have problems. That's exactly the point where it gets tricky. We don't solve the problem, however, by saying, "Oh, well, don't worry about that one. You can join the church anyway."

Mary does play an interesting part in our conversions to Catholicism. While we admit that the Marian dogmas were a difficulty, we also confess that once we opened up to Marian devotion, and said (with Mary), "Let it be to me according to your word," the way into the whole of the Catholic Church was actually eased. So, paradoxically, Mary may be a problem for converts, but she is also a part of the solution.

David: To be honest, I think that the most you can hope for is Evangelical *toleration* of some measure of Marian devotion. Perhaps that sounds condescending to you, but let's be frank: You Catholics grit your teeth and tolerate some of the things that *we* hold dear, and we know it, and you know that we know it. Sometimes toleration is the best that you can hope for—and sometimes it's enough.

Dwight: You know one of my catch phrases, "a person is most often right in what he affirms and wrong in what he denies." So toleration is better than denial, and it is a first step towards affirmation, so I guess that's progress.

Adoring Mary's son

Dwight: This book has focused on Mary. That was the point. But now that we're coming in on the home stretch, I'd like to set the balance right. I have been thinking that our whole exercise has felt distorted. I'm glad we've had a chance to discuss Mary's role in depth, but I wish we had another ten volumes to place her in proper perspective by discussing the whole divine drama of salvation. I realize that from the non-Catholic point of view, Mary looms large in Catholicism. But I also know as a Catholic that she always takes a subsidiary role. Like a proud Jewish mother she stands in the wings watching her son with adoration. Catholics love her for that, and if we have sometimes been over-enthusiastic, it is only because we love the one who has brought us so much closer to our Lord and Savior Jesus Christ.

So while I encourage our Evangelical readers to take another look at Mary and how she might play an active role in their life of prayer and worship, I would also encourage our Catholic readers never to forget the "author and finisher" of their faith, the one Mary brought into the world, and the one to whom she constantly points—Our Lord and Savior Jesus Christ. As Pope John XXIII reminded us, "The Madonna is not pleased when she is put above her Son." [209] Jesus Christ is the fountain and source of our unity, and as we draw closer to him we will invariably be drawn closer to one another as well.

David: Amen to that. You and I both long for Christian unity, the fulfillment of Jesus' prayer that we all be one. (John 17:21.) What we want, though, is a unity based on the truth—that is, both true doctrine and the Truth Himself, Jesus Christ. We abhor the variety of ecumenism that seeks a unity in form without substance, based not on affirming truth but on suppressing it.

Dwight: Jesus' passionate prayer for unity echoes throughout the New Testament. (Eph. 4:1-4; I Pt. 3:8; Phil. 2:1-3; *et al.*) Unity is so important, not only because Christ's body is broken through our division, but because we have a gospel to proclaim. How can we preach a gospel of love and reconciliation when our own house is divided? Indeed, love is not only the hallmark of our gospel, but the empowering drive of our mission. (Jn. 17:21.)

Signs of convergence

Dwight: Of course the work for Christian unity is long and hard. But that doesn't mean we give up. We continue to pray, work and strive with patience and hope that the Spirit will show the way forward. In fact, on the wider scene there are some great signs of hope for those who long for Christian unity. Along with her talks with the historic churches of the East and the mainstream Protestant groups, the Catholic Church has also participated in discussions with various Evangelical groupings like Pentecostals[210] and the Southern Baptists in the USA.[211] Often these talks stall and falter, but we must simply try again. In Europe official talks have made progress with the Anglicans[212], and in 1999 a historic agreement between Lutherans and Catholics was signed on the question of justification in which agreed on a basic formula and that this issue need not divide us any longer.[213] In 1999 the Pontifical Council for Promoting Christian Unity held three sessions with the World Evangelical Fellowship's Theological Commission.[214] Their final statement said,

> As we listened jointly to the Scriptures, prayed together and spoke the truth to one another in love, we recognized and rejoiced in the fellowship we have in Christ based on our common faith in Him. The riches of this gift are such that all who share in it cannot regard each other as strangers much less treat each other as enemies.[215]

David: I found the Catholic-Lutheran "Joint Declaration on the Doctrine of Justification" to be very encouraging and, I hope, important for the future of the Church. Evangelicals often fear that Catholics don't understand grace and that they are trying, instead, to earn their way to heaven. The joint declaration, however, proclaims a Gospel message that would reassure and please most Evangelicals.[216]

However, that joint declaration is an exception for me, and otherwise it's hard for me, as an Evangelical layman, to get very interested in most of these formal, high level talks. Maybe it's unfair, but I can't help thinking of them as negotiations by bureaucrats in competing corporations who are contemplating mergers.

Dwight: I agree. The high level talks don't interest me that much either. However, the good thing is that talks and fellowship are beginning to happen at every level of our life together, and it's right that one of those levels is official and formal.

What Will Unity Look Like?

David: I meant that I doubt whether the formal level is very important, perhaps because of my different understanding of the Church. I suspect a Catholic must presume that "unity" will mean institutional, hierarchical unity, so that ecumenical efforts must aim for the eventual enrollment of all Christians on the membership book of a single earthly entity. I admit that the unity Jesus prayed for will indeed be *visible* (since "the world" will see it and "believe" (John 17:21)), but I don't know what shape that unity might take. As an Evangelical, I am accustomed to cooperation, fellowship, and inter-communion among churches that have no legal or constitutional connection to each other but who recognize each other as part of the Body of Christ. Consequently, my notion of our future unity may be fuzzier than yours.

Although these denominational merger negotiations don't seem very relevant to me, I am more interested in the grass roots efforts and doctrinal discussions undertaken by theologians on both sides. In the mid-90s, Evangelical Charles Colson and Catholic priest Richard John Neuhaus, together with others from their camps, issued the statement *Evangelicals and Catholics Together: The Christian Mission in the Third Millennium*. The statement raised a minor storm in Evangelical circles because it was the first time that some very major conservative Evangelical players started to work openly with Catholics.

The statement recognized the already existing partnership between Evangelicals and Catholics in the areas of mission, social responsibility, sexual ethics and the defense of Christian belief. There is a growing realization among Evangelicals and Catholics that we agree on far more than we disagree on, and that we have a common cause in many areas.

Dwight: By the time of this second edition in 2017 that initiative seems to have stalled. Evangelicalism seems to have gone down the path of the "mega church" and I don't know how the new generation of church leaders perceive the Catholics. I believe the post modern Evangelicals pick and choose what they like from Catholics, but are diffident about formal co operation. Perhaps our own modest effort in this book has helped to contribute to a renewal of interest in theological discussions. If we are to move forward at all, then we must do so not only with open debate, but with genuine Christ-like humility. The only possible approach that we can have to one another as brothers in Christ is summed up beautifully by the apostle Paul, and with his majestic words I will bow out.

> So if there is any encouragement in Christ, any incentive of love, any participation in the Spirit, any affection and sympathy, complete my joy by being of the same mind, having the same love, being in full accord and of one mind. Do nothing from selfishness or conceit, but in humility count others better than yourselves. Let each of you look not only to his own interests, but also to the interests of others. Have this mind among yourselves, which is yours in Christ Jesus, who, though he was in the form of God, did not count equality with God a thing to be grasped, but emptied himself, taking the form of a servant, being born in the likeness of men. And being found in human form he humbled himself and became obedient unto death, even death on a cross. Therefore God has highly exalted him and bestowed on him the name which is above every name, that at the name of Jesus every knee should bow, in heaven and on earth and under the earth, and every tongue confess that Jesus Christ is Lord, to the glory of God the Father. [217]

David: I do hope that our discussion has had at least a small portion of that Spirit and that, where we have lacked it, our brethren will overlook our faults and will do better in their own fellowship. I can't foresee see how God will heal the great breach of the Reformation—how He will soften the hearts that need softening, correct the errors held so firmly and so sincerely, and implant the truths that are resisted so devoutly. I can't picture how it will happen, but I do believe that, as you said before, we will come into unity with one another as [218] each of us comes into unity with Jesus Christ. He will illumine the darkness, correct the faults, reconcile the enemies, and heal the wounds. To achieve the unity for which He prayed, we must each "grow in the grace and knowledge of our Lord and Savior Jesus Christ." (2 Peter 3:18.) Therefore I propose to conclude our dialogue about Mary with a prayer to that end:

On Good Friday both Catholics and Protestants sing the medieval hymn called *Stabat Mater* (Latin for "the Mother was standing"). In this hymn we recall Mary at Calvary, and we ask:

> Who, on Christ's dear mother gazing
> Pierced by anguish so amazing
> Born of woman, would not weep?
> Who, on Christ's dear mother thinking
> Such a cup of sorrow drinking
> Would not share her sorrows deep?
>
> Jesus, may her deep devotion
> Stir in me the same emotion,
> Fount of love, Redeemer kind,
> That my heart fresh ardor gaining,
> And a purer love attaining,
> May with Thee acceptance find.

Notes

Foreword / Francis Beckwith

[1]See the acounts of my journey in Francis J. Beckwith, *Return to Rome: Confessions of an Evangelical Catholic* (Grand Rapids, MI: Brazos Press, 2009), especially chapters 5-7; and Francis J. Beckwith, "A Journey to Catholicism" and "Catholicism Rejoinder," in *Journeys of Faith: Evangelicalism, Eastern Orthodoxy, Catholicism, and Anglicanism*, ed. Robert L. Plummer (Grand Rapids, MI: Zondervan, 2012), 81-114, 129-134

[2]Robert Wilken points out, that "all the ancient liturgies included prayers commemorating the 'faithful departed'. . . . [who] were not simply remembered, they were welcomed as participants in the liturgy." (Robert Louis Wilken, *The Spirit of Early Christian Thought: Seeking the Face of God* [New Haven, CT: Yale University Press, 2003], 46)

Chapter 1

[1] John Paul II, General Audience of March 21, 2001. http://www.vatican.va/holy_father/john_paul_ii/audiences/2001/documents/hf_jpii_aud_20010321_en.html

[2] Mark 3:21 even leaves open the disturbing possibility that Mary may have been among Jesus' "family" (NIV) (or "His own people" or "kinsmen" (NASV),

or "his friends" (KJV)) who "went to take charge of him, for they said, 'He is out of his mind.'" (Compare 3:21 and 3:31.)

3 John Paul II, General Audience of March 14, 2001.

4 John Paul II, General Audience of January 12, 2000.

5 Athanasius, (*Homily of the Papyrus of Turin*, quoted in L. Gambero, *Mary and the Fathers of the Church*, San Francisco, Ignatius Press, 1999, p. 106

Chapter 2

6 Irenaeus, *Against Heresies*, 5:19:1, quoted at: http://www.catholic.com/library/Mary_Mother_of_God.asp

7 Dwight Longenecker, (ed.)*The Path to Rome*, Leominster, Gracewing, 1999, p. 31.

8 Hippolytus, *Discourse on the End of the World*, 1, quoted at: http://www.catholic.com/library/Mary_Mother_of_God.asp

9 John Paul II, Address of March 4, 2000 ("Dear seminarians, love Mary, our heavenly Mother, during the years of your formation and those of your generous and holy ministry, so that one day you may honour her in heaven"). http://www.petersnet.net/research/retrieve_full.cfm?RecNum=2641

10 See our extended discussion of this problem in Chapter Nine on Veneration

11 L. Gambero, *Mary and the Fathers of the Church*, San Francisco, Ignatius Press, 1999, p.19.

12 Flannery, *Vatican Council II, Lumen gentium*, para. 66 ("after the Synod of Ephesus [in A.D. 431] the cult of the people of God toward Mary wonderfully increased in veneration and love, in invocation and imitation").

13 Ibid., pp. 20-21.

14 quoted at: http://www.newadvent.org/cathen/15459a.htm

Chapter 3

16 Ambrose, (*De virginibus* 2, 7) quoted in, H. de Romestein, *Principle Works of St Ambrose*, Oxford, James Parker and Co, 1846, p. 374

17 Cyprian of Carthage, *De Catholicae Ecclesiae Unitate, 4—7*, quoted in H. Bettenson, *The Early Christian Fathers*, Oxford, Oxford University Press, 1969, p. 265

18 See Rom. 5:12; 1 Cor. 15:21-22. Thomas Aquinas, *Summa Theologica*, First Part of the Second Part, Question 81, Article 1; available at http://www.

newadvent.org/summa/208101.htm.

[19] Origen, (*Commentary on the Letter to the Galatians,* Patrologia Graeca, 14, 1928.) quoted in, L. Gambero, *Mary and the Fathers of the Church,* San Francisco, Ignatius Press, 1999, p.73.

[20] Cyril of Jerusalem, *Catecheses,* 465 B- 468 A, quoted in, Gambero, p.133.

[21] C.S. Lewis, *Mere Christianity,* New York, Macmillan, 1978, p.7

[22] Origen, *In Matthew,* 28; Patrologiae Graecae 13, 1637, quoted in Gambero, p. 34

Chapter 4

[23] Johannes Quasten, (*Patrology,* 1:120-1), quoted at: http://www.catholic.com/library/Mary_Ever_Virgin.asp

[24] Luigi Gambero, *Mary and the Fathers of the Church,* San Francisco, Ignatius Press, 1999, p.75

[25] Ibid.

[26] Martin Luther wrote, "Christ, our Savior, was the real and natural fruit of Mary's virginal womb .... This was without the cooperation of a man, and she remained a virgin after that." Jaroslav Pelikan & Helmut T. Lehmann (eds.), *Luther's Works,* St. Louis: Concordia Pub. House (vols. 1-30); Philadelphia: Fortress Press (vols. 31-55), 1955, v.22:23 / *Sermons on John,* chaps. 1-4, (1539). Luther also wrote that "Christ ... was the only Son of Mary, and the Virgin Mary bore no children besides Him." Ibid., v.22:214-15 / *Sermons on John,* chaps. 1-4 (1539). In a sermon in 1522, the Reformer Ulrich Zwingli said, "I believe with all my heart according to the word of holy gospel that this pure virgin bore for us the Son of God and that she remained, in the birth and after it, a pure and unsullied virgin, for eternity." Max Thurian, *Mary: Mother of all Christians,* tr. Neville B. Cryer, NY: Herder & Herder, 1963, pp.76

[27] John Wesley, *A Letter to a Roman Catholic,* quoted in A.C. Coulter, *John Wesley,* New York, Oxford University Press, 1964, p. 495.

[28] Philip Schaff, *The Creeds of Christendom, Vol. I (The History of Creeds),* p. 119, Harper & Row (1931 ed.), reprinted by Baker (1990); see also Gambero, pp. 65-66, quoting Tertullian's *De monogamia* 8, PL 2, 989.

[29] Anthony Opisso, *Mary's Virginity in Light of Jewish Law and Tradition,* in *The Catholic Answer Book of Mary,* P. Stravinskas (ed.), Huntingdon, Our Sunday Visitor, 2000, p. 47

[30] The November/December 2002 edition of the *Biblical Archeological Review* reported the find of a First Century limestone ossuary (a bone-box or coffin) with the Aramaic inscription AJames, son of Joseph, brother of Jesus.@ While these

were common names at the time, two things suggest that the ossuary pertains to the New Testament characters: First, the statistical probability of the three names appearing together in these relations is small; and second, the naming of a brother on an ossuary is unusual, suggesting that the Jesus named there must have been a significant person. If this is correct, then it suggests that James, if he was indeed the son of Joseph, was not Jesus= mere cousin or kinsman but instead was Jesus= half-brother, and, therefore, a son of Mary. By these lights, Mary *did* have children after she bore Jesus, and did not remain a virgin perpetually. http://www.bibarch.org/bswb_BAR/bswbbar2806f1.html

31 Jerome, *In Evangelium Matthaei, 1, I, 25, Patrologia Latinae 26,26,* quoted in Gambero, p. 207

32 This particular argument for the perpetual virginity of Mary was put forward by many of the Church fathers, but it is most clearly expressed by Athanasius, who writes, "For if she had had other children, the Savior would not have ignored them and entrusted his Mother to someone else; nor would she have become someone else's mother." (Athanasius, *De Virginitate,* quoted in Gambero p. 104

33 Eric D. Svendsen, in *Who Is My Mother?: The Role and Status of the Mother of Jesus in the New Testament and Roman Catholicism* (Calvary Press, 2001), discusses these long-used Protestant arguments and answers recent Roman Catholic critiques.

34 See Genesis 2:24: "For this reason a man will leave his father and mother and be united to his wife, and they will become one flesh", quoted by Jesus (Matt. 19:4-6 = Mark 10:7-8). See also CCC, ¶ 1652 (citing Gen. 1:28, 2:18; Matt. 19:4; Vatican II's *Gaudium et Spes,* secs. 1, 50). See also the Roman Catholic *Code of Canon Law* (1983), Book IV, Title VII, Can. 1096 §1: "marriage is a permanent partnership between a man and a woman, ordered to the procreation of children through some form of sexual cooperation".

35 This argument is put by both Gregory of Nyssa in the fourth century and Augustine in the fifth. Gregory writes, "Mary's own words confirm the apocryphal traditions. For if Joseph had taken her to be his wife for the purpose of having children, why would she have wondered at the announcement of maternity since she herself would have accepted becoming a mother by the law of nature?" Quoted in Gambero, p. 157.

36 Jerome, *De virginitate perpetua, 7; Patrologia Latinae, 23, 200,* quoted in Gambero, p. 207

37 But see, to the contrary, Philip Schaff, *History of the Christian Church,* Vol. II (*Ante-Nicene Christianity*), Grand Rapids: Eerdman's, 1910, p. 282 & n.1, "St. Joseph certainly appears in some of the sarcophagi, and in the most ancient of them as a young and beardless man" (quoting Northcote & Brownlow, *Roma*

Sotter. (2nd ed. Lond. 1879), Pt. II, p. 141)).

38 Opisso. p. 47

39 See the Roman Catholic *Code of Canon Law* (1983), Book IV, Title VII, c. III, Can. 1084 §1 "Antecedent and perpetual impotence to have sexual intercourse, whether on the part of the man or on that of the woman, whether absolute or relative, by its very nature invalidates marriage".

40 Philip Schaff, *The Creeds of Christendom, Vol. I (The History of Creeds)*, p. 119, Harper & Row (1931 ed.), reprinted by Baker (1990) p. 119.

41 See, e.g., Pope John Paul II, General Audience, Jan. 28, 1988 ("Mary was therefore a virgin before the birth of Jesus and she remained a virgin in giving birth and after the birth. This is the truth presented by ... the Lateran Council in 649, which teaches that 'the mother of God...Mary...conceived [her Son] through the power of the Holy Spirit without human intervention, and in giving birth to him, her virginity remained incorrupted, and even after the birth her virginity remained intact", quoted by Fr. William Most, "Our Lady's Physical Virginity In The Birth Of Jesus", available at http://www.ewtn.com/library/SCRIPTUR/VIRBIR.TXT. To the contrary, see Gambero, p. 65, quoting Tertullian: "Virgin because she abstained from man; non-virgin because she gave birth.... Normally, conjugal relations open the womb. Therefore, [Mary's] womb was all the more opened, since it had been more closed. Consequently it is more accurate [after Jesus' birth] to call her non-virgin, than virgin"; see also St. Jerome's The Perpetual Virginity of Mary—Against Helvidius", ¶ 20, available at http://aggreen.net/theotokos/vir_mary2.html.

42 The New Testament uses no special vocabulary for Jesus' birth. If the "woman clothed with the sun" in Revelation 12 is Mary, then Mary "was pregnant and cried out in pain as she was about to give birth" (12:2). Moreover, after Jesus' birth, Mary underwent "the days for their purification according to the Law of Moses" (Luke 2:22) like every Jewish mother. Leviticus 12:2-7 provided that "the woman must wait thirty-three days to be purified from her bleeding" (v.4) and then, after a sacrifice, "she will be ceremonially clean from her flow of blood" (v.7). The Gospels include no hint that Mary was exempt from any of these physical or legal disabilities.

43 Isaiah 66:7 has often been read as a prophecy of the miraculous birth recorded by the *Protoevangelium* as well as *The Ascension of Isaiah (*c.70) and *The Odes of Solomon* (c.80) This view was held by the fathers, and this is still held by Catholics. Mary "remained a virgin in conceiving her Son, a virgin in giving birth to him, a virgin in carrying him, a virgin in nursing him at her breast, always a virgin" (St. Augustine, Serm. 186, 1: PL 38, 999): CCC, para. 510

44 Athanasius, *De Virginate, 42:243-244*, quoted in Gambero. p. 104

45 Basil of Caesarea, *On the Holy Generation of Christ*, 3; *Patrologia Graeca* 31,

1464 C. quoted in Gambero, p. 146

46 Ibid.

Chapter 5

47 Mormon "Apostle" Bruce R. McConkie, *Mormon Doctrine*, 1979 edition, p. 547, quoted at http://www.challengemin.org/gofm.html.

48 Thomas Aquinas, *Summa Theologiae*, 3a q. 32, a. 1.

49 Pope Paul VI, *Marialis Cultus* (1974), para. 26.

50 Protestant doctrine therefore teaches that the Church is the Bride of Christ. See the Presbyterian "Westminster Confession of Faith", chapter XXV ("Of the Church"), para. I ("The catholic or universal Church ... is the spouse, the body, the fullness of Him that fills all in all" (citing, inter alia, Eph. 5:23-32)). This is also part of Catholic doctrine; see CCC, para. 796, 1617; Pius XII, *Mystici Corporis Christi* (June 29, 1943), paras. 86, 96, 106.

51 Luigi Gambero, *Mary and the Fathers of the Church*, San Francisco, Ignatius Press, 1999, p. 117.

52 Pope Pius XII, *Munificentissimus Deus* (1950), para. 21.

53 John Paul II, General Audience of 2 May 1990, para. 6, L'Osservatore Romano, May 7, 1990, reproduced at http://www.miraclerosarymission.org/hs130.htm.

54 As the Eleventh Council of Toledo held (in 675), "we must not believe that the Holy Spirit is the Father of the Son because Mary conceived by the overshadowing of the same Holy Spirit, lest we should seem to affirm that the Son has two fathers—which it is certainly impious to say." J. Neuner and J. DuPuis, *The Christian Faith in the Doctrinal Documents of the Catholic Church*, p. 169, para. 628, New York: Alba (1982).

55 See Gen. 3:18-24: The wife will be a "helper suitable" for the husband, "bone of my bones, and flesh of my flesh". See also CCC paras. 371-372: A spouse is to be a "partner", and God made man and woman "complementary as masculine and feminine".

56 M. Wilson and J. Stek, *New International Version Study Bible*, London, Hodder and Stoughton, 1985, p. 363

57 In Ruth 3:9 "spreading the corner of the cloak" is a Hebrew word play on "wings" (the word for "cloak" is *kanaph* which also means "wing"). Another Aramaic-Hebrew word for "cloak" is *tallith*, which has its root in the word *tellal* or "shadow". Anthony Opisso, *Mary's Virginity in Light of Jewish Law and Tradition*, in *The Catholic Answer Book of Mary*, P. Stravinskas (ed.), Huntingdon, Our Sunday Visitor, 2000, p.46

58 Ibid.

59 One example will suffice: Note Luke's use of he word "shelter" (9:33) to link the Transfiguration back to the tent of meeting in Ex.29:42 and the Feast of Tabernacles (Lev.23:42). With one word the gospel writers will allude to a complex Old Testament story showing how not only particular prophecies, but whole images and themes from the Old Testament are fulfilled in the life of Christ.

60 CCC, ¶. 796

61 Thomas gives Biblical support for his view thus, "For the Holy Ghost is the Spirit of the Son, according to Gal. 4:6: "God sent the Spirit of His Son." ...the Power of God, (which is the Son Himself, according to 1 Cor. 1:24: 'Christ, the Power of God,') through the Holy Ghost formed the body which He assumed. This is also shown by the words of the angel: 'The Holy Ghost shall come upon thee,' as it were, in order to prepare and fashion the matter of Christ's body; 'and the Power of the Most High,' (i.e. Christ), 'shall overshadow thee—that is to say, the incorporeal Light of the Godhead shall in thee take the corporeal substance of human nature... The 'Most High' is the Father, whose Power is the Son." Thomas Aquinas, *Summa Theologica*, 3, q.32, reply to objection 1.

62 Br. Anthony Opisso, M.D., "The Perpetual Virginity of Mary", http:// www.ewtn.com/library/ANSWERS/TALMUD.HTM

63 H.M. Manteau-Bonamy, O.P, *Immaculate Conception and the Holy Spirit: The Marian Teachings of Fr. Maximilian Kolbe*, quoted at http://www. albertusmagnus.org/religion/theotokos/max.html

64 *Ibid.*, quoted at http://www.petersnet.net/most/getchapcfm?WorkNum= 232&ChapNum=25.

65 "The mission of the Holy Spirit is always conjoined and ordered to that of the Son. The Holy Spirit, 'the Lord, the giver of Life,' is sent to sanctify the womb of the Virgin Mary and divinely fecundate it, causing her to conceive the eternal Son of the Father in a humanity drawn from her own." CCC para. 485

66 The love of God here is defined as the dynamic force that binds the Trinity together. In the same passage Fr. Kolbe says Mary was "grafted into the Love of the Blessed Trinity" For a poetic vision of how the Virgin Mary and all the saints dwell in the very love of God see the canto 33 of *Paradiso* from Dante's *Divine Comedy.*

67 "Union with Christ is really the central truth of the whole doctrine of salvation". John Murray, *Redemption Accomplished and Applied*, Grand Rapids: Eerdmans, 1955, Chapter IX "Union with Christ", p. 161.

68 Dwight Longenecker, *More Christianity*, Huntingdon, Our Sunday Visitor, 2002, p. 13 -14

69 "The unity of Christ and the Church, head and members of one Body, also

implies the distinction of the two within a personal relationship. This aspect is often expressed by the image of bridegroom and bride." CCC, ¶ 796.

Chapter 6

70 Pope Pius IX, Apostolic Constitution *Ineffabilis Deus* (8 Dec. 1854), available at http://www.ewtn.com/LIBRARY/PAPALDOC/P9INEFF.htm.

71 John Henry Cardinal Newman, "Memorandum on the Immaculate Conception", available at http://www.cin.org/liter/memoimma.html

72 The Trinity is a synthesis of Apostolic doctrines, namely: that there is one God (see, *e.g.*, Mark 12:29); that Father, Son, and Holy Spirit are distinct from each other (*e.g.*, Luke 3:22); and that Father (*e.g.*, John 6:27), Son (e.g., John 12:3941 (quoting Isaiah 6:10)), and Holy Spirit (*e.g.*, Acts 5:34) are each God. The Scripture proofs could be multiplied many times over.

73 As to Christ's being God, see, *e.g.*, John 20:28. As to Christ's being man, see, *e.g.,* Acts 2:22. The titles "Son of man" and " Son of God" are both used frequently. As to Christ's being God incarnated in Man, see, *e.g.,* John 1:14; Php. 2:67; Heb. 2:14.

74 Luigi Gambero, *Mary and the Fathers of the Church,* San Francisco, Ignatius, 1999, p. 77.

75 Blass & DeBrunner, *Greek Grammar of the New Testament,* Chicago, Univ. of Chicago Press, 1961, p. 166. The Protestant scholar W.E. Vine says about this word, "*highly favored (endued with grace) grace implies more than favor." Expository Dictionary of the New Testament,* Old Tappan, Fleming Revell, 1940, vol.2,84. Another Protestant Greek scholar, A.T. Robertson says, "The Vulgate *gratiae plena* is right if it means 'full of grace which thou hast received.' *Word Pictures in the New Testament,* Nashville, Broadman Press, 1930, vol.2, 13. Both quoted in Dave Armstrong, *Biblical Evidence for Catholicism,* First Books, 2001, pp. 127-128

76 A form of the same verb (*charitoo*) that appears in Luke 1:28 ("highly favored"/"full of grace") also appears in Ephesians 1:6 ("he has *freely given* us"). See Francis Foulkes, *The Epistle of Paul to the Ephesians* (Tyndale New Testament Commentaries, Vol. 10), Grand Rapids: Eerdmans, 1976 (6ᵗʰ printing), p. 48.

77 Mary technically shared in the curse of original sin, but the curse was lifted by the special redeeming grace of her immaculate conception.

78 John de Satge, *Mary and the Christian Gospel,* London, SPCK, 1976, p. 74.

79 The earliest Fathers use the Eve-Mary parallel to illustrate our redemption—not to make a point about Mary. It was the later Fathers who began to understand the implications of the comparison, and by the fourth century the Eve-Mary parallel was used by virtually all the theologians. As usual, Tertullian

expresses the early patristic view most pithily: "For just as the death-creating word of the devil had penetrated Eve, who was still a virgin, analogously the life-building Word of God had to enter into a Virgin, so that he who had fallen into perdition because of a woman might be led back to salvation by means of the same sex. Eve believed the serpent; Mary believed Gabriel. The fault that Eve introduced by believing, Mary by believing, erased." *De carni Christi* 17,1-5, quoted in Gambero, p. 67.

[80] Ephrem the Syrian writes, "For on you, O Lord, there is no mark; neither is there any stain in your Mother." Ephrem the Syrian, *Camina Nisibena* 27, 8, quoted in Gambero, p. 109. At the end of the fourth century Gregory Nazianzen writes, "He was conceived by the Virgin, who had first been purified by the Spirit in soul and body." Gregory Nazianzen, *Sermon 29*, quoted in Gambero, p.162. At the beginning of the fifth century Epiphanius of Salamis writes, "Mary... never did anything wrong as far as fleshly actions are concerned, but remained stainless." *Haer.* 42.12, quoted in Gambero, p. 125.

[81] Augustine of Hippo, *De natura et gratia, 36, 42.* Quoted in Gambero, p. 226.

[82] See John MacQuarrie's, *Mary for All Christians*, London, Collins, 1992, p. 73-74.

[83] Martin Luther, *Sermon On the Day of the Conception of Mary the Mother of God*, Grisar, Hartmann, *Luther*, London, Kegan Paul, Trench, Trubner & Co, 1917, vol4, 238. Quoted in Armstrong, p. 149.

[84] Gambero, p. 77-78; *see also ibid.*, pp. 62-63 (*"Tertullian's Severity toward Mary"*); Philip Schaff, *The Creeds of Christendom*, Vol. I (*History of the Creeds*), p. 117. The patristic attitude is summarized in the *Catholic Encyclopedia* (1913), in its article "Immaculate Conception": "In regard to the sinlessness of Mary the older Fathers are very cautious: some of them even seem to have been in error on this matter [i.e., to have denied Mary's sinlessness (citing Origen, St. Basil, and St. Chrysostom)].... But these stray private opinions merely serve to show that theology is a progressive science"; reprinted at http://newadvent.org/cathen/07674d.htm

[85] Gambero, p. 77.

[86] See Rom. 5:12; 1 Cor. 15:21-22. Thomas Aquinas, *Summa Theologica*, First Part of the Second Part, Question 81, Article 1; available at http://www.newadvent.org/summa/208101.htm.

[87] *See, e.g.,* Council of Trent, 5th Session, Decree on Original Sin (1546): "This same holy Synod declares that it is not its intention to include in this decree dealing with original sin the Blessed and Immaculate Virgin Mary"; reproduced in Neuner & Dupuis, p. 139 (¶ 513).

[88] This is the view of Mary put forward by Athanasius, "Mary was a pure

virgin...she loved to do good works .... She did not want to be seen by men, but prayed God to be her judge.... She remained at home always, leading a hidden life." Gambero, p. 104

89 Thomas Aquinas argued that, if Mary had been immaculately conceived, "she could never have incurred the stain of original sin: and thus she would not have needed redemption and salvation which is by Christ, of whom it is written (Mt. 1:21): 'He shall save His people from their sins.' But this is unfitting, through implying that Christ is not the 'Savior of all men,' as He is called (1 Tim. 4:10). It remains, therefore, that the Blessed Virgin was sanctified after animation.... [T] he Blessed Virgin ... contracted original sin, since she was conceived by way of fleshly concupiscence and the intercourse of man and woman". *Summa Theologica*, Third Part, Question 27, Article 2.

90 Philip Schaff, *The Creeds of Christendom*, Vol. I (*The History of Creeds*), pp. 121-123.

91 Pope Pius IX, Apostolic Constitution *Ineffabilis Deus* (8 Dec. 1854), available at http://www.ewtn.com/LIBRARY/PAPALDOC/P9INEFF.htm.

92 Summa Theologica, Third Part, Question 27, Article 1, available at http://www.newadvent.org/summa/402701.htm.

93 Schaff, p. 121.

94 Timothy Ware, *The Orthodox Church*, London: Penguin (1987 ed.), p. 264.

95 *Catechism of the Catholic Church*, ¶ 829, quoting Vatican 2's *Lumen Gentium* 65.

96 Gambero p. 104.

97 The Archbishop of Paris, for example, thought the definition to be unnecessary and feared it would injure the Catholic faith, since the Immaculate Conception "could be proved neither from the Scriptures nor from tradition, and to which reason and science raised insolvable, or at least intractable, difficulties." Philip Schaff, *The Creeds of Christendom*, Vol. I (*History of the Creeds*), p. 109.

Chapter 7

98 The Catholic Encyclopedia's article on the Assumption (available at http://www.newadvent.org/cathen/02006b.htm) says that "The earliest known literary reference to the Assumption is found in the Greek work *De Obitu S. Dominae*.... The belief in the corporeal assumption of Mary is founded on the apocryphal treatise De Obitu S. Dominae, bearing the name of St. John, which belongs however to the fourth or fifth century." This treatise, entitled "The Transitus Mariæ: The Account of St. John the Theologian of the Dormition of the Holy Mother of God", is available at http://www.newadvent.org/fathers/0832A.

htm. Two other apocryphal accounts of the Assumption are available at http://www.newadvent.org/fathers/0832B.htm, and http://www.newadvent.org/fathers/0832C.htm.

99 *Catholic Encyclopedia* (1913), "Assumption of Mary, Feast of the", available at http://www.newadvent.org/cathen/02006b.htm.

100 John of Damascus included this miraculous assembling of the Apostles in his *Second Sermon on the Dormition*, excerpted at http://www.cin.org/liter/dormdama.html, and available in full (in a different translation) at http://www.balamand.edu.lb/theology/Jodorm2.htm.

101 Ibid.

102 Pope Pius XII, Apostolic Constitution *Munificentissimus Deus* (Nov. 1, 1950), available at http://www.ewtn.com/library/PAPALDOC/P12MUNIF.HTM.

103 When Pius XII defined the dogma of the Immaculate Conception in *Munificentissimus Deus*, he warned (in ¶¶ 45, 47): "if anyone, which God forbid, should dare willfully to deny or to call into doubt that which we have defined, let him know that he has fallen away completely from the divine and Catholic Faith.... It is forbidden to any man to change this, our declaration, pronouncement, and definition or, by rash attempt, to oppose and counter it. If any man should presume to make such an attempt, let him know that he will incur the wrath of Almighty God and of the Blessed Apostles Peter and Paul." *See also* John Paul II, *Ad Tuendam Fidem* (May 18, 1998), ¶ 4 (adding, to the Code of Canon Law, section 750 § 1), and Joseph Cardinal Ratzinger, Prefect, Congregation for the Doctrine of the Faith, *Commentary on Ad Tuendam Fidem* (June 29, 1998), ¶¶ 5, 11.

104 Gambero, pp. 125-126.

105 Ibid.

106 Pope Leo the Great, *Letter CXXXIX, To Juvenal, Bishop of Jerusalem*: Juvenal "fail[ed] in persistency of opposition to the heretics: for men can but think you were not bold enough to refute those with whom when in error you professed yourself satisfied. For the condemnation of Flavian of blessed memory, and the acceptance of the most unholy Eutyches, what was it but the denial of our Lord Jesus Christ according to the flesh?" (Available at http://www.ccel.org/fathers2/NPNF2-12/Npnf2-12-138.htm#P2319_546095.)

107 *See* William Webster's "The Assumption of Mary: A Roman Catholic Dogma Originating with Heretics and Condemned as Heretical by 2 Popes in the 5th and 6th Centuries", http://www.christiantruth.com/assumption.html. Webster argues that the belief in the Assumption came from the heretical apocryphal books, and that those books had been condemned by popes. Webster's article seems to be well-documented, but it reflects obvious anti-Catholic prejudice.

108 John of Damascus stated in his *Second Sermon on the Dormition*, "Nor were the hosts of the angels wanting. For, as we believe, obedient to the King, and honoured to stand in His Presence, it was fitting that they should stand about her, as a guard of honour to His Mother according to the Flesh…." (Excerpted at http://www.cin.org/liter/dormdama.html.)

109 J.H. Newman, *An Essay on the Development of Christian Doctrine*, Notre Dame, University of Notre Dame Press, 1989, p. 203.

110 Dave Armstrong, *Biblical Evidence for Catholicism, 1ˢᵗ Books, 2000, p. 149.*

111 Heinrich Bullinger wrote, "Elijah was transported body and soul in a chariot of fire; he was not buried in any Church bearing his name, but mounted up to heaven, so that we might know what immortality and recompense God prepares for his faithful prophets and for his most outstanding and incomparable creatures…It is for this reason we believe, that the pure and immaculate embodiment of the Mother of God, the Virgin Mary, the Temple of the Holy Spirit, that is to say her saintly body was carried up to heaven by the angels." Dave Armstrong, *Biblical Evidence for Catholicism, 1ˢᵗ Books, 2000, p. 151.*

112 *See* Hilaire Belloc, *The Great Heresies* (1938), Ch. 4 ("The Great and Enduring Heresy of Mohammed"), available at http://www.ewtn.com/library/HOMELIBR/HERESY4.TXT.

113 John Macquarrie, *Mary for All Christians*, London, Harper Collins, 1992, p. 97.

114 Anselm, *Proslogian*, ch.2, quoted in MacQuarrie, p. 85.

115 A full treatment of this Biblical type of Mary can be found in *Hail Holy Queen* by Scott Hahn, London, DLT, 2001, ch. 4.

116 *See* Jeremiah 7:18, 44:17-25. Some commentators think that the "Queen of Heaven" whose worship Jeremiah denounced was the moon, others say the sun.

Chapter 8

117 Luigi Gambero, *Mary and the Fathers of the Church*, San Francisco, Ignatius Press, 1999, pp. 160-1.

118 Divination and sorcery are forbidden in, *e.g.*, Lev. 19:26-31; Deut. 18:9-14; Mal. 3:5. *See also* CCC ¶ 2116 ("All forms of *divination* are to be rejected: … [including] conjuring up the dead …. [It] contradict[s] the honor, respect, and loving fear that we owe to God alone").

119 Concern about demonic involvement in alleged Marian apparitions is shared by Catholics and Protestants—and the Eastern Orthodox. See Miriam Lambouras, "The Marian Apparitions: Divine Intervention or Delusion?" (Orthodox Christian Information Center), http://www.orthodoxinfo.com/

inquirers/marian_apparitions.htm.

120 John J. Delaney, (ed.) *A Woman Clothed with the Sun*, New York, Image Books, 2001, p. 39.

121 *See, e.g.,* Lambouras, *supra.*

122 An excellent short study which discusses how such things should be assessed is René Laurentin's *The Apparitions of the Blessed Virgin Mary Today*, London, Veritas, 1990

123 For a Roman Catholic discussion that emphasizes the possibility of psychological explanations for the premier Marian apparitions, see Hilda Graef, *Mary: A History of Doctrine and Devotion* (London: Sheed & Ward, 1985 ed.), Part 2, pp. 85-106, 136-145.

124 The first several years' worth of messages from the Marian apparitions at Medjugorje are collected in René Laurentin and René LeJeune, *Messages And Teachings of Mary at Medjugorje*, Riehle Foundation (Milford, Ohio, 1988), which is available on-line at http://huizen.dds.nl/~jgamleus/boodschappen/messages.html.

125 The statement of the local bishops' council is reproduced at http://members.tripod.com/~chonak/documents/m19901127_zagreb.html. The bishop of the particular diocese took an even dimmer view in his letter of October 1997: "On the basis of the serious study of the case by 30 of our 'studiosi', on my episcopal experience of five years in the Diocese, on the scandalous disobedience that surrounds the phenomenon, on the lies that are at times put into the mouth of the 'Madonna', on the unusual repetition of 'messages' of over 16 years, on the strange way that the 'spiritual directors' of the socalled 'visionaries' accompany them through the world making propaganda of them, on the practice that the 'Madonna' appears at the 'fiat' of the 'visionaries', my conviction and position is not only *non constat de supernaturalitate* [the supernaturality is not proven] but also the other formula *constat de non supernaturalitate* [the nonsupernaturality is proven] of the apparitions or revelations of Medjugorje." http://members.tripod.com/~chonak/documents/m19971002_peric.html

126 The Vatican's statements are reproduced at http://members.tripod.com/~chonak/documents/m19960323_bertone.html and http://members.tripod.com/~chonak/documents/m19980526_bertone.html.

127 The Medjugorje messages are far more numerous than any others. A typical message is the one from February 2002, " Dear children! In this time of grace, I call you to become friends of Jesus. Pray for peace in your hearts and work for your personal conversion. Little children, only in this way will you be able to become witnesses of peace and of the love of Jesus in the world. Open yourselves to prayer so that prayer becomes a need for you. Be converted, little children, and work so that as many souls as possible may come to know Jesus and

His love. I am close to you and I bless you all. Thank you for having responded to my call." All the Medjugorje messages can be found at: http://www.medjugorje.org/olmpage.htm

128 The Fatima messages are collected at http://www.theotokos.org.uk/pages/approved/words/wordfati.html.

129 The Lady later says, to the same effect and more explicitly, "Tell everybody that God gives graces *through the Immaculate Heart of Mary*. Tell them to ask graces *from her*, and that the Heart of Jesus wishes to be venerated *together with the Immaculate Heart of Mary*. Ask them to plead for peace *from the Immaculate Heart of Mary*, for the Lord has confided the peace of the world *to her*."

130 The seers see a vision of Hell, and the Lady says: "You saw Hell where the souls of poor sinners go. *In order to save them*, God wishes to establish in the world *devotion to my Immaculate Heart*. If people do what I ask, many souls will be saved and there will be peace."

131 "Fatima: A Grace for Mankind" (Eternal Word Television Network), http://www.ewtn.com/fatima/apparitions/message.htm.

132 C.S. Lewis, *The Great Divorce*, Glasgow, Collins, 1988, p. 97-8.

133 Delaney, p. 60.

134 Delaney, p. 114.

135 Ibid., p. 102, 151ff.

136 Donal Anthony Foley, "Marian apparitions: Some lessons from history", Homiletic and Pastoral Review (June 2001), http://www.catholic.net/rcc/Periodicals/Homiletic/2001-06/foley.html.

Chapter 9

137 One can take a "virtual tour" of the National Shrine of the Immaculate Conception at http://www.nationalshrine.com/NAT_SHRINE/frm_tour.shtml.

138 St Louis de Montfort, *The Secret of Mary*, Rockford, TAN Books, 1998, pp. x-xi.

139 The influence of Jansenism in the Catholic Church persists today. Catholic priest Richard Fragomeni criticizes the mindset thus, "I grew up in a Jansenistic, Italian American community. Everything was a sin, God was out to get me.... That image of God couldn't hold people. So from the sixteenth century forward, our tradition developed a long, strong relationship with Mary...We prayed to her, we loved her, we had all sorts of devotions to her, because we felt within that she was the image of unconditional love.. ... She is not the source of love, but she is an enormously rich example of how to say, 'let it be done to us'" *Come to the Feast* (New York: Continuum, 2001) p.23, 26. To balance this (and I believe to balance excessive Marian devotion), the sixteenth century also saw

the flowering of devotion to the Sacred Heart of Jesus. This devotion, which emphasizes the loving and forgiving Lord was another attempt of the Holy Spirit to counter the effects of Jansenism.

140 "The object of this Consecration is to cast off the spirit of the world, which is contrary to that of Jesus Christ, in order to acquire fully the spirit of Jesus Christ." St. Louis de Montfort, *The Secret of Mary* (Rockford, Ill.: TAN Books, 1998), pp. 57-58.

141 John Henry Cardinal Newman—a convert from Anglicanism, a Marian devotee, and perhaps the greatest Catholic theologian of the 19th Century—attempted no defense of what he saw as disturbing excess in the writings of St. Louis de Montfort (among others): In reply to an Anglican critic who assembled quotations from Montfort and other Marian enthusiasts, Newman wrote: "Sentiments such as these I freely surrender to your animadversion; I never knew of them till I read your book ... They seem to me like a bad dream. I could not have conceived them to be said.... I will have nothing to do with statements, which can only be explained, by being explained away ... I consider them calculated to prejudice inquirers, to frighten the unlearned, to unsettle consciences, to provoke blasphemy, and to work the loss of souls." *Certain Difficulties Felt by Anglicans in Catholic Teaching* (1892 ed.), pp. 113-115, quoted by Hilda Graef, *Mary: A History of Doctrine and Devotion* (London: Sheed & Ward, 1985 ed.), Part 2, p. 117. For a summary of de Montfort's controversial, superlative exaltation of Mary, see ibid., pp. 57-62.

142 The Militia of the Immaculata, founded by Kolbe, encourages a particular form of consecration to Mary. Its web site is none other than www.consecration. com.

143 So Epiphanius of Salamis (d. 403) writes, "Whoever honors the Lord also honors the holy [vessel]; who instead dishonors the holy vessel also dishonors his Master. Mary herself is that holy Virgin, that is, the holy vessel." L. Gambero, *Mary in the Fathers of the Church,* San Francisco, Ignatius, 1999, p. 127. See also, CCC ¶ 964

144 Pope Pius IX, Encyclical *Ubi Primum* (2 Feb. 1849); reprinted at .

145 L. Gambero, *Mary and the Fathers of the Church,* San Francisco, Ignatius Press, 1999, p. 106-7.

146 A close reading of any papal statement about Mary must include the Catholic assumption that all devotion to Mary is inextricably linked to devotion to her Son. So, for example, all hope and salvation *do* come through her, for Jesus comes through her. Her merits are great, but the doctrine Pius is about to define makes clear that those merits are the gift of grace. Nothing has been closer to his heart than devotion to Mary precisely because she has drawn him into ever more intimate union with her Son. The foundation of his confidence is found *in*

Mary—i.e., the one who is "in" Mary is Jesus. Pius' trust in her may be "great" but he doesn't say it surpasses his trust in God.

147 Henry Thiessen, *Introductory Lectures in Systematic Theology* (Grand Rapids: Eerdmans, 1949), p. 86.

148 J.I. Packer is one of the most respected Evangelical teachers . His book *Knowing God* (Downer's Grove, Ill.: IVP, 1973), pp. 17-18, warns, "[W]e need ... to stop and ask ourselves a very fundamental question ... whenever we embark on any line of study in God's holy Book.... [W]hat is my ultimate aim and object in occupying my mind with these things? ... [T]o approach Bible study with no higher a motive than a desire to know all the answers, is the direct route to state of self-satisfied self-deception. ... [D]octrinal study really can become a danger to spiritual life. ... [The spiritual person] is interested in truth and orthodoxy, in biblical teaching and theology, not as ends in themselves, but as means to the further ends of life and godliness."

149 Catholic Answers, "Anti-Catholic Whoppers", http://www.catholic.com/library/anti_catholic_whoppers.asp; *see also* "Saint Worship?", http://www.catholic.com/library/Saint_Worship.asp ("[non-Catholics] assert that Catholics 'worship' Mary and the saints, and, in so doing, commit idolatry. This is patently false, of course"; "[non-Catholics] sometimes say that Catholics worship statues. Not only is this untrue, it is even untrue that Catholics honor statues").

150 Quoted by Hilda Graef, *Mary: A History of Doctrine and Devotion* (London: Sheed & Ward, 1985 ed.), flyleaf.

151 Pope Paul VI, *Marialis cultus*, para. 4.

152 Austin Flannery O.P., *Vatican Council II*, New York, Costello Publishing, 1984, *Lumen Gentium*, ¶ 67, p. 422.

153 Malachy Gerard Carroll (tr.), St Louis-Marie De Montfort, *Treatise On The True Devotion To The Blessed Virgin*, Langley, 1962, p. 9.

154 John Paul II, *Rosarium Virginis Mariae*, para.1.

155 Ibid, para. 4, c.f. *Lumen Gentium*, para. 66.

156 So Epiphanius of Salamis in the fourth century writes, "Yes, Mary's body was holy, but it was not God. Yes, the Virgin was surely a virgin and worthy of honor; however, she was not given for us to adore her." L. Gambero, *Mary and the Fathers of the Church*, San Francisco, Ignatius, 1999, p. 127. *Lumen Gentium*, re-iterates this: ¶ 66 reads, "The various forms of piety towards the Mother of God, which the Church has approved...ensure that while the mother is honored, the Son ... is rightly known, loved and glorified."

157 My previous footnote quoting Epiphanius was his response to this sect. Incidentally, the Collyridian's Eucharist was celebrated by priestesses. A study of this heresy might well enlighten present day controversies in the Church.

158 For example, Paul said, "flee from idolatry" (1 Cor. 10:14); John said,

"keep yourselves from idols" (1 John 5:21). For other New Testament teaching against idolatry, see Acts 7:41-43, 15:20-29, 17:16, 21:25; 1 Cor. 5:11, 6:9, 10:7, 12:2; 2 Cor. 6:16; Gal. 5:19-20; 1 Thess. 1:9; 1 Peter 4:3; Rev. 2:14, 2:20, 9:20, 21:8, 22:15.

159   See CCC ¶ 2113: "Idolatry not only refers to false pagan worship. It remains a constant temptation to faith. Idolatry consists in divinizing what is not God. Man commits idolatry whenever he honors and reveres a creature in place of God, whether this be gods or demons (for example, Satanism), power, pleasure, race, ancestors, the state, money, etc."

160   Pius XI, *Mit Brettender Sorge* (Encyclical on the Church and the German Reich, March 14, 1937), para. 8: "Whoever exalts race, or the people, or the State, or a particular form of State, or the depositories of power, or any other fundamental value of the human community — however necessary and honorable be their function in worldly things — whoever raises these notions above their standard value and divinizes them to an idolatrous level, distorts and perverts an order of the world planned and created by God; he is far from the true faith in God and from the concept of life which that faith upholds." http://www.vatican.va/holy_father/pius_xi/encyclicals/documents/hf_p-xi_enc_14031937_mit-brennender-sorge_en.html

161   C.S. Lewis, The Screwtape Letters (New York: Macmillan (17th printing, 1973), p. 22.

162   St. Augustine, *On the Morals of the Catholic Church, Against the Manichaeans*, Ch. 34, paras. 75-76, http://www.ccel.org/fathers2/NPNF1-04/npnf1-04-06.htm#P301_138769.

163   Pope Paul VI, *Marialis cultus*, para. 4.

164   Gambero, p. 127.

Chapter 10

165   Luigi Gambero, *Mary and the Fathers of the Church*, San Francisco, Ignatius, 1999, p. 79.

166   Herbert Thurston, "Hail Mary", Catholic Encyclopedia, http://www.newadvent.org/cathen/07110b.htm.

167   The Reformation-era Anglican "Articles of Religion" puts it a little less diplomatically, in Article XXII ("Of Purgatory"): "The Romish Doctrine concerning Purgatory, Pardons, Worshipping and Adoration, as well of Images as of Relics, *and also Invocation of Saints*, is a fond thing, vainly invented, and grounded upon no warranty of Scripture, but rather repugnant to the Word of God." *See also* the Westminster Larger Catechism, Question 105 ("The sins

forbidden in the first commandment [include] ... praying ... to saints, angels, or any other creatures"); Augsburg Confession, Article XXI ("the memory of saints may be set before us, that we may follow their faith and good works, ... [b]ut the Scripture teaches not the invocation of saints or to ask help of saints, since it sets before us the one Christ as the Mediator, Propitiation, High Priest, and Intercessor").

168 The Jews still believe Elijah is spiritually present with his prayers at the circumcision ceremony. (mentioned at http://www.lumenverum.com/apologetics/saints.htm).

169 A funerary inscription near St. Sabina's in Rome (A.D. 300) reads, "Atticus, sleep in peace, secure in your safety, and pray anxiously for our sins." Another reads, "Pray for your parents, Matronata Matrona. She lived one year, fifty-two days" Quoted at: http://www.catholic.com/library/Intercession_of_the_Saints.asp.

170 Origen, *Prayer 11, quoted at* http://www.catholic.com/library/Intercession_of_the_Saints.asp

171 Gambero, p. 79.

172 The precise origins of the rosary tradition are obscure, and lie in medieval popular devotions. It probably arose from an ancient practice of saying 150 Hail Marys—a number suggested by the number of Psalms. The Scriptural meditations of the Rosary were apparently added as a means of organizing and giving meaning to the 150 repetitions. (See Graef, Part 1, pp. 230-33, 249-50, 264.) If this is correct, then it suggests that the Rosary, far from being "vain repetition" or a Marian excess, has the purpose of re-directing Marian devotion onto its proper Biblical and Christ-centered focus.

173 Jerry Sinclair's "Alleluia", which I hear quite often in Evangelical worship, has a first stanza that consists solely of 8 repetitions of the word "Alleluia". On Easter 2001 my then-7-year-old counted 83 Alleluias in our service (I think he missed a few), and on Easter 2002 his count broke down when the choir sang the "Hallelujah Chorus". Some churches conclude their services with the wonderful hymn "Just As I Am" week after week without fail, and I have heard stanzas of that hymn repeated many times in a single service.

174 John Paul II, *Rosarium Virginis Maria,* para. 31.

175 Ibid., para. 26.

176 An excellent guide to the history and practice of the Jesus prayer is *The Jesus Prayer* by a Swedish Lutheran, Per-Olof Sjögren. (London, SPCK, 1974)

177 For songs that recount the course of Jesus' earthly life, *see, e.g.,* G. O'hara's "I Walked Today Where Jesus Walked"; Fannie J. Crosby's "Tell Me the Story of Jesus"; J. Wilbur Chapman's "One Day When Heaven Was Filled with His Praises"; Louis F. Benson's "O Sing a Song of Bethlehem"; Benjamin R. Hanby's

"Who Is He in Yonder Stall?"; A.H. Ackley's "Wonderful Name He Bears"; and Emily E.S. Elliott's "Thou Didst Leave Thy Throne".

178 Hilda Graef, *Mary: A History of Doctrine and Devotion* (London: Sheed & Ward, 1985 ed.), Part 2, p. 12

179 Neville Ward, *Five for Sorrow, Ten for Joy*, London, DLT, 1988

Chapter 11

180 *Mediatrix* is the feminine form of *mediator* in Latin. I see the Latin form used most, though sometimes one sees the Anglicized *Mediatress*.

181 There are further heights to which Mary might be nominated: Peter of Celle (d. 1183), who was Bishop of Chartres, "goes so far as to discuss the possibility of a Quaternity: 'O Virgin of Virgins, what is this, where are you? You approach the Trinity itself in a unique and quite ineffable, almost direct manner, so that if the Trinity admitted in any way an external quaternity, you alone would complete the quaternity." Hilda Graef, *Mary: A History of Doctrine and Devotion* (London: Sheed & Ward, 1985 ed.), Part 1, p. 253.

182 According to Catholic theology Mary, as greatest of the saints and Mother of God, *does* dwell in a unique intimacy with the Godhead. She dwells in the heart of God's love, which is the dynamic force of the Trinity. But she is *not* part of the Godhead. *Cf.* our discussion of this in ch. 5, pp. 343-7. This view is expressed poetically in Canto 33 of Dante's *Paradiso*. (Dorothy Sayers, (tr.) *Paradiso* (London: Penguin Books, 1976), p. 343-6.

183 "...[I]n comparison with the infinite majesty of the most High God, Mary is no more than a mere creature formed by his hand; that, in the light of such a comparison, she is less than an atom—nay more, that she is nothing, since only He Who Is has existence as of Himself." St. Louis de Montfort *Treatise On The True Devotion To The Blessed Virgin*, Langley, 1962, p. 9.

184 CCC, ¶ 613-616.

185 —, *A New Marian Dogma? Coredemptrix, Mediatrix of All Graces, Advocate*, Vox Populi Mariae Mediatrici Petition Centre, Santa Barbara, — p.1.

186 CCC, ¶ 618.

187 Cf. Our discussion of the Immaculate Conception, p. —.

188 In Hebrew the crucial pronoun in Gen. 3:15 is "it". So there will be enmity between the woman's offspring and the serpent, and "it" shall bruise the serpent's head. The Greek translators translated "it" as "he" thus giving the Messianic interpretation. The Latin translator said "she" thus giving the Marian interpretation. A creative solution would be to accept both the Latin and the Greek and see the offspring who defeat the serpent as both Jesus and his mother in partnership.

189 Seeing Mary as a type of the Church is rooted in Revelation 12:1, and is emphasized by the fathers of the Church from the early fourth century onward. So Ephrem of Syrian writes, "The Virgin Mary is a symbol of the Church, when she receives the first announcement of the gospel." Quoted in Gambero, p. 115. Significantly, Vatican II places its teaching on Mary in the document on the Church (*Lumen Gentium*).

190 John Saward, *The Beauty of Holiness and the Holiness of Beauty*, San Francisco, Ignatius, 1996, p. 140.

191 *Certain Difficulties Felt by Anglicans in Catholic Teaching* (1892 ed.), pp. 113-115, quoted by Hilda Graef, *Mary: A History of Doctrine and Devotion* (London: Sheed & Ward, 1985 ed.), Part 2, p. 116. Newman went on to ask, "if I hate those perverse sayings so much, how much more must she, in proportion to her love of him?"

192 *See, e.g.*, Michael J. Miller, "Mediatrix, Si! Coredemptrix, No!", Homiletic & Pastoral Review, Feb. 2001, available on-line at http://www.catholic.net/rcc/Periodicals/Homiletic/2001-02/miller.html. Mr. Miller's view is summarized, "Right now we Catholics do not need more blurred boundaries between the Creator and the creature, the Redeemer and the redeemed." In a subsequent letter to the editor, one Catholic opponent of "Co-Redemptrix" explained, "[W]hen compared with the Redemption accomplished by Jesus Christ, we find an infinite difference separating all other coredeemers, including Mary. These differences are infinite in nature, purpose and effect." http://www.catholic.net/rcc/Periodicals/Homiletic/2001-10/letters.html.

193 "[T]he formula 'Co-redemptrix' departs to too great an extent

from the language of Scripture and of the Fathers and therefore gives rise to misunderstandings.... Because Mary is the prototype of the Church as such and is, so to say, the Church in person, this [truth of Christ's] being 'with' [us] is realized in her in exemplary fashion. But this 'with' must not lead us to forget the 'first' of Christ: Everything comes from Him .... Mary, too, is everything that she is through Him. The word 'Co-redemptrix' would obscure this origin. For matters of faith, continuity of terminology with the language of Scripture and that of the Fathers is itself an essential element; it is improper simply to manipulate language." Joseph Cardinal Ratzinger, *God and the World*, Peter Seewald, ed. (San Francisco: Ignatius Press, 2000).

194 Austin Flannery, O.P. (tr.) *The Documents of Vatican II*, Lumen Gentium, ¶, 58 Costello Publishing, New York, p. 417.

195 Pope John Paul II, Speech at Guayaquil, Ecuador in 1985, quoted in *A New Marian Dogma?*, p. 2.

196 Pope Leo XIII, *Octobri Mense* (Encyclical on the Rosary), Sept. 22, 1891, ¶ 4, available at http://www.vatican.va/holy_father/leo_xiii/encyclicals/

documents/hf_l-xiii_enc_22091891_octobri-mense_en.html.

197 This theme starts early, when we teach our children to sing, "Jesus loves me; this I know, for the Bible tells me so...." Catholics join us in singing, in the same vein, St. Bernard of Clairvaux's "Jesus, Thou Joy of Loving Hearts" and "Jesus, the Very Thought of Thee".

198 Cyril of Alexandria, *Homily in Deiparum*, Patrologia Graeca 65, p. 681, quoted in *A New Marian Dogma.*

199 So St. Ephrem the Syrian says, "With the Mediator, you are the Mediatrix of the entire world." Antipater of Bostra, a father of the Council of Ephesus wrote in the fifth century, "Hail you who acceptably intercede as Mediatrix for mankind." (quoted in *A New Marian Dogma?)* St Andrew of Crete (7th c), St John Damascene (7th c.), St Germanus of Constantinople (7th c) all witness to this belief before the first millennium.

200 The New Testament word translated "Advocate"—the Greek *parakletos*—means "helper" in the broadest sense, but has the more specialized meaning of someone called alongside to aid, especially to plead one's cause. Jesus uses the word to refer to the Holy Spirit in John 14-16, where it is often translated "Comforter" or "Counselor".

201 From the Rylands Library papyrus, Luigi Gambero, *Mary and the Fathers of the Church*, Ignatius, San Francisco, 1999, p. 79.

202 St Ephrem, *Syri testim. de B.V.M. mediatione, Epheermerides Theologicae Lovaniennses, IV, fasc. 2m, 1927,* Quoted in *A New Marian Dogma?* p. 7.

203 Gambero, pp. 54-56.

204 *See* Rom. 8:34 ("Christ Jesus ... is at the right hand of God, and is also interceding for us"); 1 Tim. 2:5; Heb. 7:25 (Jesus "always lives to intercede for them"); Heb. 9:24 ("Christ ... entered heaven itself, now to appear for us in God's presence").

205 *See* Matt. 16:27, 19:28, 25:31-46 ("When the Son of Man comes in His glory, ... He will put the sheep on His right and the goats on His left"); John 5:25-30 (the Father "has given [the Son] authority to judge because he is the Son of Man").

206 *Certain Difficulties Felt by Anglicans in Catholic Teaching* (1892 ed.), pp. 113-115, quoted by Hilda Graef, *Mary: A History of Doctrine and Devotion* (London: Sheed & Ward, 1985 ed.), Part 2, p. 117. *See also* Letter to the editor, Homiletic & Pastoral Review (Oct. 2001): "our lack of enthusiasm for establishing Co-redemptrix as a formal title for Mary is simply this: Whenever one attempts to explain the term, more space has to be given to what it does not mean than what it does mean." http://www.catholic.net/rcc/Periodicals/Homiletic/2001-10/letters.html.

Chapter 12

207 Austin Flannery O.P., *Vatican Council II,* New York, Costello Publishing, 1984, *Lumen Gentium,* ¶ 67, p. 422.

208 *See* Prof. Julian Porteous, "Mary and Ecumenism", in *Mariology from Vatican Council II Until Today* (Vatican-sponsored conference, May 29, 2002), http://www.clerus.org/clerus/dati/2002-05/29-999999/09MaIn.html: "Indeed our devotion to and honouring of Mary can become precisely a source for constructive and clarifying dialogue with, particularly, evangelical Christians. It can challenge the limits of a fundamentalist approach to faith based in a narrow interpretation of the Biblical texts. It can open up the rich incarnational dimension of Catholicism. It can challenge a reluctance to explore the sacramental and ecclesial character of Christianity."

209 Quoted by Hilda Graef, *Mary: A History of Doctrine and Devotion* (London: Sheed & Ward, 1985 ed.), flyleaf.

210 The dialogue with Pentecostals has been going on quietly since 1972.

211 In 2001 the Baptists requested that these talks be terminated.

212 The Anglican Roman Catholic International Commission met over a period of thirty years from 1971. The theologians found much ground for agreement, and now a new commission (International Anglican-Roman Catholic Commission for Unity and Mission) hopes to take things further to formal agreement.

213 The Joint Declaration on the Doctrine of Justification was signed by Catholic and Lutheran leaders in October 1999.

214 Meetings took place between these groups in 1993, 1997, 1999 and 2001, and are scheduled to continue.

215 Communiqué from World Evangelical Fellowship and Pontifical Council for Promoting Christian Unity, Wisconsin, 1999. To be found at: http://www.ecumenism.org/archive/wef-pcpcu-1999.htm.

216 Paragraph 15 summarizes: "By grace alone, in faith in Christ's saving work and not because of any merit on our part, we are accepted by God and receive the Holy Spirit, who renews our hearts while equipping and calling us to good works." http://www.vatican.va/roman_curia/pontifical_councils/chrstuni/documents/rc_pc_chrstuni_doc_31101999_cath-luth-joint-declaration_en.html.

217 Philippians 2:1-11.

Bibliography

Documents of the Catholic Church

Pope Pius IX, *Ubi Primum,* 1854
Pope Pius XII, *Munificentissimus Deus,* 1950
Pope Paul VI, *Christi Matri ,* 1966
Pope Paul VI, *Marialis Cultus, 1974*
Pope John Paul II, *Redemptor Mater,*
Pope John Paul II, *Rosarium Virginis Mariae.* 2002.

—, *Catechism of the Catholic Church,* London, Geoffrey Chapman, 1994.

Books

Armstrong, Dave. *Biblical Evidence for Catholicism,* 1st Books, 2000.
Belloc, Hilaire. *The Great Heresies,* London, Ayer & Co, 1938.
Bettenson, H. *The Early Christian Fathers,* Oxford, Oxford University Press, 1969, p. 265
Coulter, A.C. *John Wesley,* New York, Oxford University Press, 1964.
de Montfort, St Louis *The Secret of Mary,* Rockford, TAN Books, 1998.

de Romestein, H. *Principle Works of St Ambrose,* Oxford, James Parker and Co, 1846.

de Satge, John. *Mary and the Christian Gospel,* London, SPCK, 1976.

Delaney, John J. (ed.) *A Woman Clothed with the Sun,* New York, Image Books, 2001.

Flannery, Austin. O.P., *Vatican Council II,* New York, Costello Publishing, 1984.

Foley, Donal. *Marian Apparitions, the Bible, and the Modern World,* Leominster, Gracewing, 2002

Gambero, Luigi. *Mary and the Fathers of the Church,* San Francisco, Ignatius Press, 1999.

Graef, Hilda. *Mary: A History of Doctrine and Devotion,* London, Sheed & Ward, 1985.

Hahn, Scott. *Hail Holy Queen,* London, DLT, 2001.

Keating, Karl, *What Catholics Really Believe—Setting the Record Straight,* San Francisco, Ignatius, 1992.

Laurentin, René, *The Apparitions of the Blessed Virgin Mary Today,* Dublin, Veritas, 1988.

Lewis, C.S. *The Great Divorce,* Glasgow, Collins, 1988.

Lewis, C.S., *Mere Christianity,* New York, Macmillan, 1978.

Lewis, C.S., *The Screwtape Letters,* New York, Macmillan, 1961.

Longenecker, Dwight (ed.). *The Path to Rome,* Leominster, Gracewing, 1999.

Longenecker, Dwight. *More Christianity,* Huntingdon, Our Sunday Visitor, 2002

Longenecker, Dwight, and Martin, John, *Challenging Catholics,* London, Paternoster, 2001.

MacQuarrie, John. *Mary for All Christians,* London, Collins, 1992.

Malachy, Gerard Carroll (tr.), St Louis-Marie De Montfort, *Treatise On The True Devotion To The Blessed Virgin,* Langley, 1962.

McManus, Jim, C.Ss.R, *All Generations Will Call Me Blessed,* New York, Crossroad, 1999.

Murray, *Redemption Accomplished and Applied,* Grand Rapids, Eerdmans, 1955.

Neuner, J. and J. Dupuis, *The Christian Faith in the Doctrinal Documents of the Catholic Church*, Staten Island, Alba House, 1982.

Packer, J.I., *Knowing God*, Downers Grove, Ill., InterVarsity Press, 1973.

Ratzinger, Joseph, *God and the World*, Peter Seewald, ed., San Francisco: Ignatius Press, 2000.

Rooney, Lucy, SND and Faricy, Robert, SJ, *Medjugorje Unfolds*, Fowler Wright Books, 1987.

Saward, John. *The Beauty of Holiness and the Holiness of Beauty*, San Francisco, Ignatius, 1996.

Schaff, Philip, *History of the Christian Church*, Vol. II (*Ante-Nicene Christianity*), Grand Rapids, Eerdman's, 1910.

Schaff, Philip. *The Creeds of Christendom, Vol. I (The History of Creeds)*, Harper & Row (1931 ed.), reprinted by Baker (1990).

Schreck, Alan, *Catholic and Christian*, Ann Arbor, Servant, 1984.

Saward, John, *Redeemer in the Womb*, San Francisco, Ignatius, 1993.

Saward, John, *Cradle of Redeeming Love*, San Francisco, Ignatius, 2002.

Staniforth, Maxwell, *Early Christian Writings*, London, Penguin, 1984.

Stravinskas, P. (ed.), *The Catholic Answer Book of Mary*, Huntingdon, Our Sunday Visitor, 2000.

Svendsen, Eric D., *Who Is My Mother?: The Role and Status of the Mother of Jesus in the New Testament and Roman Catholicism* (Calvary Press, 2001).

Thiessen, Henry, *Introductory Lectures in Systematic Theology*, Grand Rapids, Eerdmans, 1949.

Von Balthasar, Hans Urs, *Mary for Today*, San Francisco, Ignatius, 1987.

Ward, Neville. *Five for Sorrow, Ten for Joy*, London, DLT, 1988.

Ware, Timothy, *The Orthodox Church*, London, Penguin Books, 1987.